NEIGHBORHOOD POVERTY

NEIGHBORHOOD POVERTY

. . .

Volume II

Policy Implications in Studying Neighborhoods

. . .

Jeanne Brooks-Gunn
Greg J. Duncan
J. Lawrence Aber

EDITORS

Russell Sage Foundation ▪ New York

The Russell Sage Foundation

The Russell Sage Foundation, one of the oldest of America's general purpose foundations, was established in 1907 by Mrs. Margaret Olivia Sage for "the improvement of social and living conditions in the United States." The Foundation seeks to fulfill this mandate by fostering the development and dissemination of knowledge about the country's political, social, and economic problems. While the Foundation endeavors to assure the accuracy and objectivity of each book it publishes, the conclusions and interpretations in Russell Sage Foundation publications are those of the authors and not of the Foundation, its Trustees, or its staff. Publication by Russell Sage, therefore, does not imply Foundation endorsement.

Library of Congress Cataloging-in-Publication Data

Neighborhood poverty : Policy implications in studying neighborhoods / edited
   by J. Brooks-Gunn, G. J. Duncan, and J. L. Aber.
      p.   cm.
   Includes bibliographical references and index.
   Contents: v.   1. Policy implications in studying neighborhoods
   ISBN 0-87154-146-7
   1. Poor children—United States—Case studies.   2. Urban poor—
United States—Case studies.   3. Family—United States—Case
studies.   4. Neighborhood—United States—Case studies.   5. Urban
policy—United States—Case studies.   6. United States—Social
policy—Case studies.   I. Brooks-Gunn, Jeanne.   II. Duncan, Greg J.
III. Aber, J. L.
HV741.N383   1997   97-7864
362.5'0973—dc21   CIP

Text design by Suzanne Nichols.

RUSSELL SAGE FOUNDATION
112 East 64th Street, New York, New York 10021
10 9 8 7 6 5 4 3 2 1

We dedicate this volume to William Julius Wilson and to Urie Bronfenbrenner, who have inspired the serious examination of the neighborhoods and communities in which children live.

JEANNE BROOKS-GUNN
GREG J. DUNCAN
J. LAWRENCE ABER

Contents

Contributors

JEANNE BROOKS-GUNN is Virginia and Leonard Marx Professor of Child Development at Teachers College, Columbia University. She is also director of the Center for Children and Families and founder of the Adolescent Study Program at Teachers College.

GREG J. DUNCAN is professor of education and social policy and a faculty associate in the Institute for Policy Research at Northwestern University. He is also faculty affiliate of the Northwestern University/University of Chicago Joint Center for Poverty Research.

J. LAWRENCE ABER is director of the National Center for Children in Poverty at the Columbia School of Public Health, Columbia University.

DANIEL AARONSON is an economist at the Federal Reserve Bank of Chicago.

PRUDENCE BROWN is research fellow at the Chapin Hall Center for Children at the University of Chicago.

LINDA M. BURTON is professor of human development and family studies and sociology at the Pennsylvania State University.

THOMAS D. COOK is professor of sociology, psychology, education, and social policy and faculty fellow at the Institute for Policy Research, Northwestern University.

CLAUDIA J. COULTON is professor at the Mandel School of Applied Social Sciences. She is also codirector of the Center on Urban Poverty and Social Change at Case Western Reserve University.

NANCY DARLING is assistant professor of human development and family studies at the Pennsylvania State University.

SERDAR M. DEĞIRMENCIOĞLU is developmental psychologist and postdoctoral fellow at the Institute for Policy Research, Northwestern University.

FRANK F. FURSTENBERG, JR., is Zellerbach Family Professor of Sociology at the University of Pennsylvania.

MARTHA A. GEPHART is adjunct professor in the Department of Organization and Leadership at Teachers College, Columbia University. She is also senior research associate at the International Center for Cooperation and Conflict Resolution at Teachers College.

MARY ELIZABETH HUGHES is postdoctoral fellow at the Population Research Center, NORC, and the University of Chicago.

ROBIN L. JARRETT is associate professor of human and community development at the University of Illinois at Urbana-Champaign.

SHEILA B. KAMERMAN is codirector of the Cross-National Studies Research Program and professor at the Columbia University School of Social Work.

TEDD JAY KOCHMAN is an attorney in the New York office of the Chicago-based law firm of McDermott, Will & Emery, where he specializes in labor and employment law.

JILL E. KORBIN is professor of anthropology at Case Western Reserve University.

TAMA LEVENTHAL is doctoral candidate in developmental psychology at Teachers College, Columbia University. She is also graduate fellow at the Center for Children and Families.

PAUL A. MCDERMOTT is professor in the Psychology in Education Division of the Graduate School of Education at the University of Pennsylvania.

JEFFREY D. MORENOFF is doctoral candidate in the Sociology Department at the University of Chicago.

TOWNSAND PRICE-SPRATLEN is assistant professor of sociology at The Ohio State University.

HAROLD A. RICHMAN is director of the Chapin Hall Center for Children at the University of Chicago. He is also the Hermon Dunlap Smith Professor of Social Welfare Policy at the University of Chicago.

ROBERT J. SAMPSON is professor of sociology at the University of Chicago. He is also research fellow of the American Bar Foundation.

MARGARET BEALE SPENCER is the Board of Overseers Professor, Developmental Psychologist in the Psychology in Education Division of the Graduate School of Education at the University of Pennsylvania. She is also director of the Center for Health, Achievement, Neighborhood, Growth and Ethnic Studies (CHANGES) at the University of Pennsylvania.

SHOBHA C. SHAGLE is research associate at the Institute for Policy Research, Northwestern University.

LAURENCE STEINBERG is professor of psychology at Temple University.

Introduction

Martha A. Gephart and Jeanne Brooks-Gunn

The resurgence of interest in the influences of neighborhood and community contexts on the development of children, youth, and families who reside and interact in them is a welcome addition to social science. Through a new generation of studies, researchers are attempting to assess the combined effects of individual, family, and neighborhood/ community characteristics on the development of children and adolescents. An interdisciplinary group of scholars working under the auspices of the Social Science Research Council planned and undertook a research program on the influences of community and neighborhood contexts, in interaction with family processes, on the development of poor children and adolescents. The group's collaboration resulted in the two-volume *Neighborhood Poverty*. The first volume, *Context and Consequences for Children*, presents findings on the consequences of neighborhood residence on children and adolescents, drawing upon six developmental data sets. This second volume, *Policy Implications in Studying Neighborhoods*, highlights our group's approach toward, as well as other scholars' perspectives on, investigating links between child and family outcomes, on the one hand, and neighborhood residence, on the other. In this chapter we discuss the impetus for the Social Science Research Council working group collaboration, as well as the organization of volumes 1 and 2.

INTELLECTUAL AND ORGANIZATIONAL IMPETUS FOR THE RESEARCH

Several developments in social and scholarly life provided the impetus for the collaborative research described in this volume. During the late 1980s, after nearly two decades of relative neglect, issues concerning the causes and consequences of poverty reemerged on the U.S. political and intellectual agendas. Renewed public interest in the problems of urban poverty was sparked by the visibility of homeless people in American cities during the early 1980s and by journalistic accounts of social pathologies in inner-city neighborhoods. The problems highlighted in such accounts included violent crime, drug use, out-of-wedlock births, school dropout, rising and chronic unemployment, and welfare dependence. Inner-city poverty and the social disorganization thought to be associated with it were often said to be "exploding."

The perception that social problems in poor urban communities were becoming more intense and interrelated led to a concern, reflected in Ken Auletta's (1982) book *The Underclass* and in Nicholas Lehmann's series of *Atlantic Monthly* articles, that an "urban underclass" was forming in inner-city neighborhoods. Academic interest in these issues was stimulated by arguments put forward by the sociologist William Julius Wilson in a series of papers that were eventually published as *The Truly Disadvantaged* (1987). Wilson argued that severe social dislocations were occurring in some neighborhoods as a result of the increasing concentration of joblessness and poverty. Isolation from informal job networks, lack of exposure to norms and behavior patterns of the steadily employed, lack of access to effective schools, and women's lack of opportunity to marry men with stable jobs were among the "effects" that Wilson hypothesized of concentrated joblessness and poverty in the inner city (see also Wilson 1991a, 1996).

As used in the media and among scholars, the concept "urban underclass" has typically included one or more of the following characteristics: (1) persistence and/or intergenerational transmission of poverty, (2) geographic concentration, (3) social isolation from mainstream society, (4) unemployment and underemployment, (5) low skills and education, (6) membership in a minority group. In the early and mid-1980s, little was known about the overlap or interaction among these characteristics. Researchers and policy makers asked whether concentrated poverty in central cities causes or reinforces unemployment, welfare dependence, school dropout, out-of-wedlock births, and involvement in crime and drugs; and whether such behaviors, in turn, lead to the persistence of poverty and its intergenerational transmission through their effects on children.

Toward the end of the 1980s, the Committee on National Urban Policy of the National Research Committee reported that poverty appeared to be worse in many large cities than it had been ten or twenty years earlier and that poverty seemingly was becoming more spatially concentrated in inner-city neighborhoods. The committee identified the phenomenon of increasing poverty concentration in inner-city neighborhoods as the national urban policy issue most meriting further attention. Meanwhile, private foundations concerned with the plight of disadvantaged families were independently becoming convinced of the need for comprehensive community-based interventions to address the problems of urban disadvantaged children and families.

In response to these developments, and with encouragement and support from the Rockefeller and Russell Sage Foundations, the Social Science Research Council (SSRC) established a research program in 1988 to improve understanding of the causes and consequences of persistent and concentrated urban poverty and to build the knowledge base needed to design and implement better policies and programs for the persistently poor in urban areas. The program sought to establish a framework for the analysis not only of the structures and processes that generate or maintain persistent and concentrated urban poverty but also of those that help people overcome such poverty. It also sought to recruit and nurture a pool of talented, well-trained young scholars who would advance research on the topic. Under the direction of the SSRC's Committee for Research on the Urban Underclass, several working groups of scholars were established to clarify the causes, effects, and relationships among the set of social conditions that had come to be associated with the term *urban underclass*.

A significant challenge for the program was to link larger socioeconomic and political forces, the changing context of poverty at the community level, and the outcomes and experience of families and individuals. In 1989, the SSRC's committee appointed the Working Group on Communities and Neighborhoods, Family Processes, and Individual Development to improve our understanding of the ways in which neighborhoods and communities influence the development of families and the children who reside in them. The group comprised social scientists with diverse disciplinary backgrounds, as well as theoretical and methodological orientations, to facilitate the conceptualization and investigation of links that require multilevel and cross-disciplinary analysis. The members included J. Lawrence Aber (Columbia University), Jeanne Brooks-Gunn (Columbia University), Linda M. Burton (The Pennsylvania State University), P. Lindsay Chase-Lansdale (University of Chicago), James P. Connell (Institute for Research and Reform in Education), Thomas D. Cook (Northwestern University), Warren E. Crichlow (York University), Greg J. Duncan (Northwestern University), Ronald F. Ferguson (Harvard University), Frank F. Furstenberg, Jr. (University of Pennsylvania), Martha A. Gephart, (Columbia University), Robin L. Jarrett (Loyola University), Vilma Ortiz (University of California, Los Angeles), Tim Smeeding (Syracuse University), Margaret Beale Spencer (University of Pennsylvania), and Mercer L. Sullivan (Rutgers University).

CONCEPTUAL FRAMEWORK AND RESEARCH STRATEGIES

Our working group took as its mandate the following questions: Does concentrated residential poverty, along with the associated economic and social neighborhood disadvantage, place children at risk? Are diverse neighborhood characteristics mediated by family structures and processes, or do they exert a separate and powerful influence on children's lives, over and above family influences?

We began by reviewing the existing theory and research. A review of existing quantitative research (Jencks and Mayer 1990) revealed weak and inconsistent effects of neighborhood composition on individual outcomes, but many of the studies were flawed. In the early phase of our own work and of other scholars investigating the nature and effects of the changing context of urban poverty at the community level, research undertaken by scholars working in the traditions of social ecology and social disorganization theory was largely ignored. The insights from such work have subsequently been incorporated in the thinking of our group and of others studying urban poverty (see chapter 1; Gephart vol. 1).

For some time, ethnographic researchers had argued for the importance of neighborhoods and communities in understanding poverty. A number of studies (for example, Anderson 1990; Sullivan 1989; Williams and Kornblum 1985) highlighted the salience of local community factors for understanding the poor's life chances and experiences. But ethnographic research had not produced systematic analyses of the effects of neighborhoods and communities on families and the individuals in them (see chapters 2 and 3; Merriwether–de Vries, Burton, and Eggeletion 1996).

Theory and research on family structures and processes and on individual development increasingly recognized the importance of the contexts within which individuals are situated. Most existing research, however, focused on the more proximal contexts of families, peers, and social networks (see Aber et al. vol. 1). The growing literatures in these areas did not directly address the effects of neighborhood and community contexts or of concentrated and persistent poverty upon individual development.

After commissioning a review of existing research on differences among ethnic groups in the functioning of poor families and households (Jarrett 1990), we developed a conceptual framework to guide our research (figure A). This framework considers as exogenous the macro structures and processes that produce neighborhoods of concentrated disadvantage, including housing discrimination, racism, migration and contingent preferences, and institutional practices and policies. At the neighborhood and community levels, our framework specifies structural and sociodemographic characteristics, including formal opportunities and constraints, dangers, ethnicity, and persistent poverty, as the attributes of neighborhoods that may vary with the concentration of poverty and resource deprivation and that may affect developmental outcomes (see chapter 1; Gephart vol. 1). The community-level social and cultural processes are illustrated in our framework by informal networks. Such processes are assumed to mediate the effects of structural and sociodemographic characteristics on outcomes. Family structures and processes, including household demography, family theories of childbearing, and family networking to opportunities and dangers, in turn, are assumed to mediate the effects of community-level processes on individual outcomes. Individual developmental processes, such as efficacy, competence, and identity processes, mediate individual outcomes that are domain specific and

FIGURE A.   Conceptual Model

COMMUNITIES AND NEIGHBORHOODS, FAMILY PROCESSES, AND INDIVIDUAL DEVELOPMENT

EXOGENOUS FORCES

Macro structures and processes that produce neighborhoods of concentrated disadvantage

* housing discrimination
* racism
* migration and contingent preferences
* institutional practices and policies (for example, public housing)
* labor-market conditions

Attributes of neighborhoods that may vary with poverty concentration and affect developmental outcomes

Formal opportunities and constraints

Dangers

Informal networks

Ethnicity

Persistent poverty

Family responses to neighborhood conditions

Family processes

Family "theories" of childrearing

Family networking to opportunities and danger

Household "demography"

Individual developmental outcomes

(likely to be domain specific) For example:

* health and mental health
* achievement
* interpersonal relations
* depression, self-esteem, efficacy
* crime
* fertility
* "negotiating multiple worlds"

appropriate for particular developmental stages. Because developmentalists expect both ontogenetic and social-structural causes for later outcomes (such as teenage pregnancy and school dropout), our framework posits that neighborhoods will affect later outcomes by influencing relevant childhood outcomes.

Our review of existing work revealed little theory or research about the characteristics of neighborhoods and communities that affect children, youth, and families; about the nature of those effects; or about the mechanisms and mediating processes at the community, family, and individual levels through which the effects operate. Multiple theoretical perspectives, fragmented by discipline and often by method, provide partial, potentially complementary (but sometimes conflicting) guidance about the characteristics of neighborhoods that may effect the development of children, youth, and families, and about the mechanisms through which such characteristics affect families and individuals. It seemed clear that new multidisciplinary and multilevel research was needed, yet existing theory and research seemed inadequate as a basis for designing a major new data collection effort. Meanwhile, policy and program solutions were making assumptions about links across levels, but existing knowledge was inadequate to assess the links hypothesized.

Given the state of existing theory and research, we took as our major challenge the development of new theory, concepts, methods, and empirical findings that would guide future research. To address this challenge, we decided to undertake several types of collaborative research that would build on and analyze existing quantitative and qualitative data. These collaborative research activities have been undertaken with support from the Russell Sage Foundation, the Smith Richardson Foundation, the W. T. Grant Foundation, and the Rockefeller Foundation. We deeply appreciate their support.

Using a common conceptual and analytical framework, the group decided to design and undertake coordinated analyses of the separate and combined effects of families and neighborhoods on children and youth. These analyses have been undertaken using six developmental data sets that vary in the developmental outcomes and the family- and individual-level mediating processes assessed, as well as in the ages and ethnicities of the children and adolescents sampled. Most of the chapters in volume 1 are devoted to the results of these analyses.

To investigate in greater depth some of the processes through which neighborhoods and communities of concentrated social and economic disadvantage are thought to affect families and individuals, the group also established four multidisciplinary research teams. These teams focused on (1) multi-generational families, (2) household economies, (3) school/community/family links, and (4) ethnic, gender, and other identity processes. Building on ongoing research and on existing data, these teams are exploring ways of integrating quantitative and qualitative analyses to investigate the processes of mediation between the characteristics of neighborhoods and communities and the developmental trajectories of the resident families and children. These approaches are reflected in this volume.

The group's quantitative analyses have addressed three major questions: (1) Is there a meaningful underlying organization to the variation in neighborhood socioeconomic composition? (2) What are the direct effects of variation in neighborhood socioeconomic and sociodemographic composition on the development of children and youth, net of family socioeconomic factors? (3) Are neighborhood effects mediated by particular family and individual psychological variables?

One of the core activities of our working group was the collaborative examination of neighborhood effects in six different data sets, as detailed in volume 1. The group decided to use geocoded data as the unit of analysis (see Duncan and Aber vol. 1). Six data sets were selected that focused on children or youth, had address data available, and had longitudinal data collected. Three were local site studies, and two were national studies. One was an eight-site study. The Panel Study of Income Dynamics (PSID), a national twenty-five-year study, was analyzed by Duncan and his colleagues. The Children of the National Longitudinal Study of Youth (NLSY), a national study of youth started in 1979 and now including the offspring of the females in the 1979 cohort, was analyzed by Chase-Lansdale and her colleagues. The Infant Health and Development Program (IHDP), an early intervention trial for low-birth-weight premature infants and their families, was used by Brooks-Gunn and her colleagues. The upstate New York study includes African American and white children and youth from an upstate New York school district; this data set was used by Connell and his colleagues. The Atlanta study, directed by Spencer, focused on African American youth in a number of Atlanta schools. The study by Aber and his colleagues also focused on youth, but in three different cities—New York City, Washington, D.C., and Baltimore. African American, white, and Latino youth were included, and the sample was drawn from poor schools.

The investigators all agreed to analyze their data in exactly the same way—something of an anomaly in social science research. After much discussion, the group decided how to conceptualize neighborhoods and the family-level variables to include in the analyses. Results are presented in the same format to facilitate comparisons across studies in this volume. Of importance vis-à-vis the reported neighborhood effects is the fact that three samples were "local" samples, with less variability in census tracts, while three were national (or, in the case of the IHDP, an eight-site one), which resulted in more census tracts being represented. This design detail is discussed in chapter 11 of volume 1.

OVERVIEW OF CHAPTERS IN THIS VOLUME

This volume includes chapters on conceptual and framing issues, on methodological issues related to assessing neighborhoods, and on the policy implications of our focus on neighborhoods and the children who reside in them. The first four chapters present conceptual frameworks (as well as research exemplars) that are currently being employed in the study of neighborhood contexts. The research on neighborhood effects has been plagued by a plethora of definitions of *neighborhood*. Consensus is probably impossible given that *neighborhood* has different meanings as a function of historical period, geographic region, city planning, perceptions of outsiders and insiders, and characteristics of families residing in particular neighborhoods. Age, ethnicity, and gender also play a role in how *neighborhood* is constructed. Chapter 1 reviews two research traditions in urban sociology and criminology—the traditional ecological perspectives and social area analysis—and considers their implication for the study of neighborhood poverty and its contextual effects on individuals and families. The authors show how current debates on urban poverty, which are concerned with the nature and effects of changes within and between neighborhoods, would benefit from being framed within this broader theoretical tradition.

Chapter 2 provides a theoretical frame for the authors' work on neighborhood effects on family management in their Philadelphia study. They maintain that more in-depth interviews with individuals are needed to portray the neighborhoods of perceived residence and that individuals' definitions of *neighborhood* are central to an understanding of community. They contend that geocoded data may not represent neighborhoods in any form that is meaningful to individuals or families.

Chapter 3 contains a somewhat different theoretical approach to the study of neighborhood, as derived from ethnographic accounts of life in different community contexts. The author summarizes her insights from ethnographic research to assess the conceptual assumptions guiding some of the quantitative analyses reported in volume 1. She also suggests larger implications, for both future research and policy, of findings and observations from both the quantitative and qualitative research on children and families.

Chapter 4 adds a perspective linked to combining epidemiological and ethnographic approaches. The authors summarize some of the key findings from the Cleveland study of neighborhoods, in which epidemiological sampling and intensive interviews were conducted simultaneously. They illustrate how epidemiology may be used as a frame for ethnographic work, and for placing such work in a larger context.

The next chapters address methodological issues related to neighborhood analyses. Our hope is that these chapters will "ground" qualitative and quantitative findings on neighborhood effects with the appropriate cautions about interpretation. Chapter 5 describes a sibling-based procedure for controlling for possible sources of bias that jeopardize the drawing of causal inferences from the analyses of neighborhood effects.

Chapter 6 presents analyses from two studies, one in Philadelphia and the other in Prince George's County, Maryland, employing neighborhood-based designs. This chapter challenges empirical and theoretical assumptions about testing mediational models of social processes of neighborhood effects. The findings point to the striking heterogeneity within neighborhoods (as opposed to between neighborhoods) and the difficulty in distinguishing between neighborhood demographic and process variables.

Chapter 7 contains interesting analyses of community effects, using a school-based sample. From their large California study, the authors derive neighborhood-based estimates by summing parent and adolescent responses by neighborhood. Clearly, this procedure requires that sampling be clustered by neighborhood (to obtain a stable or somewhat stable neighborhood estimate). This strategy reveals a number of neighborhood-based effects that could not be obtained from the approaches used in volume 1's quantitative chapters. They demonstrate that parental norms and sanctions, as well as cohesiveness among youths' parents, are associated with youth behavior.

Measurement issues, as seen from a more contextualized approach, are addressed in chapter 8. The authors' premise is that ethnographic research can be used as a springboard for addressing more innovative ways of characterizing neighborhoods. They talk about several different properties of neighborhoods, including neighborhood of residence versus neighborhood of influence, and the discussion highlights the fluid and multidimensional nature of community of influence.

Much-needed data on an alternative approach to measuring neighborhood—the windshield observation—are presented in chapter 9. The windshield method is based on neighborhood observation of resources, neighborhood upkeep, dangerous activities, and so forth. The methodology developed in both the Atlanta and Harrisburg studies is described, as well as the measure developed in the Atlanta study. Then, the usefulness of this approach is considered, by comparing the results using geocoded data and windshield observations, vis-à-vis outcomes.

Chapter 10 focuses on the meaning of the results presented in volume 1 in terms of state and local policy. The authors provide a brief historical look at community-based initiatives, which are usually based on state and local policy and practices. They explain how the current community-based initiatives are grounded in earlier efforts and how the current programs are moving in new directions. They then describe a few of the most-promising community-based initiatives and consider how qualitative and quantitative work informs these new directions.

Chapter 11 examines the question of how we might strengthen neighborhood-based programs. Also, the authors consider the ways in which resources are allocated at the neighborhood level for children, with a special focus on poor neighborhoods in cities.

CONCLUSION

We hope that these two volumes will encourage research and evaluation studies on the neighborhoods in which children reside. Our goal also is to stimulate more contextualized research that includes innovative ways of assessing neighborhood contexts. Finally, given that extrafamilial resources, and in some cases intrafamilial ones, are distributed via neighborhoods or other more local geographic areas (such as school districts, health districts, and counties), we hope that those who evaluate changes in federal and state allocations to children and families will take seriously variations by place or neighborhood. Indeed, place has become even more important, given the passage of the Personal Responsibility and Work Opportunity Reconciliation Bill of 1996. States now are able to fashion their welfare programs in a variety of ways, with much less federal oversight than before. The first implementation of state requirements makes clear the fact that variations are occurring at the county and state levels. Obviously, we must be prepared to examine the new welfare bill's effects community by community.

1

Ecological Perspectives on the Neighborhood Context of Urban Poverty: Past and Present

Robert J. Sampson and Jeffrey D. Morenoff

Afundamental concern in current debates over concentrated urban poverty is the changing nature of social disadvantage in the inner-neighborhoods of older industrial cities. In particular, a great deal of attention has centered on the growing entanglement in urban areas of neighborhood poverty with other social dislocations such as violent crime, joblessness, family disruption, high rates of infant mortality, and a host of other factors detrimental to social development (for example, school dropout, poor health care). The changing neighborhood context of poverty was brought to the fore of the urban research agenda by William Julius Wilson in *The Truly Disadvantaged* (1987), in which he argued that poor residents of inner-city neighborhoods had become more disadvantaged in the 1970s relative to both poor residents of other city and suburban neighborhoods and to poor residents of the same inner-city neighborhoods in previous decades.

The social transformation of the inner city in recent decades has resulted in an increased geographical concentration of the most disadvantaged segments of the urban black population—especially poor, female-headed families with children. For example, whereas one of every five poor blacks resided in ghetto or extreme poverty areas in 1970, by 1980 nearly two out of every five did so (Wilson et al. 1988, 131). Urban minorities have been especially vulnerable to structural economic changes related to the deindustrialization of central cities (for example, the shift from goods-producing to service-producing industries, increasing polarization of the labor market into low-wage and high-wage sectors, and relocation of manufacturing out of the inner city). According to Wilson, the exodus of middle- and upper-income black families from the inner city also removed an important social buffer that might have deflected the full impact of prolonged joblessness and industrial transformation. This thesis is based on the assumption that the basic institutions of an area (churches, schools, stores, recreational facilities, and so on) are more likely to remain viable if the core of their support comes from economically stable families in inner-city neighborhoods (Wilson 1987, 56).

1

In short, Wilson's "social transformation" thesis invokes two principal claims at the neighborhood level of analysis: first, that substantial change has occurred over time *within* inner-city neighborhoods, resulting in environments characterized by higher levels of social and economic deprivation than in the past; and second, that contemporaneously there has been growing *between*-neighborhood inequality, so that in addition to suffering from an absolute increase in the number of poor families, inner-city neighborhoods have also become more disadvantaged relative to the rest of the city and the entire metropolitan area.

Wilson's theory also posits the existence of neighborhood effects on *individual-level* outcomes (such as employment, marriage, and crime), independent of individual characteristics. That is, the social transformation of the inner city has led to increasing social isolation and, in turn, to what Wilson (1987) calls "concentration effects"—the impact that living in an overwhelmingly impoverished neighborhood has on individuals. Concentration effects, reflected in a range of outcomes from degree of labor force attachment to degree of participation in the local community, are created by the constraints on opportunities that the residents of inner-city neighborhoods face in terms of access to jobs and job networks, involvement in quality schools, availability of marriageable partners, and exposure to conventional role models (see also Sampson and Wilson 1994).

Despite the centrality of a neighborhood framework to Wilson's (1978) theory, the contemporary urban poverty literature has not fully incorporated the rich theoretical tradition in urban sociology and criminology concerning neighborhood ecological structure.[1] In this chapter, we argue that many of the current issues facing urban poverty theorists may be better understood if they are framed within this broader theoretical tradition. More specifically, recent efforts to (1) define and measure the urban "underclass," (2) examine contextual effects of neighborhood disadvantage, (3) analyze the ecological structure of urban neighborhoods, and (4) otherwise distinguish the problems of the contemporary urban poor from those in different times and places have, for the most part, neglected some of urban sociology's most pivotal lines of inquiry. For example, how do the social and the spatial milieus of urban residents intersect one another to form the neighborhood context of urban life? What are the consequences of this intersection for ghetto residents? To what extent has this context changed over time? The notions of social transformation and social isolation are especially germane to these topics because they require an analysis of both geographical and social space, each of which represents the dominant concern of a particular urban sociological tradition—respectively, the traditional *ecological* perspective and *social area analysis.*

In the following sections we briefly outline these two traditions, consider critiques that have been leveled against them and attempts that have been made to link them, and trace the implications of this integration for the study of neighborhood poverty and its contextual effects on individuals and families. Although space constraints limit us to an overview, we hope to enhance current debate by explicitly considering the long tradition of urban ecological research and its still-relevant insights.

THE TRADITIONAL ECOLOGICAL PERSPECTIVE

The roots of the traditional urban ecological perspective are familiar to most sociologists and students of urban systems. Founded with the seminal work of the University of Chicago sociologists Robert Park and Ernest Burgess (1916, 1925), the approach was characterized by its attention to the "biotic" level of community organization. Cities were conceived as dynamic, adaptive systems motored by the free-market competition that existed between businesses for land use and between population groups for affordable and desirable housing in the different "natural" areas of the city. Park (1936), borrowing concepts from Darwinian theory, was particularly taken by the "balance of nature" and how the social order of the city seemed to transcend the competition among its subunits. In this regard, he was interested in the normative order that arises from the spatial distribution of different population characteristics in distinct enclaves. As one commentator described Park's theoretical framework: "Natural forces are seen as responsible for the initial distribution, concentration, and segregation of urban populations. Social organization derives after the fact from proximity and neighborly contact as well as the relative homogeneity of the spatially contiguous populations" (Orleans 1969, 98). According to this view, ecological neighborhoods provide the site for a developing normative order.[2]

Burgess (1984) parlayed Park's concept of the "succession" process—an orderly sequence of neighborhood change fueled by the movement of different immigrant groups—into an ideal growth model for the city. This model was characterized by a radial pattern of concentric zones emanating outward from the central business district. As these zones expanded outward at a fairly constant rate, the overall stability of the ecological system was maintained in what Burgess called a "moving equilibrium of social order" (Park and Burgess [1925] 1984, 54). Slum areas, located within "zones in transition,"[3] were viewed as temporary residences for new immigrant groups that were establishing their niches in the urban economy and that would eventually assimilate and move outward, farther away from the center city.

As articulated by Park and Burgess (1925), then, the traditional ecological framework viewed disadvantaged neighborhoods as positioned on the initial rungs of a stepladder, which the various ethnic immigrant populations were expected to climb as they assimilated into society and moved through the city's concentric zones. Under this model, the transition areas played an integral role in the overall balance of "order" and the evolutionary progression of urban expansion (see also Hawley 1950).

It would be a mistake, however, to characterize the early ecological perspective as solely concerned with order and equilibrium. Indeed, within the "classical" Chicago school, a second strain emerged that emphasized the disorderly aspects of urban life. Louis Wirth (1938), in particular, was deeply disturbed by what he saw as the socially disintegrative features of density, heterogeneity, and anonymity found in rapidly changing cities. His emphasis on the deleterious outcomes of urbanism resonates strongly with Wilson's notions of social isolation and its resulting concentration effects. Moreover, Clifford Shaw and Henry McKay (1942) integrated Wirth's theme of social dislocation with Park and Burgess's theory of neighborhood change by focusing on ecological characteristics that are associated with high levels of neighborhood crime and delinquency.

Allowing that neighborhood change may be a stabilizing force in city growth, Shaw and associates' *Delinquency Areas* (1929) emphasized its role in perpetuating social *dis*organization in certain ecologically disadvantaged areas. Shaw and McKay (1931) showed that the highest delinquency rates in Chicago occurred in low-income, deteriorated zones-in-transition next to the central business and industrial district. Rates of delinquency were found to decrease as distance from the center of the city increased, the exceptions being areas also characterized by industry and commerce. Delinquency areas were specifically characterized by three structural factors: low economic status,ethnic heterogeneity, and residential mobility (especially population loss).

In their later and most famous work, *Juvenile Delinquency and Urban Areas*, Shaw and McKay (1942, 1969) investigated further the relationship between the social systems of local neighborhoods and the growth processes of the larger city. They concluded that the structural factors of low economic status, ethnic heterogeneity, and residential mobility led to the disruption of local community social organization, which in turn accounted for variations in crime and delinquency rates (see also Kornhauser 1978). Autonomous, delinquent subcultures were hypothesized to arise in socially disorganized communities and perpetuate through a process of cultural transmission, in which delinquent traditions are passed down through generations. According to the social disorganization model, then, the ecological segregation of communities characterized by low economic status, heterogeneity, and mobility results in ineffective community culture and structure. Generally speaking, the social disorganization of an area refers to the community's inability to realize its common values (Kornhauser 1978, 63).

Arguably the most significant aspect of Shaw and McKay's research was their demonstration that high rates of delinquency persisted in certain areas over many years, regardless of population turnover. More than any other, this finding led them to reject individualistic explanations of delinquency and focus instead on the processes by which delinquent and criminal patterns of behavior were transmitted across generations in areas of social disorganization and weak social controls (1942, 1969, 320). This community-level orientation led them to an explicit contextual interpretation of correlations between race or ethnicity and delinquency rates:

> The important fact about rates of delinquents for Negro boys is that they too, vary by type of area. They are higher than the rates for white boys, but it cannot be said that they are higher than rates for white boys in comparable areas, since it is impossible to reproduce in white communities the circumstances under which Negro children live. Even if it were possible to parallel the low economic status and the inadequacy of institutions in the white community, it would not be possible to reproduce the effects of segregation and the barriers to upward mobility. (1949, 614)

Shaw's insight almost a half century ago bears directly on a chief contemporary concern regarding concentrated urban poverty in America—namely, to what extent are blacks as a group differentially exposed to structural poverty in urban areas? We still cannot say that blacks and whites share a similar environment—especially with regard to concentrated urban poverty. Although approximately 70 percent of all poor non-Hispanic whites lived in nonpoverty areas in the ten largest U.S. central cities (as determined by the 1970 census) in 1980, only 16 percent of poor blacks did. Moreover, whereas less than 7 percent of poor whites lived in extreme poverty or ghetto areas, 38 percent of poor blacks lived in such areas (Wilson et al. 1988, 130). In the nation's largest city—New York City—70 percent of poor blacks live in poverty neighborhoods; by contrast, 70 percent of poor whites live in nonpoverty neighborhoods (Sullivan 1989, 230).

The consequences of these differential ecological distributions are profound because they mean that race and individual outcomes are systematically confounded with important differences in community contexts. Hence, similar to Shaw and McKay's original position, Testa has argued that

> simple comparisons between poor whites and poor blacks would be confounded with the fact that poor whites reside in areas which are ecologically and economically very different from poor blacks. Any observed relationships involving race would reflect, to some unknown degree, the relatively superior ecological niche many poor whites occupy with respect to jobs, marriage opportunities, and exposure to conventional role models. (quoted in Wilson 1987, 58–60)

Regardless of a black person's individual-level family or economic situation, the average neighborhood of residence thus differs dramatically from that of a similarly situated white person (Sampson and Wilson 1994). For example, regardless of whether a black juvenile is raised in an intact or a single-parent family, or in a rich or poor home, he or she is not likely to grow up in a neigborhood context similar to that of whites with regard to family structure and poverty. Reductionist interpretations of race and social class camouflage this key point.

In brief, traditional ecological models have long stressed the distribution in time and space of urban poverty, residential change, and racial or ethnic composition. These neighborhood characteristics and their increasing connectedness are, of course, central to present-day concerns. Shaw and McKay's early focus on the confounding of ethnicity with ecological settings of poverty was especially prescient. An interesting question that remains is whether and how current segregation patterns have altered the relationship between urban poverty and social dislocations such as crime.

CRITIQUES OF THE TRADITIONAL ECOLOGICAL PERSPECTIVE

Because our goal is to uncover insights from the classical ecological approach that bear on contemporary neighborhood theory—and not to evaluate the whole of ecological theory—our discussion of its limitations will likewise focus on those with current relevance. In this regard, there are three weaknesses of traditional ecological theory that demand attention: (1) its sole reliance on competition and natural market forces for the understanding of neighborhood dynamics, (2) the implicit treatment of black ghettos as the ecological equivalent of other immigrant "slums," and (3) the limitations of the concentric-zone model of urban growth in accounting for contemporary patterns of neighborhood change and social transformation in particular.

Traditional ecological theory rested on the assumption that natural market forces shaped both the movement of population groups through local areas of the city and patterns of land use, resulting in a mosaic of "natural" community areas. Yet there is an extensive literature on the effect of political and institutional decision making on the ecological dynamics of the city. Hirsch (1983), for example, has provided a richly textured account of how the post–World War II expansion of Chicago's ghetto resulted from a series of concrete actions and decisions that transformed the nature of the ghetto and profoundly altered the spatial distribution of the city's class and racial structure. Public housing and urban renewal were the principal components of this story, along with real estate agents who acted as panic peddlers in an effort to induce or accelerate the pace of neighborhood change. Perhaps not surprisingly, the political economy of urban poverty has been a major focus of recent research (see, for example, Logan and Molotch 1987, Massey and Kanaiaupuni 1993).

Others have also pointed to the increasing importance of corporate and institutional decisions in determining neighborhood trajectories (see Bursik 1989, Suttles 1972, Taub, Taylor, and Dunham 1984). Bursik (1989), for example, has noted that political decision making may affect a neighborhood's delinquency rate in two ways. It can have a *direct* effect, such as when governmental actors decide to locate institutions that house delinquents within the boundaries of a given community. Political decision making can also have an *indirect* impact on an area's delinquency rate either by affecting the factors that lead to social disorganization (that is, increased levels of economic deprivation, population heterogeneity, or residential mobility) or, paradoxically, by increasing the level of social organization in the form of subversive collective action. An example of the latter occurs when a neighborhood rallies to fight off a perceived threat from an external source, a case of what Suttles calls the "defended community" (1972).

A second, and closely related, critique of classical ecology is particularly important to urban poverty research because it concerns the misleading representation of the black ghetto as just another "ethnic" neighborhood. Indeed, this criticism is relevant not only to urban analysts writing in the 1920s and 1930s but also to contemporary observers of the urban scene who subscribe to what Massey and Denton have called the "myth of the immigrant ghetto" (1993, 32). Philpott (1991), a social historian, traced the origin of this myth back to the Chicago school theorists.[4]

> Sociologists at the University of Chicago . . . constructed a map based on the 1930 census to show the spatial distribution of the city's major ethnic groups. Robert Park, Ernest Burgess, and Louis Wirth, the pillars of the Chicago school of sociology, believed and taught their students to believe that all ethnic neighborhoods were—or once had been— ghettos, like the Black Belt. They viewed Negroes as just another ethnic group, whose segregation was largely voluntary and would prove to be only temporary. They subjected Chicago's social life to "blinding scrutiny," but they never saw the difference between the ethnic enclave and the black ghetto. (141)

He also argued that black ghettos were different from other ethnic settlements in Chicago in several ways. For one, other ethnic enclaves were rarely the exclusive domain of a single nationality group, so nationalities that were associated with certain areas of the city often did not constitute a solid majority within those neighborhoods (143). Philpott used census data for Chicago in 1930 to show that for the 308 census tracts classified as ethnic "ghettos," the average number of nationalities recorded in each tract was twenty-two. Moreover, areas of the city associated with a nationality group did not contain the mass of that group's population (for example, as of 1930 only 3 percent of the Irish population lived in the area known as Little Ireland), whereas nine out of ten African Americans lived in ghetto areas whose populations were over 80 percent black (143). Ethnic clustering, where it did occur, also turned out to be transitory, whereas black segregation became a permanent feature of Chicago's social landscape (144).

The third main critique of the traditional school charged that the concentric-zone model of urban growth was both inaccurate and outmoded. Early criticism was dominated by two alternative models of urban spatial patterns that were offered in response to Burgess's theory: sectors and multiple nuclei. The *sectoral* theory, put forth by Hoyt (1939), holds that urban growth follows the pattern set by high-income households, which move outward in pie-shaped sectors along lines of existing transportation and toward both desired terrain and the homes of the elite. For example, Hoyt (1939, 42) argued that "if one sector of a city first develops as a low rent residential area, it will tend to retain that character for long distances as the sector is extended through the process of the city's growth." In another contrasting model, Harris and Ullman (1945) argued that cities developed *multiple nuclei*—functionally distinct centers of different importance—because certain types of activities benefit from being close to similar activities or require special locations and specialized facilities.

The key point, however, is that all three traditional models—whether concentric, sector, or multiple nuclei—are predicated on the assumption that cities grow in stable, predictable patterns. As Taub, Taylor, and Dunham (1984) pointed out in their study of neighborhood change, classical ecological theories assumed that cities would continue to grow as they had in the past; that this growth would be spurred by a constant influx of immigrants who would occupy the oldest and most-affordable housing left behind; and that cities would continue to revolve around a central business district, with a transportation system functioning as "spokes on a hub" (3). But conditions changed, with automobiles replacing fixed-rail systems and the availability of cheap land and federal subsidies in the suburbs resulting in increased decentralization of cities. In addition, declining rates of in-migration and changes in the political economy led the city to develop a "hollow core, as housing abandonment became a gritty fact of urban life" (4).

In any case, the traditional ecological concern with neighborhood change and urban restructuring has a clear link to recent concerns with social and economic transformation. We examine the implications of the study of change for urban poverty research in a later section, but first we must consider a second strain of urban sociological research that poses yet another challenge to the traditional ecological perspective.

SOCIAL AREA ANALYSIS

Another important development in urban ecological research was the use of social area analysis as originally formulated by researchers Eshrev Shevky and Wendell Bell (1955). The impetus appears to have been a consensus among various researchers that social area analysis offered a theoretical framework too often missing in traditional ecological research. The theoretical basis and new emphasis of Shevky and Bell's work was the concept of *social* differentiation, as opposed to the earlier Chicago school emphasis on *spatial* differentiation. Shevky and Bell attempted to relate the internal structure of cities specifically to structural changes taking place in the wider society, rather than simply focusing on the city per se.

To accomplish this goal, Shevky and Bell developed three constructs to reflect social differentiation and stratification in modern, urban industrial society: *social rank, urbanization* and *family status*, and *segregation* (1955, 3, 5). They used census-tract variables to measure these social area constructs. Social rank (that is, socioeconomic status) was measured by combinations of census variables relating to occupation, education, and rent; urbanization and family status was measured by variables relating to single-family versus multiple dwelling units, fertility, and female labor force participation; and segregation (ethnic status) was measured by the proportions of racial and ethnic groups living in relative isolation. Census tracts were identified in terms of scores on each dimension, and tracts with similar scores were grouped together (clustered) in social areas to form a typology (see also Borgatta and Hadden 1977). Criminologists have used Shevky and Bell's typological method by correlating the social rank, urbanization, and segregation constructs with indices of crime and thus have tried to delineate the ways in which social structure affects the patterning of crime across ecological areas (see, for example, Chilton 1964).

CRITIQUES OF SOCIAL AREA ANALYSIS

Although urban sociology has benefited from the use of social area analysis, its theoretical and methodological limitations should be noted. First, social area analysts tended to overstate the novelty of their own theoretical contributions by mistakenly assuming that the early Chicago school focused simply on ecological structure and spatial differentiation. To the contrary, Orleans (1969, 98) has shown that Park's work "indicates a concern for *both* the spatial distribution and the social differentiation of the population, the implications of each for the other, and of both for the total urban complex." The implication of Park's work is thus that the organization of the urban population is largely a function of the *interaction* of the differentiated attributes of the population (for instance, education) and their spatial distribution. In contrast to Park, Shevky and Bell neglected ecology and focused almost exclusively on social space. This neglect led Orleans (1969, 99) to criticize social area analysis for its "lack of any systematic specification of the relationship that social space bears to physical space."

Turning to a more substantive critique of the method itself, Baldwin (1974) attacked what he perceived to be the "theoretical hiatus" in Shevky and Bell's typology. He argued that "almost by sleight of hand, the authors move from a theoretical discussion of societal scale to the empirical analysis of how areas within cities (not within societies or countries) become socially differentiated" (152). Here, Baldwin was suspicious of the theoretical gap in moving from increasing scale of society to census variables such as rent and fertility.

In other words, Baldwin criticized Shevky and Bell for imposing a misleading theoretical structure, designed to explain differences in the scale of societies, onto an analysis of urban neighborhoods. Thus, Baldwin argued that
Shevky and Bell's choice of variables, such as rent and fertility, was somewhat arbitrary, and concluded that Shevky and Bell "thought *retrospectively*
of a theoretical system to justify the use of these variables" (152–53). In essence, Baldwin claimed that Shevky and Bell's elaborate schema was inadequate because their own theoretical discourse was not clearly related to the
empirical problems with which they were dealing.

Several empirical studies have also questioned the existence of social areas
as described by Shevky and Bell. For example, Schmid (1960) examined the
structure of ten American cities and found that four of the ten did not conform to the Shevky-Bell predictions. In fact, in two cities, fertility was found
to be more highly correlated with the social rank construct than with urbanization. Gordon (1967) also criticized the social rank construct because it
failed to include the full range of workers of low socioeconomic status (SES)
and excluded the unemployed. After reviewing social area research, Gordon
concluded that the ethnic status index, which correlated more highly with
delinquency than Shevky's SES index, "was actually the more valid indicator
of extremely low socioeconomic status" (942). Finally, Schmid (1961) found
that social area analysis was in no way superior to traditional methods of
urban analysis that relied on single census variables. They found that individual variables were as effective as, if not superior to, the more complex
Shevky-Bell typology in accounting for the areal variations of the dependent
variables.

Despite its limitations, social area analysis has had a beneficial impact on
urban sociological research, and it remains relevant to the study of neighborhood effects. Perhaps most importantly, social area researchers turned the
focus of areal research from a strict analysis of geographical and spatial influences to an examination of the broader social-structural composition of urban
communities and of the ways that social indicators (such as poverty and joblessness) coalesce in physical space. As discussed later, this refocusing parallels current attempts to investigate how macrolevel forces lead to the
clustering of social and economic factors in urban areas.

BRIDGING THE ECOLOGICAL TRADITIONS

Although the ecological and social-area-analysis research traditions have differentially emphasized geographical and social space, these traditions are not
necessarily contradictory. In fact, by integrating both lines of inquiry, we can
construct a framework for assessing the structural context of poverty. To
accomplish this unification, we need to address several basic analytical
issues: (1) A structural perspective on poverty must conceptually link the
social differentiation of cities with the idea of spatially bounded neighborhoods. (2) To provide a dynamic and historical view of urban poverty, the

perspective should shed light on how neighborhood change supports or undermines the stability of a city's social structure. (3) To examine the consequences of social isolation, we must account for the intervening mechanisms between neighborhood disadvantage and social outcomes at the individual and neighborhood levels (for example, poverty or crime). Our discussion of mediating mechanisms includes both structural conduits (such as social networks and organizations) and cultural processes.

THE INTERSECTION BETWEEN SOCIAL AND GEOGRAPHICAL SPACE

To understand fully the neighborhood context of poverty, we must begin by considering the impact of geographical constraints on social differentiation. Fortunately, we can draw on a rich, though often neglected, body of theory to address this issue. In *Inequality and Heterogeneity,* Blau (1977) took up the question of how the effects of social differentiation are mediated by spatial propinquity. Blau noted that the process of social differentiation on the individual level is reflected at the aggregate level by the concept of social structure, which he defined as the "population distributions among social positions along various lines—positions that reflect and affect people's role relations and social associations" (3).[5]

Identifying spatially bounded communities as particularly salient substructures of a society's overall social structure, Blau (1977) then argued that differentiation *among* communities has a greater effect on patterns of social association than does differentiation *within* communities:

> Despite the fact that most social associations occur within communities, group and status barriers to social associations within communities inhibit them less than such barriers among communities. The apparent paradox results from the influences of the spatial distribution on social associations. Group and status barriers to social associations within communities are attenuated by the counteracting effect of physical propinquity, whereas group and status differences among communities constitute barriers to social associations that are reinforced by spatial segregation. (168–69)

This general insight led Blau to formulate a number of more specific propositions that relate social and geographical space in a way that has important implications for the study of urban poverty. For our purposes, the most important aspect of Blau's work is that it lays down the conceptual framework for understanding the intersection between social and geographical space. It specifically suggests that inequality among neighborhoods has a significant impact on patterns of social association.

In the urban poverty literature, Blau's logic serves as a point of departure for both Wilson's work on social isolation and Massey's research on residential segregation. Although they have relied on different mechanisms to explain the process of social transformation, both Wilson and Massey have focused their attention on growing inequality at the neighborhood and community level. For example, Wilson (1987) argued that inequality within communities was more characteristic of ghetto neighborhoods during the 1950s and 1960s, while inequality among communities today has become more pronounced as a result of the increasing spatial separation of middle- and upper-income blacks from lower-income blacks. His theory that the social isolation of lower-class urban blacks leads to "concentration effects" through the decline of opportunities for social interaction with middle- and upper-income blacks can be read as an extension of Blau's (1977) proposition that inequalities among communities inhibit social associations more than do inequalities within communities.

Massey's (1990) arguments about the effects of racial segregation on patterns of social interaction emerge from the same structural logic Blau employed. Massey explained how increasing social differentiation due to economic dislocation interacts with the spatial concentration of a minority group to create a set of structural circumstances that reinforce the effects of social and economic deprivation:

> In a segregated environment, any exogenous economic shock that causes a downward shift in the distribution of minority income ... will not only bring about an increase in the poverty rate for the group as a whole; it will also cause an increase in the geographic concentration of poverty. This geographic intensification of poverty occurs because the additional poverty created by the exogenous shock is spread unevenly over the metropolitan area. ... The greater the segregation, the smaller the number of neighborhoods absorbing the shock, and the more severe the resulting concentration of poverty. (337)

Translated to Blau's terms, a racially segregated city implies that there is more racial differentiation among neighborhoods than there is within them. Massey argued that when increases in poverty are mapped onto such an environment, the result is increasing inequality among neighborhoods, which is associated with pernicious social conditions, as he and Wilson have both contended.

FACTORIAL ECOLOGY

Another method of explicating the spatial implications of social differentiation makes a more direct attempt to link the ecological approach with social area analysis. Specifically, factorial ecology involves the application of factor analytic techniques (such as principal components analysis) to both social differentiation and its spatial manifestations. Rather than specifying the dimensions of social differentiation a priori, as Shevky and Bell did, factorial ecology allows the dimensions to be determined empirically and then interpreted by the analyst (for example, Borgatta and Hadden 1977). Berry and Kasarda (1977) explained the inductive nature of this process:

> The dimensions isolated are an objective outcome of the analysis. Interpretation of the dimensions (factors) depends on the nature of the variables used in the analysis and the body of concept or theory that is brought to bear. Theory provides the investigator with a set of expectations regarding the factor structure which can be compared to the actual set of factors produced. (123)

Despite this methodological difference, many studies of American cities using the factor analytic approach have confirmed Shevky's theory that social differentiation occurs along three major dimensions: SES, family status, and ethnic status (Berry and Kasarda 1977). This type of research has led to a reconciliation of the classic spatial models because it found each one to be applicable to a separate dimension of social differentiation—SES tends to be distributed sectorally, family status can be mapped in concentric zones, and ethnic status is usually found in clusters (Berry and Kasarda 1977; White 1987). More generally, a number of researchers have examined how the factorial ecology of cities such as Baltimore, Indianapolis, and Detroit explains crime, delinquency, and other social problems (see Chilton 1964; Kornhauser 1978).

Factorial ecology has also been applied to the social transformation thesis. In their case study of Cleveland, Chow and Coulton (1992) used confirmatory factor analysis to determine whether there was a social transformation of urban neighborhoods in the 1980s. Rather than simply documenting the spread of negative social conditions and the growth of an "underclass" population, Chow and Coulton operationalized Wilson's theory of social transformation by searching for evidence of structural change in the distribution and interrelationship of adverse conditions such as violent crime, drug addiction, teenage pregnancy, and welfare dependency. They compared factor structures for a wide range of social indicators in two time periods, 1980 and 1989, and showed that the earlier period was characterized by an evenly distributed three-factor structure with the following dimensions: unruliness (for example, weakened social control of adolescents), family disruption (for example, family composition and maternal and child health), and dangerousness (for example, crime and drug arrests). By 1989, however, the set of social conditions became more interrelated, and one factor, which they called impoverishment, emerged as the dominant underlying construct (see chapter 4).

Although primarily interested in the causes of homicide, Land, McCall, and Cohen (1990), using factorially based research, have shown the relevance of Wilson's (1987) theoretical framework even at the macrolevel of cities, metropolitan areas, and states. Land and colleagues analyzed the relationships among the following structural covariates represented in twenty-one previous macrolevel studies: population size, population density, percentage of the population that is black, percentage youth (that is, percentage of the population aged fifteen to twenty-nine), percentage of divorced males, percentage of children not living with both parents, median family income, percentage of families living in poverty, the Gini index of income inequality (a statistical index that measures the degree to which the total income of a population is concentrated among a small fraction of its total families), the unemployment rate, and a dichotomous variable indicating those cities or metropolitan areas located in the South. Using principal components analysis, a factor labeled *resource deprivation/affluence* was found to consistently "hang together" over time (that is, for 1960, 1970, and 1980) *and* space (that is, for cities, standard metropolitan statistical areas, and states). This factor included three income variables—median income, percentage of families below the poverty line, and the Gini index of income inequality—in addition to percentage black and percentage of children not living with both parents.[6] Although these variables seem to tap somewhat different concepts, Land and colleagues found they could not be separated empirically. Land, McCall, and Cohen's results extend Wilson's (1987) arguments by suggesting that the clustering of economic and social indicators appears not only in 1980 and in neighborhoods of large cities, but also for the two previous decennial periods and at the level of macrosocial units as a whole. Moreover, Land and colleagues presented evidence in support of Wilson's argument that concentration effects grew more severe from 1970 to 1980 in large cities. In other words, various indicators of urban disadvantaged populations not only are highly related but are increasing in concentration (for further elaboration, see Massey and Eggers 1990).

The factorial ecology approach has thus yielded tentative support for the ecological aspects of Wilson's social transformation thesis: (1) that there is significant inequality between neighborhoods and cities, as evidenced by the clustering of various indicators of social disadvantage in multiple levels of ecological structure, and (2) that this clustering has increased over time. The second part of the thesis remains underdeveloped, however, for we have yet to consider explicitly how, in Park and Burgess's (1925) terminology, an ecological structure operates as a dynamic, adaptive system.

STABILITY AND CHANGE WITHIN AN ECOLOGICAL STRUCTURE

To this point our discussion of how to link social differentiation with spatially bounded neighborhoods has relied on cross-sectional snapshots of the city or change limited to relatively short intervals (for example, 1970 to 1980). To portray a more complete picture of the neighborhood context of poverty, we must ultimately consider changes in the social structure of the city and how they are played out geographically. Therefore, we return to Shaw and McKay's (1969) primary finding that the distributional patterns of delinquency rates across city neighborhoods remained remarkably stable over time, despite shifts in the ethnic and racial compositions of these areas. They argued that certain areas continued to serve as breeding grounds for delinquency because they were marked by the ecological characteristics associated with social disorganization—namely, economic deprivation, residential mobility, and ethnic heterogeneity.

Recent research, however, has found the assumption of ecological stability to be inadequate for characterizing neighborhood delinquency rates after World War II. Bursik and Webb (1982) have shown that while the ecological structure of Chicago was relatively stable between 1930 and 1940, neighborhood change since then has led to an ecological redefinition of some areas, principally those that underwent an accelerated invasion and succession process, after World War II.[7] Bursik (1986) argued further that significant transformations occurred in Chicago, especially after 1950, in both the ecological role played by neighborhoods on the periphery of the traditional black belt and in the velocity of the invasion and succession process. Although Bursik's historical focus was primarily on the immediate postwar era and not the 1970s—which Wilson (1987) has identified as the crucial decade for the social transformation of inner-city neighborhoods—Bursik's framework for studying changes in the ecological structure of neighborhoods and crime has important implications for the study of urban poverty.

Just as Blau decomposed social differentiation according to whether it occurs primarily within or among communities, Bursik and Grasmick (1992) have decomposed neighborhood change by distinguishing between change that occurs within a given neighborhood's longitudinal profile and change that occurs among (or between) neighborhoods with respect to their ecological positions. This distinction means that poverty can increase within a neighborhood over time, but if the overall poverty rate for the city also increases, and this change is equally distributed across all neighborhoods, then the relative position of that neighborhood vis-à-vis other neighborhoods does not change (that is, there is no change between neighborhoods). This formulation rests on the notion of an ecological structure wherein each neighborhood holds a position that is defined by its relationship to other neighborhoods in the city along a given parameter.[8] Change can either stabilize or disrupt the ecological structure, depending on how it affects the interrelationships among neighborhoods.

The point we wish to stress is that both types of change are important to the study of urban poverty. Change within neighborhoods captures increases or decreases in the levels of neighborhood poverty over time, while change between neighborhoods implies an increasing ecological stratification, as levels of social and economic deprivation increase disproportionately in certain neighborhoods. Under Wilson's social transformation thesis, we would expect to find a substantial amount of change in poverty occurring between neighborhoods as ghetto areas that were previously home to both middle-

and lower-income African Americans experience an ecological redefinition by becoming areas of severely concentrated poverty and social disorder.

A more thorough treatment of neighborhood change would address one of the major weaknesses of the urban poverty literature: a historical shortsightedness that is often manifested in the implicit assumption that processes of social transformation began no earlier than 1970. Indeed, the emergence of an "underclass" poverty population is usually traced to the 1970s. Urban poverty scholars' reluctance to extend their focus back to the 1960s (or earlier) is puzzling when one considers that many of the behavioral characteristics assigned to the underclass in current debates were noted in the Moynihan report on the negro family (Moynihan 1965) and the early ethnographic studies of the 1960s (see Wilson 1987). Also, many of the social and political foundations for the emergence of an underclass that Wilson and others have pointed to—such as the construction of public housing projects, the passage of civil rights legislation, the expansion of social welfare programs, and an increase in urban violence—were laid down in the 1960s.

In analyzing the historical timing of neighborhood change, we also need to consider how the effects of change vary over the different stages of a neighborhood's life cycle. "Tipping-point" and "threshold" models of neighborhood change that explain the collective impact of individuals' decisions concerning staying in or moving from a given neighborhood, suggest that critical transitions in neighborhood trajectories may occur *before* the onset of high levels of poverty and associated ecological characteristics. (See the models employed by Taub, Taylor, and Dunham [1984], and see Tienda [1991]). Hence, many neighborhoods that became poverty or "underclass" areas in 1970 may have reached these critical transitional junctures in the 1960s. By leaving the 1960s and earlier decades out of their analyses, urban poverty researchers may have missed an important part of the story of neighborhood change.

THE MEDIATORS OF CONCENTRATED POVERTY: A SYSTEMIC APPROACH

In the structural-ecological approach described thus far, an important question has gone unanswered: What social processes determine the impact of concentrated urban poverty? Previous research in social disorganization theory provides one answer by specifying the social mechanisms that *intervene* between the structural clustering of neighborhood disadvantage and the life experiences of individual residents. Specifically, social disorganization may be seen as the inability of a community structure to realize the common values of its residents and maintain effective social controls. The structural dimensions of community social disorganization refer to the prevalence and interdependence of social networks in a community and in the span of collective supervision that the community directs toward local problems. Social organization is reflected in both informal networks (for example, in the density of acquaintanceship, intergenerational kinship ties, and mutual guardianship) and formal institutions (as with organizational density or institutional stability).

This social disorganization approach is grounded in what Kasarda and Janowitz (1974) called the systemic model, where the local community is viewed as a complex system of friendship and kinship networks, plus formal and informal associational ties rooted in family life and ongoing socialization processes. From this view social organization and social disorganization are seen as different ends of the same continuum with respect to systemic networks of community social control. As Bursik and Grasmick (1993) noted, social disorganization, when formulated in this way, is clearly separable not only from the processes that may lead to it (such as poverty and residential mobility) but from various outcomes that may result (such as crime). For example, both Bursik (1986) and Sampson and Groves (1989) have explicated the intervening dimensions of community social organization that bear on adolescence and the control of delinquency. Among others, these include local friendship ties, density of acquaintanceship, social cohesion, organizational density, local participation in formal and voluntary organizations, and the ability of a community to supervise and control teenage peer groups—especially gangs. Recent research has also established that crime rates are positively linked to community-level variations in family "disruption" (for example, the percentage of single-parent households or the divorce rate), and rates of community change (see also Byrne and Sampson 1986; Reiss 1986). As Sampson and Groves (1989) hypothesized, family disruption, urbanization, and the anonymity accompanying rapid population change all undercut a community's capacity to exercise informal social control, especially of teenage peer groups in public spaces.

Perhaps more relevant to urban poverty literature, recent research has shown that variations in community social organization—especially informal social control—appear to mediate the effect of structural disadvantages (such as concentration of poverty or family disruption) on crime and delinquency rates. Also, community-level variations in social cohesion and informal social control have significant effects on individual-level variations in delinquent outcomes as mediated by family management. For example, the monitoring of youth activities, networks between parents and their children's friends and parents, and the effective and consistent discipline of children appear to be fostered in neighborhoods characterized by high levels of social cohesion and informal social controls. In turn, strong family social controls reduce the probability of delinquent outcomes (see chapters 2 and 4; Sampson 1993; Simcha-Fagan and Schwartz 1986).

The systemic model considered by Sampson (1988) also pointed to the role of community-level residential stability in promoting an individual's social integration into the community—regardless of his or her own length of resi-dence. In particular, Sampson found that community residential stability had significant contextual effects on individual-level local friendships and partici-pation in local social activities (such as visitation and leisure entertainment). Consistent with the predictions of the systemic model, these findings suggest that factors such as residential mobility and sparse friendship ties are impor-tant social forces that undermine an individual's integration into the local com-munity, regardless of urbanization and the compositional factors (for example, age, social class, or life-cycle stage) suggested by traditional theory.

In short, the structural dimensions of social organization and systemic the-ory (Bursik and Grasmick 1993) are directly relevant to urban poverty. Local social networks, informal social control, organizational strength of ghetto institutions, and other features of neighborhood systemic structure are all part of the agenda in current debates on the underclass and neighborhood-level processes. What seems especially relevant is the relationship between the systemic base of community social organization and various forms of struc-tural disadvantage, such as concentrated poverty and racial segregation.

SOCIAL ISOLATION AND NEIGHBORHOOD CULTURE

Traditional ecological inquiry also emphasizes the ways in which structural characteristics of neighborhoods persist over time and are transmitted, in part, through patterns of cultural learning. A recognition of the cultural context of neighborhood life is brought out in a passage from *The Gold Coast and the Slum*, in which Zorbaugh ([1929] 1976) argued that the structural features of the slum persist because they pervade the personal lifestyles of residents:

> It is apparent that the slum is more than an economic phenomenon. The slum is a sociological phenomenon as well. Based upon a segregation within the economic process, it nevertheless displays characteristic atti-tudes, characteristic social patterns which differentiate it from adjoining areas. And it is this aspect of slum life that is especially significant from the standpoint of community organization. The slum sets its mark upon those who dwell in it, gives them attitudes and behavior problems pecu-liar to itself. (151)

Whereas Park and Burgess emphasized the assimilation process through which immigrant groups were able to escape the slum and eventually inte-grate into "mainstream" society, both Zorbaugh and Shaw and McKay described a pattern of neighborhood change more consistent with the notion of an underclass that remains trapped in the ghetto, geographically and socially isolated from the mainstream values of the larger society.

Although social disorganization theory is primarily structural, it too focuses on how the ecological segregation of communities gives rise to what Kornhauser (1978) termed cultural disorganization—the attenuation (but not rejection) of societal cultural values. Poverty, heterogeneity, anonymity, mutual distrust, institutional instability, and other structural features of urban communities are hypothesized to impede communication and obstruct the quest for common values, thereby fostering cultural diversity with respect to nondelinquent values. For example, an important component of Shaw and McKay's theory was that disorganized communities spawned delinquent gangs with their own subcultures and norms perpetuated through cultural transmission.

As reviewed elsewhere (Sampson 1992), ethnographic studies generally support the notion that structurally disorganized communities are conducive to the emergence of diverse value systems and attitudes that seem to legitimate, or at least provide a basis of tolerance for, crime and deviance. For instance, Suttles's (1968) account of the social order of a Chicago neighborhood characterized by poverty and heterogeneity supports an emphasis on age, sex, ethnicity, and territory as markers for the ordered segmentation of slum culture. Suttles found that single-sex, age-graded primary groups of the same ethnicity and territory emerged in response to threats of conflict and community-wide disorder and mistrust. Although the community subcultures Suttles (1968) described were provincial, tentative, and incomplete[9] (Kornhauser 1978) they nonetheless undermined societal values against delinquency and violence.

A renewed appreciation for the role of cultural adaptations is congruent with Wilson's (1987) notion of *social isolation*, defined as the lack of contact or of sustained interaction with individuals and institutions that represent mainstream society. According to this line of reasoning, the social isolation fostered by the ecological concentration of urban poverty deprives residents not only of resources and conventional role models but also of cultural learning from mainstream social networks that facilitate social and economic advancement in modern industrial society (Wilson 1991b). Social isolation is specifically distinguished from the culture of poverty, by virtue of its focus on adaptations to constraints and deviant opportunities rather than internalization of norms (Sampson and Wilson 1994).[10]

As Hannerz (1969) noted in *Soulside*, it is thus possible to recognize the importance of macrostructural constraints—that is, avoid the extreme notions of the culture of poverty or culture of violence and yet see the "merits of a more subtle kind of cultural analysis" (182). This led Wilson (1991b) to hypothesizes a difference, on the one hand, between a jobless family whose mobility is impeded by the macrostructural constraints in the economy and the larger society but who nonetheless lives in an area with a relatively low rate of poverty and, on the other hand, a jobless family who lives in an inner-city ghetto neighborhood that is influenced not only by these same constraints but also by the behavior of other jobless families in the neighborhood (see also Hannerz 1969). The latter influence is one of culture—the extent to which individuals follow their inclinations as they have been developed by learning or influence from other members of the community (Sampson and Wilson 1994; Wilson 1991b).

The concept of social isolation captures this process by implying that contact between groups of different class or racial backgrounds is either lacking or has become increasingly intermittent, and that the nature of this contact enhances effects of living in a highly concentrated poverty area. Massey and Denton (1993) have gone even further by proposing that racial segregation, which isolates blacks living in ghetto communities from contact with whites, leads to the formation of distinct speech patterns among blacks and, more generally, to the evolution of an "alternative status system" in the ghetto. They have argued that this status system is defined

> in opposition to the basic ideals and values of American society. It is a culture that explains and legitimizes the social and economic shortcomings of ghetto blacks, which are built into their lives by segregation rather than by personal failings. This culture of segregation attaches value and meaning to a way of life that the broader society would label as deviant and unworthy. (167)

Although the question of cultural differences by neighborhood context remains to be answered, it is clear that recent formulations can be distinguished from earlier accounts like the culture of poverty. Social isolation does not mean that ghetto-specific practices become internalized, take on a life of their own, and therefore continue to influence behavior, no matter the contextual environment. Rather, it suggests that reducing structural inequality would not only decrease the frequency of these practices but also make their cultural transmission less efficient. In this sense, the urban sociological literature suggests a renewed appreciation for ecological constraints in shaping patterns of cultural learning.[11]

CONCLUSION

The focus of urban ecology on the many facets of cities and neighborhoods—for example, social change, the clustering of economic and family disadvantage, segregation, the confounding of race with urban poverty, city growth and economic restructuring, social area classification, integration of social and physical space, social isolation and local culture, social disorganization, informal social control, and systemic organization—bears directly on current concerns with neighborhood effects and the concentration of urban poverty. As a result, many of the debates now dominating the urban poverty literature tend to recapitulate the themes that urban sociologists have been discussing since the time of the Chicago school. As but one example, the question of how to define or measure the concept of an "urban underclass" directly relates to the broader issue of conceptualizing the intersection between social and geographical space.

This is not to say that the classical school of ecological research envisioned the future or somehow eclipsed present activities. Quite to the contrary, the emphasis by Wilson (1987) on large-scale macrostructural changes in the economy during the 1970s and 1980s suggests that recent transformations of urban poverty may be unique in their causes and consequences. Nonetheless, the ideas, methods, and constructs from urban ecology and the literature on social disorganization retain much promise as a guide to ongoing research.

We thank Mercer Sullivan for helpful comments on an earlier draft.

NOTES

1. One important exception to this individualistic emphasis is the literature on residential segregation, which we discuss

2. The idea of a neighborhood, as used by Park, Burgess, and other members of the Chicago school (see, for example, McKenzie in Park and Burgess ([1925] 1984), refers to a subsection of a community—a collection of both people and institutions occupying a spatially defined area that is conditioned by a set of ecological, cultural, and political forces. Communities vary in size and are always nested within successively larger communities. Although Park and Burgess laid most of their explanatory emphasis on ecological forces—"those which have to do with the process of competition and the consequent distribution and segregation by residence and occupation" (147)—it is important to note that they were also aware of the cultural and political dimensions of neighborhoods. Park recognized these multidimensional aspects of a community's organization: "The cultural and political organization of the community rests upon the occupational organization, just as the latter, in turn, grows up in, and rests upon, the ecological organization" (116–17).

3. These zones were "transitional" in that the dominant mode of land use was changing from residential to commercial. They consisted of neighborhoods with deteriorating housing stocks that would soon be converted to commercial use because of their adjacency to the expanding central business district.

4. The exception, as just noted, would seem to be the work of Shaw and McKay (1942), who clearly recognized the unique ecological characteristics and differential status of black communities in Chicago.

5. More specifically, Blau (1977) argued: "To speak of social structure is to speak of social differentiation among people, for social structure, as conceptualized, is rooted in the social distinctions people make in their role relations and associations with one another. These social distinctions give rise to differences in roles and positions, which in turn influence subsequent social intercourse. What is meant here by social structures is simply the population distributions among these differentiated positions" (3).

6. The other factors were divorce rate and urbanization. In terms of explaining homicide rates, resource deprivation had the largest effect, generally followed by the male divorce rate and population structure.

7. The invasion and succession process is the replacement of one group by another in a residential neighborhood.

8. Our usage of the word *position* derives from McKenzie's definition: "The word 'position' is used to describe the place relation of a given community to other communities, also the location of the individual or institution within the community itself" (in Park and Burgess [1925] (1984): 64). We use it here to indicate the place relation of a given neighborhood.

9. We emphasize that our discussion in this paper refers only to the neighborhood context of learning patterns, not to the potential role of such factors as gender, ethnicity, and family in shaping processes of cultural transmission.

10. That is to say, they did not constitute an unqualified rejection of the cultural values of the larger society.

11. This is the notion that poverty breeds a value system, or way of life that becomes internalized and is passed down through generations.

2

The Influence of Neighborhoods on Children's Development: A Theoretical Perspective and a Research Agenda

Frank F. Furstenberg, Jr., and Mary Elizabeth Hughes

A s noted in the previous chapters, the influence of neighborhoods on children's development has recently become a hot topic among researchers in the social sciences, largely due to the issues raised in Wilson's seminal book *The Truly Disadvantaged* (1987). Wilson's thesis about the devastating impact of economic stagnation and urban disintegration put poverty research back on the social science agenda. A good deal of this renewed interest in poverty has identified the neighborhood as a critical element in the reproduction of social disadvantage, echoing themes emphasized earlier in this century by Chicago school sociologists (for instance, Park and Burgess 1924; Shaw and McKay 1942; Tannenbaum 1938; Thrasher 1927). Whether and by what means the characteristics of communities influence children's well-being are questions not only of theoretical interest to social scientists but also of immense importance to policy makers addressing social inequality (Jencks and Peterson 1991; Lynn and McGeary 1990).

A few years ago, Jencks and Mayer (1990) surveyed the literature on the social consequences of growing up in a poor neighborhood. Into the late 1980s, they could locate only a handful of studies that met their methodological standards for providing reliable, quantitative evidence on the impact of neighborhoods on children's life chances. Moreover, virtually none of the studies in their review examined *how* neighborhoods affect children's lives— that is, explored the processes by which communities shape children's development. Noting several alternative explanations of how neighborhoods could influence children's chances, Jencks and Mayer lamented the tendency of researchers to rely on a "black box" model of neighborhood effects.

It is no exaggeration to state that more studies have been completed in the past few years on the relationship of neighborhood characteristics to children's life chances than were included in the entire Jencks and Mayer review. However, when considered as a whole, the results of this new crop of studies are inconclusive (see Gephart vol. 1). Furthermore, a disappointing amount of attention has been devoted to opening the black box containing the processes by which neighborhoods influence children's lives. A skeptical reader might easily conclude on the basis of the available research that neighborhoods matter little, if at all. Yet even the skeptic would likely agree that it is much too soon to draw any conclusions about the importance of neighborhood influences on children's development. In this chapter we assess the state of neighborhood research and suggest research strategies for furthering our understanding of the influence of neighborhoods on children's well-being.

THEORETICAL ORIENTATIONS ON NEIGHBORHOODS AND CHILD DEVELOPMENT

In their review, Jencks and Mayer (1990) classified into four broad models the potential mechanisms by which neighborhoods may influence children's experience. The epidemic model emphasizes the normative system that develops in enclosed communities of like-minded individuals (see, for instance, Case and Katz 1991; Crane 1991). Residents of a confined geographical space are likely to share the same attitudes, beliefs, and behaviors and hence to adopt and adhere to common ways of doing things. These subcultural practices develop from what the criminologist Edwin Sutherland (1937) referred to as the "differential association" that typically occurs among neighbors and friends or within local collectivities. The more exclusively people interact with members in segregated social milieus, the more alike will be their beliefs and behavior. The epidemic model postulates the social contagion of norms or prescribed practices transmitted primarily by peers.

In contrast is a second source of neighborhood influence, which Jencks and Mayer referred to as collective socialization. The essential feature of this explanation, according to Jencks and Mayer, is the role of community adults—not just a child's parents—in promoting certain types of behavior for children. Socially approved behavior is reproduced by the presence of role models and mechanisms of social control employed by adults, thereby discouraging alternative forms of behavior. This explanation also has a long and honored tradition in criminological research (see, for example, Cohen 1955; Matza 1964).

The presence of institutional resources—in the form of schools, police protection, strong neighborhood organization, and community services—provides a third model of community influence on children. Jencks and Mayer argue that the benevolent intrusion of agents into the community is a potential source of influence distinguishing good and bad neighborhoods. The availability of these resources both promotes opportunity and prevents problem behavior (Cloward and Ohlin 1960).

All three of these models predict that disadvantaged children will do better when they reside in affluent neighborhoods where, presumably, they have access to conforming peers, successful adult models, and abundant resources. The fourth model outlined by Jencks and Mayer suggests that the proximity of well-off neighbors may have the perverse effect of creating further problems among the less advantaged. If children perceive that they are at a disadvantage relative to their peers, this may diminish their motivation to conform. Alternative cultures may arise that sanction deviant behaviors. Competition for scarce resources may also limit the chances of the less advantaged with respect to the more advantaged. Finally, poor children could be at a comparative disadvantage in neighborhoods where they are in the minority if they are subject to negative labeling by their more-affluent peers (Clinard 1964; Lemert 1951).

The processes that Jencks and Mayer identified need not be viewed as discrete or alternative mechanisms of neighborhood influence. Rather, they could be complementary processes. Theoretical orientations within sociology that posit links between children's well-being and characteristics of the spatial communities in which they grow up typically include several of these mechanisms.

One such theoretical orientation is social disorganization theory, which originated with the insights of Shaw and McKay (1942) and has since been elaborated by others (see chapter 1; Bursik 1988; Kornhauser 1978; Sampson and Groves 1989). Shaw and McKay's interest was in explaining the existence and persistence of ecological patterns in rates of delinquency and crime. Based on their empirical finding that areas with high rates of deviant behavior were also characterized by low economic status, ethnic heterogeneity, and high population turnover, they argued that these conditions led to social disorganization, which in turn led to deviant behavior among individuals. The level of social organization in the community, or the degree to which residents are able to realize common goals and exercise social control, is seen as a reflection of both systems of social relationships within the community and the content and consensus of values. The structural aspects of communities identified by Shaw and McKay are expected either to promote or to inhibit social organization along these dimensions. The likelihood of deviant behavior among individuals is higher where the community is relatively disorganized, a view that encompasses several of the mechanisms just discussed. Shaw and McKay's empirical findings have been confirmed in more recent work, which has also demonstrated other ecological correlates of high rates of deviance; however, detailing and testing the intervening mechanisms remains an important topic for future research (Elliott et al. 1994; Sampson 1992).

Wilson's (1987, 1991a) argument regarding the causes and consequences of concentrated poverty is another comprehensive theory of the influence of communities on individuals. Wilson built on important ingredients of the Chicago school tradition regarding ecological patterns within urban areas to explain how disadvantage may be socially reproduced from one generation to the next. Differentiating his theory from alternative explanations that either rely exclusively on cultural or structural conditions, Wilson instead argued that persistent poverty is created and sustained by a unique amalgamation of economic, social, and cultural elements that are fused together, creating specialized local environments. Macroeconomic conditions have reduced the demand for unskilled labor and limited the chances of those less equipped by education and background to compete for scarce jobs. Institutional resources within poverty neighborhoods have declined with the exit of middle-class residents seeking more desirable locations and the limited commitment of government to sustain inner-city institutions. Declining rates of marital stability due to the lack of marriageable males has decreased the availability of role models within the family. These forces have in turn permitted the spread of ghetto-specific cultural beliefs that undermine commitment to conventional norms. Children raised in these areas of concentrated poverty are therefore isolated from the conventional values and networks that would support their mainstream development.

While not specifically focusing on the influence of neighborhoods, Coleman's (1988) concept of social capital does suggest the potential importance of local communities in shaping children's life courses. Coleman used the term *social capital* to refer to social relationships that serve as resources for individuals to draw on in implementing their goals. He identified three forms of social capital: norms, reciprocal obligations, and opportunities for sharing information. The neighborhood is clearly a potentially important reservoir of social capital (Furstenberg 1993). Sampson (1992) argued that the concept of social capital dovetails with social disorganization theory in that the lack of social capital is one of the distinguishing features of individuals in socially disorganized communities. The presence or absence of social capital—or at least social capital that is useful in achieving mainstream goals—in a community is thus a further link between the structure of communities and the development of children.

Social disorganization theory, Wilson's theory on the impact of concentrated poverty and social isolation, and Coleman's concept of social capital may be conceived as overlapping, rather than competing, explanations. They each hypothesize links between the socioeconomic composition of communities—ethnic diversity, poverty rates, residential stability—and the development of children via intervening social processes such as those outlined by Jencks and Mayer. The differences among them are largely differences of emphasis in the particular compositional features considered important and the roles of various intervening mechanisms. But they are each based on a causal framework that considers the socioeconomic composition of communities the ultimate source of community influences.

While the explanations just described share the view that the characteristics of the local community are a potent influence on individual experience, they place relatively little emphasis on the developing child or even the family dynamics that may contribute to children's acquisition of values, skills, and practices. They focus instead on how the community context influences the developing child, more or less assuming uniformity in the response of families and children to their immediate environments. Wrong (1961) once referred to this sociological vision as "the oversocialized view of man."

A contrasting, but complementary, approach to community influences is taken by psychologists. Within social psychology, an important tradition of research exists that has attempted to connect community influences to the developing child. First established by Lewin (1951), applied and elaborated by Barker (1968) to the study of children, and more recently developed by Bronfenbrenner and his students, environmental or contextual psychology examines the ways that parents and children organize, adapt to, and shape their immediate environments (Bronfenbrenner 1979, 1986; Garbarino 1992; Steinberg 1990). Psychologists have studied context as a socially constructed system of external influences that is mediated by individuals' minds. This is not to say that environments are merely epiphenomenal—a perspective that invites considerable opposition in some sociological quarters—but that whatever influences local environments have on children must be seen a product of how these environments are perceived and interpreted by parents and children (for comparison see Medrich et al. 1982). In this respect, the neighborhood is very much like the family itself, a context in which the members live in different, albeit overlapping, psychological worlds (Dunn and Plomin 1990).

This perspective adds a further dimension to the complexity of investigating contextual influences, for it implies that in the course of growing up, children encounter and respond to a changing set of environments that both affect and are affected by their experiences. A feature of socialization within any culture is that cnvironments are socially arranged—more or less deliberately— for children's acquisition of knowledge and skills. However, especially in the adolescent years, children may be granted considerable discretion to select environments even though their elders may maintain considerable indirect control on their options. This observation closely parallels sociological and anthrophological perspectives examining how social niches are organized, discovered, and cultivated by parents and children during childhood (Fine 1987; Thorne 1993). These processes proceed in tandem with the children's acquisition of knowledge, beliefs, and competencies that shape their future prospects and personal well-being.

If we apply this perspective to neighborhoods, it is obvious that community influences represent a subtle and changing blend of social and individual processes. Parents, to the extent possible, locate and select desirable environments for their children, channeling their access to favorable settings or at least segregating them from undesirable locales (Furstenberg 1993). The parents' abilities to do so depend both on their material, social, and personal resources and on their skill at gaining compliance from their children (Walker and Furstenberg 1994). Their success at implementation is also affected by characteristics of their children that make them more or less receptive to adult or peer influences. Like their parents, children actively participate in organizing their environments. Furthermore, they change in their capacity to do so as they get older and respond differently to past experiences and present circumstances.

Encounters with neighborhoods are not only shaped by parenting processes and children's experiences but also by gender, class, and ethnicity. Like age, the child's gender is likely to result in sharply divergent experiences that modify the impact of neighborhoods on development. Girls typically are granted less autonomy and are subject to greater domestic control. Especially in low-income areas, boys often have more access to street life, and at younger ages. Thus, neighborhood influences may operate differently for different age groups by gender.

A great deal of evidence testifies to the way that social class differences mark the character of neighborhood organization and culture (Baumgartner 1988; Gans 1962; Kornblum 1974). How these features of local environments influence the developmental process has been the focus of numerous ethnographic studies. It is less clear from the abundant literature on class and community to what extent neighborhoods are simply a product of class composition or take on an emergent character due to the density of particular social class groupings. Even less is known about how ethnicity alters class cultures in ways that create distinctive environments, which in turn may shape the course of children's development.

It is not only children and their families who interpret characteristics of neighborhoods. The residences of children might also affect how they are perceived by others who may influence their success, such as teachers or employers. Neighborhoods might reify or concretize race and class distinctions both internally through socialization and externally through labeling. Thus, the meaning of neighborhood distinctions may only be experienced by children as they begin to recognize their place in the social order.

Recognizing that parents and children are not passive recipients of neighborhood influence but people who interact with their environments also focuses attention on the manner in which parents and children *create* their environments. For instance, residential mobility is a key means by which parents choose the environment their children experience. Because of changes in residence, a child may be exposed to a variety of neighborhoods while growing up. The impact of a particular community on a child will likely depend on the child's duration of exposure to the characteristics of that community, the ages at which it occurs, and, perhaps, the types of neighborhoods that precede and follow it. Even more important, residential mobility is also an important strategy that parents can and do use to select suitable environments for their children. Neighborhoods with particular constellations of characteristics—including child outcomes—may be created by family mobility rather than the effects of emergent properties of neighborhoods on children. In this perspective, the relationship between neighborhoods and children's outcomes is the opposite of that assumed by the mechanisms discussed thus far.

However, spatial communities are not merely created by the residential stability of mobility of families. Any theory of neighborhood influence assumes some degree of social interaction among members of the neighborhood. However, the quantity and quality of social interaction within a neighborhood are the result of investments in social relationships by those living in the neighborhood. Given limited resources, parents may choose not to invest in community building. Parents—especially women, who are the traditional community builders—may simply be too busy with the demands of jobs and family care to devote themselves to nurturing relationships with community members (Walker and Furstenberg 1994). Residential mobility may reduce attachment to the local community and the perceived incentive to invest in social relationships. Finally, parents may devote their attention to alternative communities, which may then become more relevant to their children's chances than the local community. Particularly important in this regard may be schools, churches, and parents' networks of kin and friends outside the neighborhood. Children themselves, especially as they grow older, may relate to alternative reference groups, such as school communities or peer groups. The extent to which these alternative groups replace neighborhoods as communities of reference depends on the extent to which they are separate or overlapping social worlds.

The ability of families to choose their residential communities and their networks of interaction suggests that understanding the manner in which communities are formed is essential to understanding the influence of neighborhoods on children's outcomes. Recognizing whether and by what means parents can and do select their neighborhoods of residence to maximize their children's well-being is central to comprehending the effect of spatial communities on children's development (Tienda 1991). Likewise, the ways in which parents trade off investments in the local community with investments in other resources such as income or alternative communities is a key aspect of the relationship of neighborhoods to children's well-being.

Given these considerations, demonstrating the "effect of neighborhoods" on children's experiences may be a far more daunting challenge than many researchers believe. If we are to demonstrate that the content and process of socialization is altered by conditions in local environments, then we must be prepared to show exactly how conditions within neighborhoods influence normative expectations, social control, links to opportunities, and exposure to dangers and how these influences vary by the child's age, gender, class, and ethnicity. Moreover, we need to be aware of the ways in which local differences will be mediated by how parents and other important figures in the child's life interpret and respond to these conditions and how the children themselves define the environment and react to those who mediate it. Any explication of neighborhood effects must also take account of the children's changing exposure to and construction of their environments as they grow older, implying a need to consider the developmental trajectories of children, rather than statuses at a single point in time. Finally, understanding of neighborhood effects must be based on an appreciation of the ways in which parents and children create their communities, through mobility and through investment in social relationships.

If neighborhoods are a significant factor in children's development, different trajectories of development should emerge in different contexts, depending on the child's characteristics and his or her experience with and exposure to the positive and negative features of local environments. When we are able to demonstrate this pattern, then and only then do we begin to approach a convincing case for the influence of neighborhoods on development.

ASSESSING EXISTING RESEARCH ON NEIGHBORHOODS AND CHILDREN

Empirical research on the links between neighborhood characteristics and children's development has made limited progress on the broad agenda previously described. In part, this reflects the newness of interest in neighborhood effects; despite a spate of new analyses, a critical mass of scholarship has yet to accumulate. For instance, most existing analyses of neighborhood effects focus on the adolescent, rather than the childhood, years (Gephart vol. 1). The relative newness of the endeavor has also led to conceptual gaps as researchers grapple with formulating questions, especially in light of the cross-disciplinary connections that both enrich and complicate approaches to research (Cook et al. 1994; Elliott et al. 1994; Tienda 1991). However, the primary impediment to progress in understanding the effects of neighborhoods on children continues to be the lack of data sources that contain information on neighborhoods, families, and children. Until recently, there were no studies explicitly designed to answer questions of neighborhood influence on parents and children (Jessor 1993). Thus, quantitative researchers have perforce had to rely on secondary analysis of existing sources of data not well suited to address these questions. While some existing qualitative and ethnographic studies of neighborhoods have spoken more directly to some of the issues that we have touched on, this research has not usually been designed to contrast the experiences of children living in different communities.

Typically, quantitative research on neighborhood effects has used existing administrative areas, usually census tracts, to represent neighborhoods. One strategy has been to link individual records from a survey with sociodemographic characteristics of the census tract in which the individual resides. Individual statuses are then modeled as a function of both census-tract characteristics and individual and family characteristics (see, for example, Aber et al. 1993; Brooks-Gunn et al. 1993; Clark and Wolf 1992; Duncan, Brooks-Gunn, and Klebanov 1994; Hogan and Kitagawa 1985). Another approach has related aggregated data on children's outcomes to census-tract characteristics (see, for example, Aber et al. 1992; Coulton and Pandey 1992; Garbarino and Sherman 1980; Sampson and Groves 1989; Simcha-Fagan and Schwartz 1986).

When considered as a whole, the research using these approaches has produced mixed results. Some analyses have shown moderate correlations between census characteristics and outcomes, while in others the associations have been weak or nonexistent. Interpreting the findings is complicated by differences in the neighborhood characteristics employed in different studies, as well as variations in the number and type of individual and family control variables, or in the case of aggregate-level studies, the absence of individual controls. It is difficult to argue, based on existing evidence, that children living in neighborhoods with particular sociodemographic profiles differ in obvious ways, even controlling for individual characteristics. Thus, despite the intensity of interest in neighborhood influences, the conclusion that Jencks and Mayer reached several years ago remains: quantitative research has not demonstrated a convincing association between neighborhoods and children's development, much less established the causal pathways between characteristics of neighborhoods and child development. (See Gephart vol. 1 for a comprehensive review of recent research.)

Even if the results of these types of studies were to converge to a consistent pattern of associations, they would be of limited utility in understanding the complex pathways of influence among neighborhoods, families, and children. No matter how well executed, studies such as these can only demonstrate an association at a point in time between sociodemographic characteristics of neighborhoods and children's statuses. That is, they do not open the black box containing the causal directions between neighborhood conditions and children's lives. The inclusion of only neighborhood sociodemographic information obscures not only intervening mechanisms between neighborhoods and individuals but also the relationships among neighborhood characteristics. Both of these restrictions impede the evaluation of competing theories of neighborhood effects. The use of cross-sectional data does not permit dynamic analyses of neighborhoods and children. It is thus virtually impossible to assess theories of neighborhood effects against theories arguing that observed differences in outcomes across neighborhoods are due to differential selection into neighborhoods (Tienda 1991). Later on, we discuss alternative strategies for measuring neighborhood processes through social surveys.

Ethnographers have taken quite a different tack from quantitative researchers in their efforts to demonstrate connections between neighborhood conditions and children's development. With relatively few exceptions, they have adopted a case example approach, examining in detail how the social organization of a particular community orders family life, socialization practices, and child outcomes. Mostly, they have relied on a time-honored anthropological practice of providing vivid evidence suggesting differences (or sometimes similarities) between "them" and "us." Comparisons are often implicit, and explanations rely more on assembling configurations of interrelated practices and their meanings (two exceptions are Sullivan [1989] and Burton, Obeidallah, and Allison 1996).

Much of what we know—or at least suspect we know—comes from the persuasive accounts of urban sociologists and anthropologists (see, for example, Anderson 1990; Burton 1990; Hannerz 1969; Rainwater 1970; Stack 1974; Williams and Kornblum 1994). In an impressive metareview of a large body of qualitative research on poor and near-poor neighborhoods, Jarrett (1992) attempted to identify how the availability and quality of institutional resources, particular mechanisms of social control, and the social climate support conventional behavior or tolerate departures from mainstream norms. Her findings suggested that family processes and socialization practices may indeed differ across communities, depending on their economic status and racial composition.

In summary, while there is no lack of real-world motivation and theoretical speculation for exploring the effects of neighborhoods on children's development, the existing body of empirical work provides little evidence for or against the effects of neighborhoods—especially in the childhood years. Recent quantitative research on the links between neighborhoods and development has not demonstrated convincing associations between neighborhoods and development, much less addressed the particular pathways of influence by which neighborhoods influence children and youth. Ethnographic research, while providing tantalizing suggestions of community dynamics, lacks the generalizability to provide solid evidence.

Some progress in understanding the influence of neighborhoods on children may be made by continuing to link existing surveys with administrative data, especially if this work exploits the longitudinal aspects of surveys. While these models will not untangle the processes by which neighborhoods influence children's development, they may be considered a logical starting point for assessing the impact of neighborhoods on children's outcomes. Determining whether associations exist between neighborhoods of various types and children's statuses will demonstrate whether there is anything to be explained by more-detailed models that do open the black box. These associative models will be most helpful when processual theories are used to guide the characterization of neighborhoods and model building. It is also important that studies estimate models both with and without available processual variables. The failure of existing research to find a consistent pattern of associations is due in part to differences across studies in the extent to which variables measuring mediating processes are included.

However, real progress in understanding the relationships among neighborhoods, families, and children will require initiating research explicitly designed to address these questions (Furstenberg 1992; Jessor 1993). In the remainder of the chapter we outline issues of design and measurement that we believe researchers need to consider in planning primary research in this area. Because the most powerful tools for disentangling the effects of neighborhoods on individuals are not statistical, but conceptual, we emphasize the importance of grounding both design and measurement in theoretical orientations.

ISSUES IN DESIGNING STUDIES TO TEST FOR NEIGHBORHOOD INFLUENCES

We believe five issues are important in planning data collection to address the relationship between neighborhoods and children's development.

MULTILEVEL DESIGNS

The first consideration in designing neighborhood research is the need for studies to be *multilevel*—that is, to include and analyze data on both neighborhoods and individual children within these neighborhoods. In addition, because family management strategies may be an important link between communities and children, data on family processes should be collected as well (Furstenberg 1993; Sampson 1992). In this framework, children may be perceived as nested within families and families within neighborhoods.

With this approach, the structure of the data mimics the structure of the general theoretical proposition that properties of communities affect families and children, enabling both logical tests of the proposition and assessments of competing explanations (Smith 1989). The central question in neighborhood research is whether families and individuals with similar characteristics behave differently in distinct environments (Jencks and Mayer 1990). In the absence of true experiments assigning individuals to neighborhoods at random, research designs must approximate the experimental design by comparing similar individuals living in different areas. Detailed individual- and family-level information is necessary to statistically examine similarities and differences in individuals across neighborhoods, while neighborhood-level information is necessary to describe the properties of neighborhoods that account for any observed spatial differences. In fact, this is only a poor approximation of an experiment. But continuing evidence that families and individuals respond in patterned ways to different contexts establishes plausible evidence of neighborhood effects.

Clearly, researchers are aware of the utility of multilevel analyses, as the existing research linking census-tract characteristics to individual data attests. We discuss this approach here to underscore the need to undertake projects that are explicitly designed to collect data at multiple levels.

SPECIFICATION OF NEIGHBORHOODS

A second consideration in designing neighborhood research is the manner in which the relevant geographic community is defined. As just indicated, most of the recent research on the effects of neighborhoods on development has used census tracts as a proxy for neighborhoods, an approach dictated by cost and convenience, rather than by empirical evidence that tracts represent neighborhoods. While census tracts may be a convenient starting point for measuring neighborhood differences, researchers must consider other ways of sampling communities that take into account local definitions of neighborhoods that may be either more or less geographically circumscribed. Census tracks clearly capture some important elements of geographical and social space, but they may not depict the neighborhood as it is experienced by residents, who may relate to smaller areas within census tracts or areas that fall outside the boundaries (Elliott et al. 1994).

However, delineating geographic neighborhoods is difficult, because the concept of "neighborhood" is not precise (Chaskin 1994). There is growing evidence that residents in close geographical proximity often do not agree on the boundaries of their neighborhood. In research undertaken by the MacArthur Network on Adolescents at Risk, very different levels of agreement among residents about the size of their "neighborhood" have been discovered. There is also evidence of large differences within census tracts on definitions of the neighborhood (Cook et al. 1994; Elliott et al. 1994; Furstenberg et al. forthcoming). Furthermore, adults and youth—even adults and youth in the same household—do not necessarily share the same definition of the neighborhoods. Geographical neighborhoods are not highly relevant entities for many parents, as their ties extend beyond their neighborhood (Medrich et al. 1982; Wynn et al. 1988). Important social institutions are often located beyond the confines of the neighborhood—however defined—implying that many residents are weakly attached to the areas where they reside (Walker and Furstenberg 1994). Like "family," "neighborhood" is a highly malleable concept full of personal meaning but often idiosyncratic and not invariably consequential for behavior. An added complication is that neighborhoods, however defined, are themselves nested in broader communities. Especially as children grow older, their behavior may reflect the influence of local labor market conditions or public policy mandates that apply to larger geographical areas.

While we offer no simple solutions to these difficult issues, we believe recognition of the ambiguity of neighborhood boundaries has several implications for designing research. First, it may be valuable for researchers planning primary data collection to do a small-scale preliminary investigation of the definitions of *neighborhood* that are relevant to their area of examination. Second, including several overlapping definitions of *neighborhood* in one study would enable comparison of relationships under different definitions (see, for example, Brooks-Gunn et al. 1993). Third, by querying neighborhood residents about their social ties outside their residential communities, researchers might be able to test the extent to which individuals within communities are relatively more or less isolated from competing reference groups that influence them and their children. Finally, researchers should be sensitive to the idea that we may not find neighborhood effects precisely because internal definitions of sociospatial communities are so variable across individuals. These considerations are all the more important, as it is likely that even new data collection efforts will have to rely on administrative boundaries, at least to some extent. Building in one or two of the first two features may permit testing the fourth possibility.

SAMPLING STRATEGIES

As we have argued thus far, data collection will be most useful when it is conducted in a multilevel framework. However, it is important that the data include both a sufficient number of neighborhoods and a sufficient number of families and children within each neighborhood to support adequate statistical tests of hypotheses. This implies a strategy whereby neighborhoods are sampled first and then families and individuals are sampled within neighborhoods in a manner that yields approximately equivalent numbers of families and individuals per neighborhood.

To test hypotheses about the influence of neighborhood characteristics on children, researchers must statistically compare children with similar personal characteristics across neighborhoods. Since neighborhood characteristics tend to cluster together, it is impossible to disentangle the effects of particular mechanisms of influence on children without large samples of both neighborhoods and children. Moreover, as we noted earlier, it is also of interest to examine the interaction of neighborhood characteristics and family processes as they influence children, further raising the sample-size demands.

Comprehensive samples of neighborhoods would also provide an opportunity for a baseline description of how much variability there actually is in neighborhood conditions (see Cook et al. this volume). Similarly, much of the interest in neighborhood effects has come out of the interest in poverty, yet it is as important to ascertain whether effects of neighborhoods exist for affluent neighborhoods as well. In particular, nonlinearities or threshold levels in the effects of neighborhoods on children are important from a policy perspective (Crane 1991; Jencks and Mayer 1990). Finally, dense samples of families and individuals within neighborhoods would enable researchers to generate reliable measures of neighborhood characteristics by aggregating individual responses.

LONGITUDINAL APPROACHES

As we noted earlier, all of the published research on the relationship of neighborhoods to children's development has employed cross-sectional data, limiting the casual inferences that may be drawn from the analyses. Longitudinal designs are called for in which neighborhoods and individuals are followed over time—either in separate studies or, ideally, within the same study.

Neighborhood research on children has thus far tended to view neighborhoods as relatively static entities. However, neighborhoods also have developmental trajectories, and the rate and manner in which a particular neighborhood is changing may have important implications for child development. Neighborhood change might be a particularly salient force if the change is rapid and dramatic, such as gentrification or an influx of immigrants. The Chicago school tradition of research explicitly considered the influence of transitional neighborhoods on children's life chances. To our knowledge, no recent study has mapped how changes in neighborhoods relate to the changing circumstances of children, though this notion is central to Wilson's theory of neighborhood influence (Tienda 1991). In general, attention to the research traditions on community organization and change would help inform current research on the influences of neighborhoods on children (for comparison see chapter 1).

At the individual level, the need for longitudinal data follows directly from our emphasis on children's development. Demonstrating neighborhood influences, we have argued, requires demonstrating the processes in the immediate milieu that affect the cumulative experience of children as they develop over time. Thus, we must attend to the slope of life-course trajectories, not simply to the level of outcomes or statuses at a point in time. Such a strategy requires tracking the same individuals using repeated measures of different domains of development as they encounter distinctive neighborhood environments over time. Furthermore, one of the strongest ways of demonstrating neighborhood influence on children's development would be to link the length of *exposure* to neighborhood conditions to specific paths of development (Tienda 1991). Longitudinal research would permit analyzing neighborhood effects by duration of exposure.

Most important of all, longitudinal research on both neighborhoods and individuals would illuminate the causal relationships among neighborhood change, family management processes, and children's well-being. A principal ingredient of several of the sociological theories relating neighborhoods to children's life chances is the stability of the neighborhood. This is most notable in social disorganization theory, in which residential instability is one of the main structural correlates of high delinquency rates. However, it is unclear from this association just which way the causal arrow runs. For instance, the principal competing explanation for any net differences observed among individuals in separate neighborhoods is nonrandom selection into neighborhoods. That is, observed differences in behavior across neighborhoods are argued to be due to the presence in separate neighborhoods of individuals with distinct but unobserved characteristics. The differential pattern of residence is due to the dynamics of residential mobility, as the qualities of neighborhoods attract or expel migrants with particular characteristics. However, residential mobility is also one strategy that parents might employ to obtain the environment they desire for their children. Thus, there is a complex relationship between the stability and characteristics of neighborhoods and local migration, a relationship that is at least partially mediated by processes of family management. Sorting out this tangle requires longitudinal data that trace family management and mobility within the context of changing communities.

COMBINING QUANTITATIVE AND QUALITATIVE APPROACHES

As we reported earlier, most ethnographic studies have focused on documenting the influence of single communities. We believe a much larger role exists for qualitative researchers to carry out their studies both across place and over time. Indeed, we share the view of a growing number of urban ethnographers that fieldwork can be embedded into research designs that include both systemic surveys and observations. Many researchers currently use fieldwork for hypothesis generation rather than hypothesis testing, a condescension to the potential of qualitative methods to detect and document processes not easily captured by survey procedures. We have at least as much hope that qualitative methods will illuminate neighborhood effects as quantitative methods, but we believe that studies employing both procedures in tandem have the greatest possibility of collecting convincing evidence of how neighborhood influences operate to affect human development.

MEASURING CONCEPTS RELEVANT TO NEIGHBORHOOD RESEARCH

Having sketched elements of research design that are important for researchers in exploring potential neighborhood influences on child development, we now consider how to conceptualize and measure relevant features of large communities, neighborhoods, families, and children. We devote most of our attention to issues in measuring neighborhood conditions and processes, as these are both critical to neighborhood research and conceptually underdeveloped. We include a short discussion of broad opportunity structures as a reminder that neighborhoods, families, and children are embedded in economic markets and local cultures that affect children's life chances. Family and child measures are routinely collected in other research; therefore we only discuss aspects that seem to us unique to the study of neighborhoods.

MEASURING BROADER OPPORTUNITIES AND CONSTRAINTS

While our focus is the impact of neighborhood conditions on children, neighborhoods are themselves embedded in broader geographic communities whose properties also shape behavior. These include labor, marriage, and housing markets; levels of welfare benefits; structure of property taxes; and other similar conditions that constrain or promote local attitudes and practices. As children grow older, these conditions begin to permeate their perceptions of opportunities and shape their adaptations and decision strategies. The qualities of the broader environment may also condition the influence of neighborhood characteristics (Case and Katz 1991). This level of community, while not as indistinct as neighborhoods, is also difficult to circumscribe. However, here we conceptualize it as the metropolitan area or, in nonmetropolitan areas, the county.

A variety of data characterizing the demographic composition, economic climate, housing context, and health and educational resources for metropolitan areas and counties is available from the Bureau of the Census (see, for example, U.S. Bureau of the Census 1991). Other information may be more difficult to assemble, especially if the aim is to build a data set that includes all areas in the United States. Thus, building a data set that includes all theoretically relevant aspects of metropolitan or county contexts is a potentially arduous task. If the aim is to characterize a specific area or county, recourse could be made to local administrative records and sources to obtain not only a characterization of the context at a point in time but its recent history as well (see, for example, Coulton and Pandey 1992).

MEASURING NEIGHBORHOOD CONDITIONS, PROCESSES, AND TRAJECTORIES

Complete evaluation of neighborhood influences on children would require obtaining direct measures of all the community characteristics relevant to how one or more theories explain the influence of neighborhoods on the developing child. For instance, social disorganization theory posits a causal chain from the sociodemographic composition of the neighborhood, through the social organization of the neighborhood, to children's outcomes. Testing the theory requires measuring both neighborhood sociodemographic composition and the neighborhood social processes hypothesized to mediate its effects on children's behavior. However, researchers are only beginning to include direct measures of these social processes in tests of social disorganization theory (see, for example, Sampson and Groves 1989; Simcha-Fagin and Schwartz 1986). Including all dimensions of neighborhoods hypothesized to have effects on child development not only enables more complete tests of theories but also illuminates the causal structure among neighborhood-level variables, suggesting which aspects of neighborhoods are potential targets for policy manipulation.

Collecting direct measures of neighborhood conditions, processes, and trajectories involves careful consideration of the attributes of communities considered central to various theories of neighborhood influence. We specify and discuss four broad dimensions of neighborhood conditions that arise in theories of neighborhood influence. These dimensions of neighborhoods are likely to be highly interrelated. Indeed, any strong neighborhood effects are likely to occur when neighborhood conditions are favorable on many dimensions. Although we discussed earlier the difficulty of defining neighborhoods in geographic terms, here we sidestep this thorny question and assume that the relevant unit is known. However, it must be recognized that measuring the neighborhood and measuring the properties of the neighborhood must actually occur together.

Characterizing neighborhoods requires not only greater conceptual specification but also more precision in how these constructs are measured. Developing techniques to measure neighborhoods' properties adequately is an important area for future work (Cook et al. 1994). Reference to existing literatures in overlapping areas, such as community psychology and urban sociology, would be helpful both for developing community concepts and the techniques to measure them (see, for instance, Shinn 1988). Careful attention to meaning and measurement is especially important in light of the methodological constraints inherent in identifying social effects (Manski 1993).

NEIGHBORHOOD INFRASTRUCTURE   At the neighborhood level, local infrastructure provides the physical reality in which social life and individual development occurs. Features such as the types and quality of housing, the use and arrangement of space, and the level of deterioration are fixed over short periods of time and thus provide boundaries of community development and change. Physical characteristics may also represent important constraints to social relationships (Williams and Kornblum 1994). For instance, an area composed mainly of rental apartments may have a very different character than one composed of owner-occupied single-family row houses. This may be due to the attributes of the people who choose to live in each area, the levels of residential mobility, the ways in which the arrangement of space fosters or inhibits social exchange, or a combination of all three. In this manner, infrastructure may be the ultimate cause of neighborhood influences on children or, alternatively, the selection of certain families into certain neighborhoods. If this is indeed the case, policy might then be fruitfully focused on changing infrastructure.

Data on infrastructure may be the simplest neighborhood-level information to assemble. In situations where tracts or other census designations are used to approximate neighborhoods, some information may be obtained from the Census of Housing, which contains extensive information on housing infrastructure. To supplement these data, or in cases where census definitions are not used, fieldworkers could directly record the physical features of neighborhoods, supplementing their observations with detailed maps and data available from local administrative sources, such as zoning boundaries and conditions of streets. Developing specific indicators would be relatively straightforward, since the concepts are concrete. For example, measures could include the percentage of various types of buildings—row homes, apartments, or detached houses; the presence of open spaces such as parks or vacant lots; the presence of graffiti and vandalism; the presence of vacant and boarded-up buildings; the distance of detached houses from each other; and even architectural details such as whether homes have porches or stoops. Combined indices may be constructed that gauge the potential for social exchange in a given combination of infrastructure.

NEIGHBORHOOD DEMOGRAPHIC COMPOSITION   Sociodemographic composition has been used by virtually all recent census-tract-based studies as a general indicator of neighborhood conditions, as we have noted. While we have emphasized the limits of this approach, our comments should not be interpreted as an argument to leave demographic characteristics out of neighborhood analysis. To the contrary, as central components of several theoretical stances, they must be included. Under the rubric "demographic" we include several attributes of the neighborhood population: age, household structure, racial composition, educational level, income level, and mobility status. Each of these characteristics represents an aspect of the local population that may affect children's well-being. For instance, a neighborhood in which the local population is highly educated may provide role models for educational attainment, increasing children's attachment to school. A neighborhood with a high concentration of well-off individuals may be better able to mobilize political resources in order to defeat legislation or policy that may threaten the neighborhood's safety or integrity. Each of these effects is the result of the demographic structure, in contrast to an effect of another type of characteristic for which demographic structure is a proxy.

Obviously, studies using census tracts or other census units to circumscribe neighborhoods will have the resources of the Census of Population, with its myriad items describing local populations. To the extent that other definitions of *neighborhood* are used, obtaining data about demographic composition may be more difficult. Responses from surveys of families and individuals may be aggregated, but if the sampling frame includes only households with children, the results may be seriously distorted. Basic aspects of population structure may be calculated using small-area methods for demographic estimation (see, for example, Myers and Doyle 1990). However, this technique relies on precise information about housing composition within the area, which may not be readily available. Furthermore, using this approach then confounds demographic composition with housing infrastructure. A final, but difficult, possibility is a neighborhood census.

NEIGHBORHOOD INSTITUTIONS   The importance of local institutions is also highlighted in theories of neighborhood effects. Wilson (1987, 1991a) assigned an important role to the absence of middle-class-sponsored institutions in isolating the underclass. Jencks and Mayer (1990) cited institutional resources as mechanisms of socialization and social control. None of these theorists specified exactly what types of institutions may be most important to children's development. Here we distinguish two types of institutions. One represents commitment and attention from outside the neighborhood, and to some extent may link the neighborhood to the broader community. Examples of these types of institutional resources include police protection, social welfare agencies, public health clinics, libraries, and the advocacy of local politicians. The second type of institution is indigenous to the community: local businesses, churches, and community centers. Of course, especially important are any institutions that specifically target children or their parents.

In order to assess the salience of institutions to the development of children, it would be helpful to collect two sorts of data: an objective inventory of all agencies with a presence in the neighborhood, and parents' and children's perceptions and actual use of these institutional resources (Wynn et al. 1988). Objective presence may not matter as much as the residents' knowledge of and opinion about the institutions' salience to their lives. For instance, knowing about the presence of a community center may not be illuminating unless the researcher also knows that residents consider it viable only for a particular ethnic group.

We know of no data sources that provide inventories of institutions across various neighborhoods, no matter how defined. Therefore, considering the presence of institutions requires original data collection. Listings of neighborhood institutions can be collected by fieldworkers through observation and use of the administrative sources previously suggested for measuring infrastructure. In the case of institutions, however, interviews with local informants and leaders of institutions will be important to determine the institution's mission and actual presence in the community. Residents' knowledge of the existence of institutions and their participation in them can be ascertained through survey procedures (Cook et al. 1994) If the survey follows the institutional inventory, it will be possible to ask respondents about particular institutions specifically.

Indicators might include the presence of specific types of institutions or a summary measure indicating the general level of institutional resources in the community. The specific institutional measure would be important to use if the institution was directly related to an outcome of interest—for instance, a family planning clinic when studying school-age childbearing—or was directly aimed at parenting processes. Both the general and specific indicators could be discounted or inflated by data on residents' perceptions. Alternatively, aggregated measures of individual responses on awareness, use, and opinions of institutions could be used independently.

NEIGHBORHOOD SOCIAL ORGANIZATION   While many of the theories discussed thus far refer to physical, demographic, or institutional properties of neighborhoods, the fundamental expectation is that the qualities of the social environment are the proximate determinants of child development. Each of the three dimensions of neighborhood life discussed thus far is anticipated to indirectly affect children's development via its effects on social relationships within the neighborhood. The mechanisms that Jencks and Mayer (1990) referred to are essentially *social* processes by which the content and qualities of social interaction shape the behavior of individuals. Thus, measurement of concepts related to neighborhood social organization is central to advancing research on neighborhoods' influence on children.

Along with Sampson (1992), we argue that the importance of neighborhood social organization is its role in generating social capital for individuals. Characteristic patterns of social organization in neighborhoods either facilitate or inhibit the creation of neighborhood-based social capital, which in turn affects family management and children's well-being. Coleman (1988) elaborated three forms of social capital: shared norms, reciprocal obligations, and information channels. To the extent that parents and children possess social capital in the neighborhood, the neighborhood may be more or less of an influence on their lives.

In varying degrees, neighborhoods are normative communities representing common values that are reinforced by social control. The extent to which adults and youth in the neighborhood subscribe to and promote mainstream norms is a component of several theories suggesting neighborhood effects. Networks of reciprocal obligation and exchange are particularly important to child development when they exhibit intergenerational closure, which occurs when parents of children who are friends are themselves friends. The existence of informal networks of association in the neighborhood ensures that children are monitored by adults other than their parents, facilitating collective socialization. Dense social networks within the community may also connect children to opportunities for modeling, mentoring, and sponsorship. The opportunity for information acquired in social relationships is also an important aspect of neighborhood-based social capital. The density of child contacts with adults who can offer social guidance and support is an important aspect of the child's position in the opportunity structure. This is especially the case if these adults can inform children of opportunities outside the neighborhood.

We recognize that the existence of norms, networks, and information need not imply a prosocial or conventional orientation (Cloward and Ohlin 1960; Sullivan 1989; Sutherland, 1939). Neighborhoods can provide normative support for disengagement from conventional behaviors, mentoring for criminal roles, and opportunity structures for illicit activities. Thus, studies of neighborhood influence should measure the availability of social support for underground activities or tolerance for behaviors outside the mainstream.

While social organization is the most critical element in most theories of neighborhood effects, it is also the most elusive to measure. In order to gauge the extent to which the neighborhood facilitates the formation of social capital among individuals, we need to measure the extent to which the neighborhood is a normative community, the extent to which there are informal networks in the community (and the density and closure of these networks), and the opportunities for information that exist in social relationships within the neighborhood.

Information on neighborhoods' social organization could be gathered in either structured or qualitative interviews with individuals. In fact, a scenario in which qualitative and quantitative interviews are employed, not as alternatives or in sequence but in a series of feedback loops, would likely yield the optimal measures of neighborhood social fabric. Using individual reports, researchers could build multivariate scales that summarize aspects of neighborhood social organization (see, for example, Cook et al. 1994). However, individual evaluations of neighborhood social organization tend to be distorted, as respondents apply internal, nonstandardized yardsticks in their responses to an interviewer's questions. Assessment of neighborhood social processes by outside observers would help to correct for the difficulty that individuals have in standardizing their perceptions of their local environment.

MEASURING PROPERTIES OF THE FAMILY SYSTEM

It is beyond the scope of this chapter to discuss in any detail the dimensions of family systems that are relevant to the developing child. However, we would like to emphasize three aspects of family life that are critical to assessing the effects of neighborhoods on children and should therefore be included in any data collection efforts.

First, information on residential mobility must be collected, including length of time in the neighborhood, reasons for moving, and, when possible, characteristics of the previous neighborhood. In cross-sectional studies this information can be collected in a retrospective residence history; in longitudinal studies it may be collected prospectively. Second, we cannot ignore the importance of how parents relate to their local environments, how they draw on resources in their communities, and how they manage and shape the child's milieu. Of particular importance is the degree to which parents possess neighborhood-based social capital. The neighborhood may present a favorable environment for the generation of social capital, but individual parents may or may not exploit these resources. We know relatively little about how neighborhoods influence the creation and management of social capital.

Finally, parents' ability to create and sustain a normative system in the household and generate reciprocal obligations with their children can be thought of as a form of family-based social capital. Simply put, parents who invest in their children by establishing and maintaining expectations and obligations are likely to gain a greater degree of compliance or adherence to their values. Family-based social capital has features similar to the capital that inheres in community ties. Consequently, we want to measure shared norms within the family, social connectedness of family members as indicated by the strength and salience of bonds, and the sense of reciprocal obligations.

MEASURING CHILDREN'S DEVELOPMENT

We also do not discuss measures of child development that might be included in neighborhood studies, as there is ample information on this issue available elsewhere (see, for example, Hauser, Brown and Prosser, forthcoming). However, we would like to emphasize two features of children's lives that we think are of particular importance in assessing neighborhood effects. First, it would be helpful to measure children's acquisition of social capital during childhood—for example, children's contacts, identification with and respect for adults within the neighborhood, and involvement in and service to community institutions. Such measures provide an indication of the extent to which children are increasingly bonded to and regulated by norms outside the family and their ability to call on support and sponsorship by figures other than parents. Second, many of our surveys collect data on aspirations and attainment. Yet we know relatively little about children's changing knowledge of and competency with the social world. For example, little is known about what children know about what it takes to go to college, what employers look for when they are hiring, how to obtain medical information (like getting an abortion), and the like. Such information on how youth read and interpret the social world is an important indicator in dealing with children's position in the opportunity structure.

CONCLUSION

We have argued that progress in understanding the influences of neighborhoods on children's development will require designing primary research aimed explicitly at addressing the complex questions generated by current theoretical orientations. To this end, we outlined issues of both design and measurement that we deemed important in planning such research. However, we recognize that it is impossible, and probably not desirable, to combine all the elements we suggest in a single study. Throughout our review, we have ignored the very real constraints of cost, time, and manageability. Therefore, we propose several types of projects that suggest potential ways in which the elements we have discussed may be practically implemented.

While we have criticized approaches that combine demographic information about census tracts with survey data, we recognize that this strategy is often the best available. We believe these approaches could be fruitfully elaborated in two ways. First, the longitudinal nature of many of the surveys can be exploited more fully. This strategy is likely to be most informative when the study contains both census-tract data over time and repeated measures of development. This conjunction of information makes it possible to calculate intervals of exposure to varying contexts and to examine cases that migrate across contexts. The relatively low cost of augmenting existing longitudinal data sets makes this a promising strategy for several large-scale longitudinal surveys containing developmental outcomes, such as the Panel Study of Income Dynamics, the National Longitudinal Survey of Youth, and the National Survey of Families and Households.

A second strategy that builds on the tract-survey combination approach is to add additional tract-level information to the data set, such as information on infrastructure or institutions that may be available from administrative sources. We recognize that this may well be impossible with the national data sets that include a large number of census tracts; thus, this strategy may be most feasible with locally concentrated samples. If this is the case, direct observation could be used to supplement data from administrative sources. To the extent that the data sets are also densely sampled within areas, individually based measures may also be constructed. Including other measures of census-tract characteristics has the distinct advantage of permitting investigators some way of testing how demographic profiles are related to theoretically relevant features of local milieus. Again, this is a budget-conscious strategy to approaching our ideal design.

As we have argued, new data collection aimed at disentangling the influences of neighborhoods must be multilevel and must sample at the neighborhood level first, as the unit of comparison is fundamentally the neighborhood. Elements on which more compromise is possible include what definition of neighborhood is employed, whether the study is longitudinal, and how extensively quantitative and qualitative work are combined.

A broad program of research undertaken by the MacArthur Foundation Research Network on Successful Adolescent Development among Youth in High-Risk Settings has sponsored a series of studies involving this strategy. In a number of different sites, the influence of neighborhood is being assessed by following dense samples of families and youth, each of which represents a number of neighborhoods or communities with contrasting social characteristics. Several of these studies are carefully assessing the individual and added influence of families, schools, peers, and neighborhoods. (Furstenberg and colleagues [forthcoming] have been conducting a comparison of urban neighborhoods in Philadelphia. In ongoing research, Cook and colleagues and Eccles, Sameroff, and colleagues are studying the influence of neighborhoods, schools, families, and peer groups on youth in Prince George's County, Maryland. Elliot and colleagues [1994] are examining neighborhood influences in Denver and Chicago. Finally, Elder and Conger [1994] have been looking at community influences in rural Iowa.) Studying neighborhoods within a single area has not only the advantage of lower costs and ease of management but also the theoretically attractive property of holding broader opportunity structures constant. This type of study could include all or some of the following elements: a survey of *neighborhoods* that characterizes all neighborhoods in the city and that may or may not contain a component aimed at determining the boundaries of neighborhoods; dense sampling in enough neighborhoods toprovide data for quantitative analysis; selection of a subset of these neighborhoods for extensive ethnographic comparison to add depth and richness to the statistical comparisons. The study could be extended to be longitudinal by tracing individuals and neighborhoods over time. Finally, a comparative dimension could be added if similar studies were being conducted in other cities. A second broad category of project would incorporate national samples of neighborhoods, selected either strategically or probabilistically. These studies would resemble the efforts of a series of Russell Sage Foundation–funded studies that are examining the influence of macroeconomic conditions on family life and the marital and economic transitions of young adults. The potential components would be essentially similar to those suggested for city-based studies.

Finally, too little research on neighborhood effects has capitalized on planned and natural experiments. The Gautreaux study stands as a major exception, wherein Rosenbaum and his colleagues examined the effects of random assignment to geographical mobility among low-income families in Chicago (Rosenbaum and Popkin 1992). Evaluation of different types of housing policies on families and children provides an attractive route for examining neighborhood effects on low-income families. Studies of communities in rapid transition also afford an opportunity to examine how families react to community change and how different cohorts of children may fare over time in different environmental conditions. Careful inspection of housing projects that undergo change may also provide another avenue for looking at the mechanisms that affect children's development. Of course, these strategies require a timely awareness of local conditions and the cooperation of local players.

In closing, we note that Jencks and Mayer (1990) argued powerfully that understanding neighborhood influences on children would require a long-term commitment from both the research and funding communities. Their argument remains true today, with the added urgency that we are exhausting the possibilities of existing data without advancing our understanding of how neighborhoods influence children's development. Significant progress in combining the rich insights of sociological and psychological theories of whether and how neighborhoods shape the course of development requires a greater commitment to designing and executing more innovative investigations. This process will be neither easy nor inexpensive, but the potential rewards to researchers and policy makers justify a bolder approach in the future.

This chapter was prepared for the conference Indicators of Children's Well-Being sponsored by the University of Wisconsin Institute for Research on Poverty, the Department of Health and Human Services Office of the Assistant Secretary for Planning and Evaluation, Child Trends, Inc., the NICHD Family and Child Well-being Network, and the Annie E. Casey Foundation, Bethesda, Maryland, November 17–18, 1994. The authors acknowledge the helpful comments of Greg J. Duncan, Donald Hernandez, Christopher Jencks, Susan Mayer, Ronald Mincy, and Karen Walker and the ongoing advice of Julien Teitler and Lynne Geitz. This research was supported in part by the MacArthur Foundation Research Network on Successful Adolescent Development among Youth in High-Risk Settings. The paper reflects many ideas gained in collaborative research and discussions with committee members, including Albert Bandura, James Comer, Tom Cook, Jacquelynne Eccles, Glen Elder, Del Elliott, Norman Garmezy, Robert Haggerty,Beatrix Hamburg, Dick Jessor, Arnold Sameroff, Marta Tienda, and Bill Wilson.

3

Bringing Families Back In:
Neighborhood Effects on Child Development

Robin L. Jarrett

Recent discussions of the underclass have directed attention to the impact of growing up in poor neighborhoods. Focusing primarily on African Americans, demographic data document the concentration of the most impoverished individuals and families within inner-city neighborhoods. Increases in various indices of social disorganization—crime, joblessness, welfare dependency, school dropout, and out-of wedlock childbearing—parallel these changes in neighborhood composition (chapter 1; Gephart vol. 1). In light of these compositional and organizational changes, a negative association between residence in impoverished neighborhoods and child and youth development has been posited. Several explanations—including neighborhood resource, collective socialization, contagion, competition, and relative deprivation theories—have been proposed to identify the mechanisms by which neighborhoods impair cognitive, economic, and social outcomes (Brooks-Gunn et al. 1993; Crane 1991; Jencks and Mayer 1990; Tienda 1991; Wilson 1987).

QUANTITATIVE AND QUALITATIVE APPROACHES TO STUDYING YOUNG CHILDREN AND NEIGHBORHOODS

This larger intellectual debate drives the analyses presented in chapters 4 and 5 of volume 1. Testing neighborhood resource and collective socialization theories, these authors used data from the Children of the National Longitudinal Survey of Youth (NLSY) and the Infant Health and Development Program (IHDP) to examine the relative effects of neighborhood and family factors on the intellectual and behavioral competence of preschool and early school-age children. Their work integrates the sociological literature on neighborhood effects (for an overview, see Jencks and Mayer, 1990) and the psychological literature on parenting and child development (see, for example, Bronfenbrenner 1979; Bronfenbrenner, Moen, and Garbarino 1984; Moen, Elder, and Lusher 1995) and addresses gaps in each. Chase-Lansdale, Klebanov, Brooks-Gunn, and Gordon focus on young children, who have been all but ignored in the study of neighborhood effects. And these researchers place parenting and child development within the context of neighborhoods (Brooks-Gunn, Denner, and Klebanov 1995).

The findings are relatively consistent across data sets. Both of the studies carried out in chapters 4 and 5 of volume 1 underscore that family effects are more prominent than neighborhood effects for both preschool and school-age children. Yet when neighborhood effects are significant, the findings seem to be counter to what many neighborhood models would predict. Family residence in affluent neighborhoods affects children. No negative effects of living in poor neighborhoods are found when controlling for family income and maternal education. Thus, neighborhood effects are due to high, not low, income and associated sociodemographic characteristics. Further, family residence in ethnically diverse neighborhoods negatively affects children, both before and after adding family-level controls. Racial comparisons indicate that ethnic diversity of neighborhoods affects white children more negatively than black children.

The focus on neighborhood contexts as represented in chapters 4 and 5 of volume 1 reflects a major shift in how urban poverty is studied. Current studies use statistical analyses of survey data to explore the organizational and compositional characteristics of neighborhoods and their impact on various outcomes (chapter 1; Gephart vol. 1; Jencks and Mayer 1990). Past studies of urban poverty, in contrast, had included ethnographic case studies to examine interpersonal dynamics within the context of inner-city neighborhoods (see chapter 2; Baca Zinn 1989, 1990). Relying on quantitative data alone ignores the roles of microlevel interactions and social processes that transpire within poor neighborhoods (Newman 1996). Such interactions and processes might further explain the quantitative findings from chapters 4 and 5.

My goal is to demonstrate how qualitative data enhance quantitative discussions of neighborhood effects. Focusing primarily on the experiences of African American families and children, observations from existing qualitative studies highlight family and neighborhood processes that could influence child outcomes. Quantitative studies alone offer an incomplete understanding of family life and child development in impoverished neighborhoods. As an addendum to quantitative approaches, qualitative studies offer a dynamic view of interactions within families, as well as those that occur between families in specific neighborhoods.

FAMILY PROCESSES AND NEIGHBORHOOD DYNAMICS

Qualitative findings provide possible reasons why family influences predominate over neighborhood effects (see chapters 4 and 5 of volume 1). Qualitative studies of low-income African Americans identify and describe family and parenting strategies that are used to counteract the problems of living in poor neighborhoods. Criminal behavior, nonmarital childbearing, welfare dependence, drug use and selling, incivility, overcrowded schools, deteriorated housing, inferior medical facilities, and the like characterize impoverished neighborhoods. Yet not all families exhibit negative behaviors, nor are all families adversely influenced by the absence of basic resources. Four types of strategies—family protection strategies, child-monitoring strategies, parental resource-seeking strategies, and in-home learning strategies—play a role in facilitating conventional family patterns and child development outcomes.

FAMILY PROTECTION STRATEGIES

Qualitative studies provide insights on how some poor families create family stability in the midst of neighborhood impoverishment. Family protection strategies consist of several behaviors that families use to manage their daily lives, including avoidance of dangerous areas, temporal use of the neighborhood, restrictions on neighboring relations, and ideological support of mainstream orientations (Anderson 1990; Burton 1991; Burton and Jarrett 1991; Clark 1983; Furstenberg 1993; Hannerz 1969; Jarrett 1995; Jeffers 1967; Kostarelos 1989; Merry 1981; Williams 1981).

Consider the example of Don and Angela Carter-Williams (Kostarelos 1989). Residents of a severely impoverished Chicago neighborhood, they circumscribe their movements within the local impoverished neighborhood based on their perceptions of neighborhood dangers:

> [They] are fearful and cautious when moving about the West Side. When Don and Angela are not working and the children are not in school they stay home, are in church, or visiting the homes of church friends or relatives. . . . They avoid social relationships with people who do not go to church. (235)

Clearly, the entire neighborhood does not make up Don and Angela's social world. The location of gang territories, high-crime areas, and street loiterers may further construct, if not constrict, neighborhood boundaries (Anderson 1990; Merry 1981).

Some families in poor neighborhoods selectively use neighborhoods at different periods, reflecting a perception of safe and dangerous times. This behavior insulates different lifestyles and individuals from one another. Burton (1991) observed this temporal pattern in an impoverished neighborhood in a northeastern city:

> [N]eighborhood residents who are not involved in the local drug trade (which are the majority of families) use the safe morning hours to do their grocery shopping and banking, visit with friends in the neighbor-

hood, attend church activities, deliver and pick up children from school, and take toddlers and preschool children out for walks. (35)

Thus, for community residents, like shift workers, the late-afternoon hours mark the transition to different personnel and a different pattern of activities.

Another behavior reflecting neighborhood protection strategies is the restriction of relationships with neighbors. Some families limit, through avoidance, relationships with neighbors who have different lifestyles. While living side by side, conventionally oriented families evade interactions with those whose lifestyles are different, associating instead with other like-minded families. The Johnson family (Merry 1981) provides an example:

> The Johnsons' acquaintances are all among the respectable blacks in Dover Square, families that similarly value stability, work, and church and condemn criminality. . . . Although he knows the local street youth by name and knows where they live, [Mr. Johnson] is not friendly with them and does not say hello when he sees them. . . . Mrs. Johnson also knows who the youths are, but carefully minds her own business when she sees them. (67).

Social distance is achieved in poor neighborhoods not only by physical barriers but by ideological defenses. Symbolically, an ideology of distinctiveness based on the family's perceived respectability and adherence to mainstream lifestyles distinguishes local families (Hannerz 1969; Williams 1981). According to Irene Mack (Burton and Jarrett 1991):

> We are different than the people around here. We are special. We do things different like with Christmas and birthdays. These are special times. We make sure that the kids understand they are different . . . not better than anyone but just striving for a better life. (38)

In general, family protection strategies allow residents to create distinct social, and in some cases physical, worlds within the larger neighborhood.

CHILD-MONITORING STRATEGIES

Qualitative data identify specific parenting strategies that buffer children from neighborhood dangers. Monitoring or supervisory strategies reflect the efforts of parents to limit their children's exposure to larger neighborhood influences. Two key strategies—isolation and chaperonage—have been identified.

Isolation or "lock-up" is used to segregate children from nonparental influences and disapproved peers and activities. In the most extreme form, concerned parents attempt to confine children to the household. Cynthia, a young mother, emphatically stated:

> I keep my kids up inside with me all the time. I never let them out even if it is 120 degrees inside. I will protect them from the stuff out there

until I can do better . . . until I can get out of this project. (Burton and Jarrett 1991, 42)

While physical lock-up at all times is impractical and becomes increasingly more difficult as children leave the family circle (for example, to attend school), the strategy is feasible for very young children, as they have few social contacts outside of the family circle (Rainwater 1970).

Yet isolation is often more subtle. Jeffers (1967), for example, observed that some parents selectively discourage their children from playing with "bad" peers (see also Anderson 1990; Silverstein and Krate 1975):

Certain children were tagged as "bad" and some mothers warned their children not to play with them. Some of the more protective mothers did not let their children play in the court because of their fears about the aggressive behavior of some of the other young children. (107)

Often isolation is supplemented by creating parentally approved play groups consisting of "desirable" children, including siblings (Tatje 1974).

Chaperonage, or the adult accompaniment of children on their daily rounds in the neighborhood, is the second child-monitoring strategy some poor parents use to mediate the effects of living in impoverished neighborhoods (chapter 2; Clark 1983; Furstenberg 1993). Sam, a sixty-five-year-old retired factory worker who cares for his three nieces, illustrates the chaperon role:

I take them to school. Then I go and hang out with my buddies until it's time to pick my babies up. We hurry up and walk home because I want to be in the house by three o'clock. . . . I don't want them to turn out like the low-life drugheads their momma and daddy are. (Burton 1991, 36)

Sheila, an outstanding high school senior, has avoided the risks associated with her impoverished neighborhood. Retrospective child-rearing data from her mother suggests the important role of family chaperoning. In the Johnson family, multiple kin members provided this function for young Sheila:

As a young girl, Sheila was allowed to attend recreational activities, games, and social events only when accompanied by a relative. Usually these relatives were Sheila's older sisters, two nephews whom Mrs. Johnson considers "trustworthy," and Mrs. Johnson herself. Sheila was never allowed to walk to school alone. Her two older sisters accompanied her to school through eighth grade. Mrs. Johnson would tell Sheila to accept their guidance because "I know what's best for you." (Clark 1983, 89)

This example also indicates that the most effective parents begin their monitoring efforts from their children's birth through their adolescence. Like family protection strategies, parental monitoring strategies allow parents to control neighborhood influences on their children.

PARENTAL RESOURCE-SEEKING STRATEGIES

In addition to protective monitoring strategies that insulate children from neighborhood dangers, parents, on behalf of their children, must be able to garner resources for their development. Qualitative data indicate that competent parents make use of both local and extralocal resources and opportunities. Despite limited resources in poor African American communities, some parents are able to locate the limited good-quality resources that exist. Not only do these parents identify local resources, but they also challenge them to fulfill specific functions.

Parents expect schools to emphasize the "three Rs," which set the foundation for later school success. One parent had clear expectations for the Head Start program in her community (Ogbu 1974). She asserted:

> I feel that to upgrade a person is to teach him at Headstart. At Headstart . . . they should be learning them to write their name . . . teach them to say their numbers, a little bit of their "ABC." . . . They should learn these children something better than going there and eating some food and laying about on the floor and rolling over and playing with balls and all that crap. . . . But your parents at home is not educated and so are not going to teach you how to write your name, or your numbers, or your "ABC." This is where the schoolteacher play his part. (154–155)

This parent seems to be aware of the importance of concrete learning skills, particularly for children with parents of limited education. Consequently, the hidden curriculum of play is less valued.

Mrs. Todd, a Washington, D.C., housing-project resident, sought opportunities through the local recreation center. Observations suggested that she was aware of the limitations of local schools and sought compensatory activities:

> [Mrs. Todd] acted upon her belief that every child should have some preschool training by putting her children in the half-day nursery school that was operated by the Recreation Department. She said she wanted much more than the school could give. (Jeffers 1967, 77)

Clearly, caregivers must allocate significant portions of time and energy to ferret out such resources for their children (Clark 1983; Furstenberg 1993; Jarrett 1995; Jeffers 1967; Tatje 1974). However, some parents do locate them and use them to enhance their children's development.

Resources outside of the neighborhood are frequently accessed through kinship connections. Caregivers who live in impoverished communities, by virtue of their network ties to "better-off" kin, have access to affluent communities with a wider array of institutional, informational, and economic assets. Extended-kin members can link children into institutions and networks that facilitate greater opportunities (chapter 2; Aschenbrenner 1975; Zollar 1985). It is not uncommon to send children to school in a relative's neighborhood as a way to take advantage of better schools and recreational activities (Jarrett 1992, 1995).

Cara, a young mother, described the advantage of ties to economically secure kin who live outside of the neighborhood: "We are lucky that we have family who live in other neighborhoods here. We can send our children to their houses to play with other, nicer kids" (Burton and Jarrett 1991, 35).

Another young mother took advantage of ties to her geographically dispersed extended kin. Her young daughter Tracey benefited as a result of this connection:

> Brenda is the only member of [the Niles] family who is dependent on welfare payments. . . . They continue to make sure that she has her rent paid, some food to eat, and clothes for herself and her two children to wear. (43)

Further:

> Neither does Brenda have to look far to find a baby-sitter. Her sister Louise is generally more than willing to keep her daughter, Tracey. Louise says that the big backyard behind her single family home is a much better place for Tracey to play than the inside of Brenda's studio apartment. (Zollar 1985, 26–27)

Moreover, kinship ties, across as well as within neighborhoods, underscore the importance of other kin in the lives of some young children, particularly during family crises. An example comes from a community in an eastern city. In Northton community, one overwhelmed by drugs, a resident observed the critical role played by grandmothers:

> If it wasn't for grandmom, the kids wouldn't survive. The grandmoms have to take over from the mom. See, I talk with a lot of grandmoms, and they be tellin' me, "Lawd, I got to take care of my grandchild since this thing [drugs]." . . . And if it wasn't for a lot of the grandmothers, a whole lot of kids wouldn't be able to eat, or sleep neither. (Anderson 1990, 90)

In another eastern city, Mary, a grandmother, cared for her grandchildren, who too had lost their parents to drugs. She described her daily routine:

In the morning, I get up early, get the babies ready, and hits the streets. At 7:00 in the morning, I let the kids go out to play—them that don't have school. Then about 10:00 o'clock, I pack up the babies, and we go to the store and the doctor. I'm always home by 2:00 in the afternoon so we can all go inside. That's when shit starts to change around here. Them no-good women and men dope dealers takes over the streets. I done lost one child to dope. I ain't letting her babies get lost too. (Burton 1991, 36)

These examples (see also Jarrett 1994; Martin and Martin 1978) suggest many of the problematic effects of neighborhood impoverishment and some of the ways kin ties are activated as a response.

IN-HOME LEARNING STRATEGIES

Qualitative studies describe parenting behaviors that facilitate the intellectual development of young children in poor neighborhoods. These parents institute in-home learning activities with their young children that are directly related to competencies and tasks desired in school settings. Consider the interactions between Mrs. Todd and young Elsie:

She said that she used to play with her children a lot, teaching them various things, and she would always read to them at night before they went to bed. The result of her instruction showed. Her oldest daughter, Elsie, could read at a third-grade level when she completed first grade. . . . She was very alert. (Jeffers 1967, 77–78)

One high school senior, Marie Chivers, recounted similar in-home learning experiences that were undoubtedly reflected in her academic success. She recalled:

[My mother] would let us go off and do our stuff and she'd be talking to us then—like she'd be standing in the kitchen cooking and be saying, "OK, one plus one is what?" If we say 3, she'd say, "No, you know it's not 3, it's 2," you know. (Clark 1983, 42)

These parenting behaviors suggest the ways in which the home learning environment reinforces school expectations. Enhancing the congruence between home and school learning patterns may be an important strategy for mediating the limitations of impoverished inner-city schools.

Lincoln and Lillie Harrison illustrate the importance of indirect parental behaviors as well. While some parents concentrate on specific learning tasks that mirror the school curriculum, others provide encouragement and support:

> Like many ghetto parents Lincoln and Lillie place a great value on education for their children. . . . The Harrisons have translated their concern into several positive steps aimed at encouraging their children to stay in school and excel. This is one area in which the use of positive emotional rewards is most apparent. Both parents make it a deliberate point of complimenting and praising each effort of their children—good report cards, special honors, even satisfactory homework assignments are celebrated. (Tatje 1974, 185–186)

While expressive strategies sometimes reflect limited parental education, they nevertheless play a critical role in keeping children attached to school authority, classroom routines, teacher directives, and conventional peers.

The qualitative data highlight additional skills untapped by conventional measures that poor children learn (see also Burton 1991; Hippler 1971; Ladner 1971; Rainwater 1970; Schulz 1969; Stack 1974; Valentine 1978; Williams 1981). Mrs. Todd assisted her children with in-home literacy skills and taught them important independence skills. The fieldworker observed:

> At less than a year, Shirley was seated at the table with her brothers and sister with a plate of food before her just like the rest. . . . [A]t the ages of two and three, Mrs. Todd's children had made considerable progress in dressing themselves. (Jeffers 1967, 63)

Similarly, Harriet Jones provided formal educational experiences that were supplemented with a real-world education. The fieldworker observed:

> She took her children everywhere: to plays, to museums, to the park. . . . Often, Daniel came to Harriet's place of work, bringing Carla, and she took them somewhere after work—to the zoo, shopping, or to their grandparents' house. . . . Harriet believed that her children should learn responsibility early in life. . . . She put her children on the bus and sent them anywhere in the city. . . . [She believed] they should not be too sheltered. . . . She often sent Daniel, who was ten years old, on errands. He and Carla [age 4] knew how to dry clothes at the laundromat. . . . At home, both children answered the phone for Harriet and were taught how to take messages when she was not there. (Aschenbrenner 1975, 81)

In both the Todd and Jones families early independence training allowed the children to manage in the multiple contexts in which they had to live. These examples also suggest that poor children assume skills and behaviors typically associated with later developmental stages. Early independence training is, in part, related to family and neighborhood characteristics. Within poor neighborhoods, the lack of family resources often encourages parents to accelerate some aspects of their children's development. Similarly, some parents recognize that children will need skills that will help them navigate in the local community as well as in the larger society and its institutions.

ETHNIC DIVERSITY AND FAMILY FUNCTIONING

Brooks-Gunn, Chase-Lansdale, Gordon, and Klebanov (see chapters 4 and 5 of volume 1) have identified circumstances under which neighborhood effects are prominent. According to their findings, neighborhood ethnic diversity negatively impacts white children, and high neighborhood socioeconomic status (SES) does not positively affect African American children (see also Brooks-Gunn et al. 1993; Klebanov, Brooks-Gunn, and Duncan 1994). Qualitative descriptions of the social climate, or the nature of social relations between residents of different races and social classes, provide clues as to the processes underlying the quantitative findings.

Two ethnographic studies have described how some white residents respond to local or nearby African American families, suggesting why ethnic diversity negatively affects white children. In Garrison Heights, a working-class white neighborhood in a northeastern city, a general climate of hostility and intimidation permeated social relations:

> Garrison Heights, and other neighborhoods like it, are held together by a fierce racism that helps contain the almost constant internal frictions and political infighting within the community. Heighters are brought up from early childhood to defend their territory from the encroachment of blacks, who reside nearby. (Furstenberg 1993, 245)

A similar pattern was found in Clarendon Heights, another working-class white neighborhood. According to a local teen, Shorty:

> [O]nce more and more black families moved in, they said, "Wow, we can overrun these people. We can overpower them." That's what their attitude was (Macleod 1995, 43).

Frankie, a friend of Shorty, provides a more disturbing account:

> [W]hen I grew up here, when I was [sic] fucking second, third, grade, there was racial riots right in front of my window every night. My brothers I have seven brothers, were all out there . . . stabbin' niggers, beating niggers up. I was brought up thinking fucking niggers suck. Went over to the Hoover School, no fuckin' black people there at all. . . . [W]e had one black kid. His name was Sonny. . . . [E]veryone fucked him up. . . . I was brought up to hate niggers. (MacLeod 1995, 37).

These examples suggest that some white residents view neighborhood change as a challenge to ethnic group dominance and control (see chapter 4).

The presence of African American families connotes to long-time white residents a decline in neighborhood quality. This perception appears to have implications for parenting behaviors. Observations from Kerryville, a neighborhood in an eastern city and Norman Street, in Brooklyn, New York, two white working-class neighborhoods undergoing varying stages of racial transition, describe how white residents segregated themselves and their children from minority families:

> Families who remain behind . . . bemoan the breakdown of social ties and the loss of community consensus. Kerryville parents feel that they have been invaded by outsiders and deserted by insiders. . . . Many now refuse to allow their children to participate in recreational programs that attract Puerto Ricans or African Americans, complaining that they will be exposed to drugs or threatened by violence. (Furstenberg 1993, 251)

The process of segregation potentially has negative consequences for white children, whose neighborhood activities are constricted as a result of parental fears (see also DeSena 1990; LaRuffia 1988; Susser 1982; Wrobel 1979).

Qualitative studies offer clues as to why residence in an affluent neighborhood might not positively affect African American children (over and above issues related to the proportion of affluent black and white neighbors; see chapter 11 of volume 1). Although the experience of low-income African Americans in affluent neighborhoods has been poorly documented in qualitative studies, Anderson's (1990) observations of a multiclass, multiethnic gentrifying neighborhood suggests critical social dynamics. The following example is particularly insightful. A white, middle-class resident described his interaction with Marvin, an African American child who lived in the nearby African American ghetto. He said:

> My son Jonathan has a young black friend named Marvin. . . . I had met Marvin a few times because I had been involved in the school. He's a bright, energetic kid, you know, a very good student. He popped up at the door the other morning at about 8:00. . . . A lot of things went through my mind at first. . . . Why is he here? . . . Should I let Marvin in? And I feel this fear. And I say, Why am I afraid of letting a six- or seven-year-old black child come in? . . . [T]hese feelings go against what I've been saying I want for my child, you know, to be in an integrated school, and his friends should be black and of all different nationalities, but here I am a little bit nervous about it. I think, well, is Marvin going to be connected up with drugs when he gets older? Is Jonathan going to be a friend of a child who is going to be connected up with drugs? (Anderson 1990, 147–48)

While clearly self-conscious about his own preconceptions, this middle-class father, like residents in working-class neighborhood, holds fears about his son's friendship with African American children. Already at the age of six or seven, Marvin is considered likely to engage in criminal behavior at some point.

Tatum's (1987) study of middle-class African American families in a predominantly white and affluent neighborhood provides another example. Her work suggests a social climate that potentially reduces the positive benefits of residence in affluent neighborhoods. Further, Tatum's work highlights how race is more important than social class in the treatment of families in this particular neighborhood. An African American father commented on his children's experiences in the neighborhood. He said:

> Well, my kids came and told me that my neighbor won't let her kids play with my kids. And my little daughter, she don't know anything about being prejudiced . . . so she comes and tells us this. We know what's going on. . . . They are teaching their kids resentment or making them think that they're better than so-and-so's kids (Tatum 1987, 70).

A more blatant example of racism was recounted by another parent:

> Imagine the dismay of a newly-arrived mother when the school official she has called for information advises her in no uncertain terms to avoid those schools with black children in them. Assuming this mother, whose child has been in a private Montessori kindergarten, must, of course, be white like himself, he makes no effort to hide his racism. She does not inform him of his error, but instead listens with amazement to what he has to say. (Tatum 1987, 57–58)

Like the African American families in white working-class neighborhoods, middle-class African American families also confront racism. While examples of direct violence and intimidation appear to be less prominent in more-affluent neighborhoods, African American families' access to resources is circumscribed in all cases. Although more-affluent neighborhoods have better resources, including schools, playgrounds, and better-educated families, an antagonistic social climate negates to some degree the benefits of residence. African American residents are excluded from neighboring relations that potentially include communal child-care assistance; they are also excluded from long-standing social networks that provide information and access to local resources. The examples from Anderson's and Tatum's works, as well as examples from the experiences of white working-class neighborhoods undergoing racial change, suggest another critical point: poor African American families experience stressors in both poor and more-affluent neighborhoods.

CONCEPTUAL AND THEORETICAL IMPLICATIONS
OF THE QUALITATIVE DATA

The key constructs (neighborhood, family, and child competence) and guiding theories (neighborhood resource and collective socialization), in light of the qualitative observations, warrant examination.

CONSTRUCTS

NEIGHBORHOOD-LEVEL CONSTRUCTS   In volume 1, the authors of chapters 4 and 5 used geographic and demographic dimensions—as conceptualized by census tracts and SES of neighbors, concentration of families, ethnic diversity, and male joblessness—to measure neighborhoods. The qualitative examples expand on geographic definitions by revealing how social relationships shape neighborhood boundaries. Family definitions of neighborhoods do not always conform to census tracts. For some families, *neighborhood* is defined by perceptions of personal danger and their ability to manage it. Such perceptions can contract neighborhood boundaries, discouraging the use of the larger geographic area. For other families, *neighborhood* is defined by kinship and the institutional attachments they generate. Such bonds can expand neighborhood boundaries, encouraging the use of multiple census tracts.

The qualitative data also expand on demographic profiles by describing the social dynamics behind key dimensions. Demographic profiles—the number of people in a neighborhood and their ethnicity, or social status—reflect only one aspect of neighborhoods. Equally important are how these composite factors interact to create particular neighborhood climates. More precisely, neighborhoods' demographic features influence the nature of relationships that residents have with one another. Neighborhoods characterized by ethnic diversity and socioeconomic variability, for example, can generate intergroup tensions that constrain the quality of parenting and child development.

These qualitative insights encourage broader conceptualizations of neighborhood that include geographic, demographic, and social dimensions. An expanded formulation more accurately captures intraneighborhood dynamics, interneighborhood linkages, and specific local neighborhood conditions (see also Olson 1982; Wireman 1984).

FAMILY-LEVEL CONSTRUCTS   The authors of chapters 4 and 5 in volume 1 used demographic characteristics of the mother—including school-completion level, family structure (female headship or two parents), maternal age at giving birth, maternal employment, and family income-to-needs ratio—to measure family conditions. The qualitative illustrations expand on compositional variables by identifying internal family dynamics embedded in these demographic dimensions. They explicate key processes that families use to manage in impoverished neighborhoods, including neighborhood protection strategies, parental monitoring strategies, and resource-seeking strategies. Qualitative studies reveal internal dynamics that allow families to strategically respond to neighborhood impoverishment. These qualitative insights encourage a broader conceptualization of families that includes their internal processes. An expanded formulation reveals precisely what it is about particular family compositional variables that leads to specific child outcomes.

CHILD COMPETENCE   In volume 1, cognitive functioning and behavioral functioning—as assessed by the Wechsler Preschool and Primary Scale of Intelligence, the Peabody Picture Vocabulary Test, and problem behaviors—were used to measure child developmental competence. The qualitative data expand on these indicators of developmental competence by highlighting parent–child interactions and family processes that support intellectual abilities. In-home learning strategies, both instrumental and expressive, foster cognitive development for some poor African American children, as demonstrated in the quantitative work involving the Home Observation for Measurement of the Environment (HOME) scale (Brooks-Gunn, Klebanov, and Duncan 1996; Chase-Lansdale et al. vol. 1; Klebanov, Brooks-Gunn, and Duncan 1994, vol. 1). Moreover, the qualitative data reveal a range of child developmental skills untapped by preselected measures.

These qualitative insights encourage broader conceptualizations of child competence that include conventional indicators of child development, as well as those specific to impoverished neighborhood settings. Indeed, *competence* takes its meaning from the specific setting in which it occurs. Different settings have different demands, leading to a variety of child development abilities and skills. Competencies that are relevant to mainstream settings, as well as those specific to the local community, should be examined (see Aber et al. vol. 1).

THEORIES OF NEIGHBORHOODS

NEIGHBORHOOD RESOURCE THEORY   Neighborhood resource theory argues that the quality of local resources available for families and their children affects developmental outcomes. Neighborhoods with an extensive array of good, accessible services, such as parks, libraries, and child-care facilities, provide more extrafamilial experiences, which in turn are associated with better cognitive and behavioral outcomes. Conversely, neighborhoods lacking good, accessible services restrict extrafamilial experiences, which in turn are associated with poorer cognitive and behavioral outcomes (Brooks-Gunn, Denner, and Klebanov 1995).

Qualitative insights refine and expand on neighborhood resource theory by identifying social processes in impoverished and affluent neighborhoods that contradict expected outcomes. These include parental strategies that foster positive child outcomes in poor neighborhoods and intergroup relations that impede optimal child development in affluent neighborhoods.

Unquestionably, as resource theory hypothesizes, impoverished African American neighborhoods have fewer institutional and social resources than more-affluent neighborhoods (Brooks-Gunn et al. 1993; Gephart, vol. 1). Further, there is ample reason to expect better development outcomes based on residence in affluent neighborhoods than in impoverished ones. However, as the qualitative examples indicate, neighborhood protection strategies, parental monitoring strategies, and parental resource-seeking strategies in low-income neighborhoods obviate the deleterious effects of neighborhood impoverishment on child development. Some parents can generate good-quality experiences and resources that positively affect child outcomes. Further, racial group tensions that lead to restricted neighboring relations, withdrawal from neighborhood activities, and exclusionary social networks in affluent neighborhoods diminish the positive effects of neighborhood affluence on child outcomes. Racial tensions generate an antagonistic neighborhood climate that negatively affects parenting and child development (see chapter 4).

These examples suggest that it is not merely the absence or presence of resources, or the quality or quantity of resources, within neighborhoods that influences parenting and development (although clearly they are still important). It is access to resources as mediated by parenting skills, family resources, and social relationships that may prove to be most important. In impoverished neighborhoods, competent parents can identify and access local resources, and affiliated parents can use network contacts to access extralocal resources. In more-affluent neighborhoods, antagonistic interclass and interracial neighboring relations can constrain access to high-quality resources.

COLLECTIVE SOCIALIZATION THEORY   According to collective socialization theory, impoverished neighborhoods with more unemployed adults and single-parent households provide role models that eschew conventional emphases on school achievement, work skills, family organization, future orientations, and self-efficacy. In contrast, affluent neighborhoods with more working adults and two-parent families provide stronger normative support and conventional role models for school achievement, work skills, family patterns, future orientations, and self-efficacy. In both settings, albeit with different outcomes, local adults are major influences on the lives of parents and their children. In impoverished neighborhoods, parents receive little communal support for child rearing. To the contrary, the presence of adults who are involved in unconventional lifestyles and behaviors poses physical and moral risks to children's development. In affluent neighborhoods, parents receive multiple sources of support for child rearing. The presence of cooperating adults who are involved in conventional lifestyles and behaviors reinforces conventional paths for child development.

Qualitative insights refine and expand on key tenets of collective socialization theory by identifying processes in impoverished neighborhoods that challenge expected outcomes. These include parental strategies that mediate the negative role-modeling effects of unconventional neighbors and family coalitions that function in the absence of communal child support.

Parents in poor communities use neighborhood protection strategies, child-monitoring strategies, and restricted neighboring relations to buffer themselves and their children from ghetto-specific neighborhood influences and role models. These interaction strategies allow some poor families and their children to lead mainstream lives within impoverished neighborhoods, despite the presence of neighbors who participate in unconventional lifestyles. These residents literally inhabit the same physical space, but coexist in separate social worlds. While residential propinquity is one condition associated with role modeling, it is not a sufficient basis for asserting causality. Residential propinquity is not a clear-cut indicator of social interaction.

Qualitative insights also expand on the issue of communal support for parenting in impoverished neighborhoods. Recent qualitative studies indicate, like neighborhood socialization theory, a decline in the availability of local adults who provide additional care, support, and supervision of children. However, the qualitative observations suggest that families respond to limited adult support by greater reliance on individual parents or greater reliance on extended kin. In the absence of wider neighborhood support, parents adapt an individualistic parenting style (see, for example, chapter 2), whereby they alone are responsible for child care, or a communal parenting style, in which kin members jointly are responsible for child care. The neighborhood collectivism that reportedly characterized the care of African American children in the past, for some families, is reduced to family and kin networks (Anderson, 1990; Wilson 1987). These examples suggest that while broad neighborhood support that reinforces parenting efforts is desirable, alternative parenting strategies can effectively foster positive child outcomes as well.

IMPLICATIONS FOR STUDYING NEIGHBORHOODS AND CHILDREN

As discussed thus far, the quantitative data identified important variables, frequencies, and patterns derived from statistical associations, while the related qualitative data identified social processes and meanings embedded in these statistical relationships (see, for example, Rank 1992). Together, these data yielded a broader and more detailed understanding of neighborhood effects. However, new qualitative research is needed that explores African Americans' experiences in affluent settings, since the bulk of qualitative information on family and neighborhood processes derives from low-income populations and settings. Comparative studies that focus on family experiences in a variety of neighborhood settings can help isolate family and neighborhood influences. Moreover, comparative designs should include the family and neighborhood experiences of various ethnic and racial groups.

Further, new qualitative research is needed that focuses on contemporary families and neighborhoods. The studies discussed in this chapter indicate that increasing neighborhood impoverishment has placed greater management pressures on families. Yet many of the same management strategies remain constant over time. What is unclear, however, is the effectiveness of these patterns in light of new environmental constraints. New ethnographies can update older baseline studies, highlighting continuity and change in neighborhood conditions and family adaptational strategies and capabilities.

Future qualitative research concerned with neighborhood effects on family life and child development will also need to focus on the experiences of young children. Studies of adolescents are relatively more plentiful. Yet we need to know more about the antecedent stages of development of young children in impoverished neighborhoods. Ethnographic observation of young children is strongly indicated, reflecting not only the paucity of information but also the constraints in interviewing young children.

Finally, more qualitative research is needed to address family variability within neighborhoods. While this discussion concentrated on families that obviate the negative effects of neighborhood impoverishment, similar attention should be given to families that are faring less well. In particular, research should concentrate on specific family processes that amplify families' vulnerability.

The observations from this paper suggest the need for collaborative multimethod studies as well. Research concerned with neighborhood and family influences on child development should include both qualitative and quantitative approaches. Qualitative case studies can specify relevant variables, describe neighborhood dynamics, reveal parenting processes, and elucidate child outcomes. Informed by qualitative insights, quantitative research can address the representativeness and generalizability of case study observations. The study of child development within the context of neighborhood settings signals a new and challenging area of inquiry. Clearly, parenting processes and individual development cannot be understood independent of the context in which they occur. Within this intellectual arena, collaborative qualitative and quantitative studies will be the most substantively and theoretically insightful. These types of studies suggest the promise of truly multimethod research.

This paper was funded by awards from the William T. Grant Foundation; a National Science Foundation Award for the Study of Race, Urban Poverty, and Social Policy; a grant from the Social Science Research Council's Program on the Urban Underclass; and a Visiting Scholar Award from the Russell Sage Foundation. Jeanne Brooks-Gunn, Geraldine Brookings, Linda Burton, Thomas Cook, Greg J. Duncan, Martha Gephart, Katherine Newman, Margaret Spencer, and members of the Social Science Research Council's Working Group on Communities and Neighborhoods, Family Processes and Individual Development made helpful comments on earlier drafts of this paper. Deanne Orput and Robin Draper expertly assisted in the review of the qualitativestudies, and Denise Daniels skillfully assisted in preparation of the manuscript.

4

Understanding the Neighborhood Context for Children and Families: Combining Epidemiological and Ethnographic Approaches

Jill E. Korbin and Claudia J. Coulton

In this chapter we report on our ongoing research in Cleveland, Ohio, that has combined epidemiologic and ethnographic methods to examine the impact of neighborhood factors on families and children. Specifically, we will focus on the relationship between the aggregate data analysis and findings from the ethnographic component of our research. The aggregate data analysis is reported in detail elsewhere (Coulton et al. 1995), as are other findings from the ethnographic study (Korbin and Coulton 1994, 1996). For the purposes of this chapter, findings from the ethnographic study will be linked to the major factors identified in the aggregate analysis. As noted in previous chapters, the impact of neighborhood conditions on children and families is experiencing a resurgence of interest (see, for example, Brooks-Gunn et al. 1993). An ecological perspective has been an important paradigm in child development theory and research (see, for example, Aber et al. vol. 1; Belsky 1980; Bronfenbrenner 1979, 1988; Cicchetti and Lynch 1993; Garbarino 1977; Pence 1988). Developmentalists using an ecological perspective have viewed neighborhoods as part of the exosystem affecting child development. Among other things, this exosystem is seen as being a source of both stressors and resources. Bronfenbrenner has expanded his vision of an ecological perspective to encompass both neighborhood ecology as experienced (1979) and as objectively measured (1988).

Anthropological and cross-cultural research on child rearing and socialization has traditionally examined the impact of the larger social and environmental context (see, for example, LeVine, Miller, and West 1988; Super and Harkness 1980; Weisner 1984; Whiting 1963; Whiting and Edwards 1988; Whiting and Whiting 1975). In addition to using cross-cultural work, anthropologists and sociologists have applied an in-depth, in-context approach to the study of poverty and urban settings, with the neighborhood context either implicitly or explicitly included. Few ethnographic studies, however, have focused directly on understanding the impact of differing neighborhood contexts on children and families. A notable exception in this regard is Furstenberg's (1993) research on parenting strategies in neighborhoods that pose different risks for children and youth. Anderson (1990, 1994), while not comparing different neighborhoods, has described two distinct and competing sets of roles for teens within neighborhoods—a more-conventional, middleclass, "decent" role and a "streetwise" role.

The study of neighborhood influences on children and families has been approached through aggregate statistical analyses, multilevel regression models, and ethnographic studies. All of these approaches have their strengths and limitations. Only occasionally have these approaches been combined, as in the work of Garbarino and colleagues (Garbarino and Crouter 1978; Garbarino and Kostelny 1992; Garbarino and Sherman 1980) on child maltreatment and the work of Maccoby, Johnson, and Church (1958) on neighborhoods with varying rates of juvenile delinquency.

Ethnographic descriptions of neighborhoods and their inhabitants have provided in-depth, contextual portraits of the realities of daily life. Ethnographic studies frequently have involved a relatively small number of individuals within a circumscribed geographic location (see, for example, Liebow 1966; Whyte 1955) or social network, as with the kin and friendship networks of African American women (see, for example, Stack 1974) or groups such as gangs (see, for example, Keiser 1969). Jarrett's (1994) recent ethnographic portrait of poor women underscored the importance of women's dynamic role in responding to the structural constraints of poverty (see also chapter 9). Ethnographic research has furthered our understanding of such diverse topics as the coping strategies of mentally retarded individuals living in the community (Edgerton 1993), terminally ill children (Bluebond-Langner 1978), health care, and low birth weight (see, for example, Boone 1989). Ethnographic portraits are rich, contextual, and aimed specifically at eliciting the perspective, understanding, and experience of those being studied. Ethnographic studies often provide insights that elude statistical measurement. At the same time, questions about the representativeness of the neighborhoods and individuals studied and the difficulties of replicating labor-intensive ethnographies challenges the generalizability of ethnographic findings.

Aggregate statistical measures of neighborhood conditions have contributed to our understanding of the association between poverty and related structural conditions and negative outcomes for children (see, for example, Brooks-Gunn et al. 1993; Duncan, Brooks-Gunn, and Klebanov 1994). These analyses, in which neighborhood is usually represented by census tracts, are powerful in their large sample size and generalizable findings. They also employ data that are readily available at the census-tract level, making replication feasible. On the other hand, statistical analyses at the census-tract level cannot elaborate the processes involved as neighborhood residents negotiate their living circumstances. Poor neighborhoods differ from one another in many subtle but important ways (Coulton and

Pandey 1992). Furthermore, children and families influence one another as they respond to their community surroundings.

STUDY METHODS

Our research has sought to actively combine multiple methods and approaches. This chapter reports on research combining aggregate-level analysis of the association between macrostructural factors and outcomes related to families and children at the census-tract level with ethnographic study of census tracts representing different rates of outcomes related to families and children including child abuse and neglect reports.[1]

AGGREGATE ANALYSIS

The units of analysis for the aggregate component were the 177 residential census tracts in Cleveland. A census tract has an average of two thousand residents and was chosen because it is the unit of analysis for which numerous types of data are readily available. It is also large enough to allow the calculation of rates, yet small enough to approximate a neighborhood reasonably. Unfortunately, census tracts do not necessarily represent the neighborhood as it would be defined by residents and may be more heterogeneous than would be true of the residents' perceived neighborhood.[2]

The aggregate analysis used available measures (see table 4.1) of outcome variables, including child maltreatment, violent crime, drug trafficking, juvenile delinquency, teen pregnancy, and low-birth-weight births. Indicators of community structure were also drawn from available data at the level of the census tract. Principal components analysis revealed three orthogonal factors. We have labeled them impoverishment, instability, and child-care burden (Coulton et al. 1995; see chapter 1 and Duncan and Aber [vol. 1] for a discussion of other factor analytic descriptions of neighborhoods).

ETHNOGRAPHIC STUDY

Thirteen census tracts were included in the ethnographic study. Census tracts were selected to represent high, medium, and low child abuse and neglect report rates, as defined by being one standard deviation above or below the mean report rate for Cleveland's 177 residential census tracts of 36.3 per thousand children ($SD = 20.7$). Predominantly African American and predominantly white neighborhoods were included in the high-, medium-, and low-rate types.[3]

The ethnographic component included interviews with neighborhood residents and with owners and managers of local businesses; informal observations of and structured discussions with various personnel at churches, libraries, recreation centers, and other organizations such as block clubs in

TABLE 4.1   Variable Definitions for Aggregate Analysis

Variable	Definition	Source
Indicators of community structures		
Poverty rate	% poor persons, 1990	1990 Census, STF3
Unemployment rate	% residents unemployed	1990 Census, STF3
Vacant housing	% vacant housing units	1990 Census, STF1
Population loss	% 1980–1990 population	1990 Census, STF1
Movement, 85–90	% who moved between 1985–1990	1990 Census, STF3
Tenure <10 years	% households in current residence less than 10 years	1990 Census, STF3
Recent movement, 89–90	% households that moved in one year	1990 Census, STF3
Family headship	% households with children that are female-headed	1990 Census, STF1
Child/adult ratio	# of child(0–12)/# of adults(21+)	1990 Census, STF1
Male/female ratio	adult male(21–64)/adult female(21–64)	1990 Census, STF2
Elderly population	% population that is over 65 years old	1990 Census, STF1
Percent black	% residents classified as black	1990 Census, STF1
Contiguous to concentrated poverty	Contiguous to poor or non-poor tracts (0 = borders no poor tracts, 1 = borders one or more poor tracts)	1990 Census, STF3
Behavioral outcomes		
Child maltreatment rate	maltreatment children/1000 children population (0–17 years old)	1991 Cuyahoga County Department of Human Services
Violent crime	FBI index crimes against persons/1000 population	1990 Cleveland Police
Drug trafficking	drug arrests/1000 population	1990 Cleveland Police
Juvenile delinquency	juvenile filings/1000 teenagers (12–17)	1990 Cuyahoga County Juvenile Court
Teen childbearing	births to teens (12–17)/1000 teen females (12–17)	1990 Birth Certificate Tape, Ohio Department of Health
Low birth weight births	low birth weight (≤2,500 gm) births/1000 live births	1990 Birth Certificate Tape, Ohio Department of Health

Source: Coulton et al. 1995.

the neighborhoods. This chapter focuses primarily on ethnographic interviews with neighborhood residents (*n* = 121). Ethnographic interviews are generally open-ended and are designed both to obtain in-depth answers to questions posed and to elicit additional information not directly sought (Bernard 1994; Spradley 1979).

Neighborhood residents (*n* = 121) were contacted through churches, block groups, community organizations, libraries, and recreation centers. While the sample is not representative of all neighborhood residents, we sought individuals who were involved in and knowledgeable about their neighborhood. We termed these people "knowledgeable neighbors." Ethnographers were matched by ethnicity with neighborhoods, and, to reduce bias, were not informed of neighborhood rates of child maltreatment reports. Because all of the neighborhoods were low- to moderate-income urban neighborhoods, the ethnographers had little factual basis from which to guess rates of child maltreatment reports.

CHILD-CARE BURDEN AND THE SUPERVISION AND CONTROL OF NEIGHBORHOOD CHILDREN

The aggregate analysis indicated the importance of a factor we termed child care burden, which reflects the ratio of children to adults. In the ethnographic interviews, the issue of supervision of and intervention with neighborhood children emerged as among the most important concerns of neighborhood residents and amplified the findings from the aggregate analysis.

AGGREGATE ANALYSIS

In the aggregate analysis of our child maltreatment study, the factor termed child-care burden had a significant effect (but a somewhat weaker effect than impoverishment) on all child outcomes. This factor included the ratio of children to adults, the ratio of males to females, and the percentage of the population that is elderly. Areas that had the combination of many children per adult, few elderly residents, and a low proportion of adult males were at the highest risk of adverse child outcomes. These were the areas in which the number of adults available to supervise, care for, and support children, and to involve themselves in neighborhood social institutions, may have been low. In Coleman's (1987) terminology, they may have had insufficient levels of social capital.

ETHNOGRAPHIC INTERVIEWS

In the ethnographic interviews, we sought to elaborate on the meaning and impact of a high ratio of children to adults from the perspective of neighborhood adults. This domain was of particular interest to us because of its tie to Coleman's (1987) concept of social capital and Furstenberg's (1993) analysis of differences in parenting strategies in response to neighborhood conditions. Connections among adults and the perceived abilities of adults to affect the behavior of neighborhood children quickly emerged as an important theme in ethnographic interviews. Residents of neighborhoods with high rates of child maltreatment reports and other adverse outcomes perceived their neighborhoods as settings in which they and their neighbors were the least able to intervene in or control the behavior of neighborhood children.

Most of these residents believed that they were living in vastly changed circumstances from their own childhoods. The overwhelming majority (88 percent; n = 107) felt that someone would have made them, as children, behave if their parents were not present. The tenor of their remarks was that any adult had the authority to enforce good behavior. Other adults could reprimand or physically punish, and certainly would inform the parents about their child's misbehavior. A common response was that when they were children, they would have been disciplined twice, first by the intervening adult and then again by their parents for behaving badly enough to warrant another adult's attention. To paraphrase one resident, "The parent would punish the child and thank the neighbor."[4]

In contrast, 32 percent of residents (n = 36) reported that someone would intervene nowadays if a child was misbehaving. A number of themes emerged as residents explained why they would not intervene in child misbehavior in their neighborhoods. First, residents expressed the belief that parents would take the child's side. Some residents expressed bewilderment as to why parents would believe a misbehaving child over a responsible adult. To paraphrase a woman in her early eighties living in an African American neighborhood with a medium child maltreatment report rate:

Parents stick with what their children say. A mother will even bring the child to your door and ask the child right in front of you if they did what you said they did. The child will lie and say no, and the mother will believe the child.

Second, residents alluded to a situation in which parents have very different standards about child care and child behavior. Bad behavior in their eyes, then, was not necessarily bad behavior in the eyes of the child's parent. For example, residents reported that young children were outside unattended and unsupervised, even after dark. This was a particular concern in the neighborhoods with medium and high child maltreatment report rates. Residents assumed that if the parents did not care where their children were, they certainly would not care what they were doing or if they were misbehaving. In the high-rate neighborhoods, leaving a child unsupervised was less likely to be viewed as abusive or neglectful than in the medium- or low-rate neighborhoods (Korbin and Coulton 1994).

Third, residents were concerned that the child's parents would be angry with them for becoming involved at all with their child, disrupting relationships among neighborhood adults. Residents expressed the ethic of neighbors minding their own business and of child rearing being a family matter. Residents were concerned that anger among neighbors made day-to-day living more unpleasant.

Fourth, residents expressed frustration that past intervention not only had been unsuccessful at resolving problems but also could exacerbate the situation. A woman in her early twenties in a white neighborhood with a low child maltreatment report rate recounted such a string of incidents (paraphrased):

> Our neighbors have two young boys who are very destructive, they break windows and everything. I've tried saying something to the mother, but she says that she can't do anything about it. He's snuck down into the basement [at a business in the neighborhood] and broken the windows. If you try to talk to him, it aggravates him and he does worse things.

And fifth, residents were concerned about retaliation from parents and children. Residents commented that parents would yell or swear at them, or come after them with knives or guns. Disturbingly, a degree of the hesitancy to intervene also was tied to fear that children and adolescents would verbally assault or physically retaliate. The following comments (paraphrased) of a male resident in his mid-forties in a white high-rate neighborhood illustrate this point:

> Before, neighbors treated all children like their own. Now no one would step in. People don't want to step on other people's toes. And if they do step in, sometimes the kids or even the parents get nasty. Just a few days ago, there was a woman walking down the sidewalk by our house. She had a little boy with her who was throwing rocks at our dogs. I told the boy to stop it, and the mother turned around and said all kinds of words I can't repeat. Then the little kid repeated exactly what she said.

Residents of neighborhoods with high (n = 10; 26.3 percent), medium (n = 10; 26.3 percent), and low (n = 9; 20.0 percent) rates of child maltreatment reports were similar in expressing fear of retaliation by parents. However, residents of neighborhoods with high rates of child maltreatment reports (n = 10; 26.3 percent) more frequently expressed concerns that children or adolescents would verbally or physically retaliate than did residents of neighborhoods with medium (n = 3; 7.9 percent) or low (n = 4; 8.9 percent) rates.

Verbal retaliation by children included swearing, telling the neighbor that he or she was not their parent and therefore had no right to interfere, and threats that the children or their parents would sue the neighbor. Threats of physical harm or property damage also were made by children and adolescents. A few examples paraphrased from interviews illustrate this point:

A teenage grandson of a woman in her mid-fifties in an African American neighborhood with a high child maltreatment report rate interrupted his grandmother to explain to the interviewer that nobody would step in because (paraphrased): "[The child] might pull out an Uzi and call one of his boys and put you on a hit list."

Similarly, in a high-rate white neighborhood, a male resident in his late thirties explained that people were reluctant to reprimand other people's children because (paraphrased): "[The children] might try to burn the house down or something like that."

Several residents reported incidents in which children and adolescents had retaliated against them for trying to intervene in their behavior. A woman in her mid-thirties in a medium-rate white neighborhood recounted the following story:

> A few years ago there was a fourteen-year-old boy who lived on my street who collected weapons like nunchuks [martial arts weapons] and switchblade knives. I caught him throwing his switchblades at trees, and he was teaching my son, who was six, how to do it. I asked him to stop throwing at trees and told my son he wasn't allowed to play with him anymore. But the boy's parents said that he could do whatever he wanted, and he continued knifing my trees. I ended up going to court. The parents of the kid said that he wasn't doing anything wrong. The police confiscated his weapons. Then the boy and his older friends starting hanging around my house to intimidate me. I went back to court and got a restraining order so that he had to cross to the other side of the street to even go past my house.

While fear of child retaliation was reported more often by residents of neighborhoods with high child maltreatment report rates, residents in low-rate neighborhoods were not immune. To paraphrase a female resident of a low-rate African American neighborhood in her mid-fifties:

> They would yell vulgarities at you. I heard they would hit you, I've never seen it, but it's enough to scare you. And I know youth carry weapons. It's very intimidating.

The aggregate analysis found that neighborhoods with high rates of child maltreatment reports also had high rates of crime, drug trafficking, teen childbearing, and juvenile delinquency (Coulton et al. 1996). The ethnographic interviews mesh with this finding in suggesting that residents view themselves and their neighbors as unable to control child and adolescent behavior. While residents of Cleveland's neighborhoods are expressing a wider public concern about crime, including the fear of young criminals, the high- and medium-rate neighborhoods were the most fearful of child and adolescent retaliation.

Ethnographic interviews, then, suggest that residents of neighborhoods with high child maltreatment report rates believe that they and their neighbors have great difficulty in controlling child behavior. While residents of all neighborhood-rate types reported fear of retaliation by parents if they intervened in child misbehavior, residents of high-rate neighborhoods were also fearful of the children and adolescents. A high proportion of children to adults found in the aggregate analysis, then, was coupled with increased hesitancy and fear about intervening in the children's behavior identified in the ethnographic component of our study.

In the ethnographic interviews, however, we directly explored only the issue of intervention in child misbehavior. The nature of ethnographic research is to facilitate discussion about unasked matters from the perspective of those being studied. While hesitant to intervene in child misbehavior, some residents also expressed the notion that adults still had a responsibility to come to the aid of children needing help in the neighborhood. A lost and wandering child or a child needing attention became the subject of anecdotes related by residents.

The theme of helping children in need arose again when residents were asked what neighbors could do about child abuse and neglect. More than half of the residents across all neighborhood-rate types (n = 71; 59 percent) said that neighbors should report child abuse and neglect. The second most frequent response (n = 53; 44 percent) was that neighbors should intervene and try to help one another. Proposed intervention by neighbors took the form of talking to the parent, child, or other neighbors or of offering help to the parent (Korbin and Coulton 1994, 1996).

Further, similar to Furstenberg's findings (1993), the ethnographic interviews yielded a theme of the importance of parental vigilance in dangerous neighborhoods. As an example, a male resident in his mid-forties in a white neighborhood with a high child-maltreatment report rate expressed this concept (paraphrased):

> You need to do more parenting here because of the crime. Other things like all of the broken glass in the streets also make it difficult. If the kids go out into the street they get cut. . . . We can't let them play outside alone. In the suburbs you don't have as many blatant hazards like broken glass.

IMPOVERISHMENT, GEOGRAPHIC-ECONOMIC ISOLATION, AND NEIGHBORHOOD RESOURCES

The strongest predictor in the aggregate analysis was a factor we termed impoverishment. Additionally, the aggregate analysis indicated the importance of the geographic-economic isolation of neighborhoods. The ethnographic study with both neighborhood residents and neighborhood businesses further explained these findings along the dimension of resources available in the neighborhood.

AGGREGATE ANALYSIS

In the aggregate analysis, the impoverishment factor had the greatest effect on adverse outcomes for children (Coulton et al. 1995). The impoverishment factor comprised six variables: poverty rate, unemployment rate, vacant housing, population loss, female-headed households, and race. This factor represented the overall economic disadvantage experienced in neighborhoods that are disinvested, have high joblessness, and have many one-parent families. Segregation and discrimination have resulted in these areas being disproportionately African American. In other words, areas with the highest rates on all outcomes were those with the intertwined conditions of poverty, unemployment, female-headed households, segregation of African Americans, abandoned housing, and population loss (see Duncan and Aber vol. 1). These are the kinds of neighborhoods that have proliferated during the past two decades and have caused considerable debate about whether these areas are becoming home to a so-called underclass (Ricketts and Sawhill 1988; Wilson 1987).

Another factor in the aggregate analysis (Coulton et al. 1995), the geographic-economic isolation of the tract relative to concentrated poverty areas, also suggested an association between the resources available in a neighborhood and the rates of adverse conditions for children. Because resources in an area can be affected by resources available in nearby areas, we constructed a measure to determine whether each census tract was contiguous with other high-poverty census tracts. Areas that were contiguous to other high-poverty areas had higher maltreatment and delinquency rates, independent of their values or the structural factors associated with community social organization. These two factors of impoverishment and geographic-economic isolation, then, may indicate differences among neighborhoods in the resources that neighbors can access or that they have to offer one another (see chapter 1).

ETHNOGRAPHIC STUDY

The ethnographic interviews also suggested the importance of neighborhood resources. However, objective and subjective impressions did not consistently match. For example, an objective measure of neighborhood quality for children and families might be the presence of a playground with modern play equipment in good repair. One would expect parents and young children to cluster around such a playground resource, becoming acquainted, forming play groups, and sharing information. However, residents in neighborhoods with perceived high crime, delinquency, and drug trafficking extended their vision beyond the state of repair and quality of playground equipment. They viewed the playground as dangerous due to crime, drugs, and gangs and therefore avoided it. Whether or not groups of teenagers represented actual gangs, parents perceived danger in groups of teenagers. This perception was possibly intertwined with the adults' perceived inability to control the behavior of other children and teens, as discussed earlier. Conversely, a dead-end alley or a vacant lot within sight of a well-regarded adult might have been classified as an eyesore by an objective measure but might have been viewed as a neighborhood asset by caregivers of young children. In the ethnographic interviews, a dead-end alley was viewed as a protected, restricted environment, one in which children could experience the freedom of being outdoors without being exposed to danger from traffic or from the neighborhood's deleterious conditions. Parents, too, could accomplish their household chores while being vigilant about their children, as when washing dishes while looking out their kitchen windows.

Along similar lines, small food and convenience stores in some neighborhoods were a mixed blessing. On the one hand, prices were generally higher than in larger grocery or discount stores, thereby draining household resources. On the other hand, these small stores provided a number of advantages to residents. First, and most obviously, they were often within walking distance, increasing access. Second, these small businesses were often responsive to fluctuations in individual neighborhood and family situations. Owners and managers of small food and convenience stores reported that they gave credit to neighborhood residents, letting customers pick up necessities such as a loaf of bread, milk, or baby formula on credit near the end of the month. These small stores also broke packages to sell individual items, making them at once more expensive (and therefore profitable) and more affordable (and therefore accessible). Cigarettes were the most common example. Storeowners or workers sometimes answered our direct question by saying they did not sell single cigarettes, even when displays of single cigarettes were clearly visible. Occasionally, this was explained away as an aberration, as a package having broken earlier in the day. On one occasion, we observed a neighborhood store selling single tampons.

The absence of neighborhood resources had important meaning for residents. Neighborhood residents in some high-rate African American communities took it as a substantial insult, not merely an inconvenience, that there were no banks in the vicinity. They acutely felt the racism that they attributed to banks' fear of crime and skepticism about making a profit in their neighborhoods. Similarly, the lack of other amenities, such as postal drop boxes, indicated a larger societal antipathy toward and neglect of them beyond the inconvenience of having nowhere to mail bills and letters.

INSTABILITY AND POPULATION MOVEMENT

The aggregate analysis indicated the importance of population instability as reflected by movement into, out of, and within the community. Ethnographic interviews suggested that the meaning of population movement for the residents of these neighborhoods was more important than the quantity of movement that was measured statistically.

AGGREGATE ANALYSIS

The factor labeled instability represented the degree to which the area could be characterized by movement of residents, and it included the percent of residents who had moved to, or from, a different house within the past five years, the percent of the households who had lived in their current homes for less than ten years, and the percent of households who had lived in their current homes less than one year.

The instability factor generally had the weakest effect, even though the trends were in the expected direction. However, the harmful effects of instability were almost negligible in the most-impoverished areas, but more significant in better-off areas.

ETHNOGRAPHIC STUDY

Ethnographic interviews elaborated on the meaning of residential mobility. It was not movement alone but the composition of the movement that was salient to residents. There was a difference in whether instability reflected an increase in renters or an increase in homeowners and known individuals. Renters were viewed as a detriment, as individuals who were uncommitted to the neighborhood, and therefore as unpredictable and unreliable. Turnover of renters also meant that neighbors had diminished opportunities to get to know one another. On the other hand, homeowners and known individuals moving back into the neighborhood signaled individuals who would be invested in the community. Home owning had particular symbolic value and salience to residents. Individuals in very impoverished neighborhoods in which new homes were being built clearly saw this construction as an important positive feature of their surroundings.

The ethnographic interviews yielded differences in the nature of transience, or residential movement, particularly in medium-rate African American, versus medium-rate white neighborhoods. Anecdotal data suggested that in the medium-rate African American neighborhoods, adult children of current residents were moving back into the neighborhood with their families. These returning new residents, then, were known to longtime residents, who had known them when they were growing up and who had seen them visiting their parents. They also represented a continuation of home owning, as ownership passed to them directly from their parents. And finally, these returning new residents represented proof that the neighborhood was on a positive trajectory if children of current residents, who could have chosen to live elsewhere, instead were moving back "home."

In contrast, in the predominantly white medium-rate neighborhoods, new neighbors were likely to be unknown to current residents and were regarded suspiciously. New neighbors were likely to be renters, who were viewed as having little commitment to the area. Renters also were regarded with some suspicion as having come from worse circumstances. These new neighbors, then, represented a negative trajectory for the neighborhood. In other white medium- and high-rate neighborhoods, new residents represented gentrification. In this situation the new residents, with more resources, were suspicious of their poorer neighbors, while the longer-term residents viewed the newer residents as a threat to their living conditions. The gentrification was not seen as a benefit by those already living in the neighborhood. They had little expectation that they would benefit by having upscale restaurants and shops. Instead, they viewed these developments as the first step in being pushed out of their homes and neighborhood.

CONCLUSION

The combination of ethnographic and aggregate findings enhances our understanding of the factors that influence children and families in neighborhoods, beyond what would be possible with either methodology alone. This combination of approaches assists us in minimizing errors of interpretation due to either the ecological fallacy, that relationships found at the aggregate level necessarily occur at the individual level, or aggregation effects, that relationships found at the individual level will necessarily occur at the aggregate level (Bronfenbrenner 1979, 1984). A challenge to interpreting macrolevel associations is the possibility that they are merely aggregation effects (Bronfenbrenner, Moen, and Garbarino 1984). For example, it is possible that a community characteristic such as poverty rate, which is presumed to measure an attribute of the community structure, actually operates to influence an outcome at the family level. Researchers could mistakenly conclude that poverty exerted a structural effect when its influence on children actually occurred within each poor family. Aggregation effects are the opposite of the ecological fallacy. However, individual-level explanations can be equally flawed when what seems to be an individual problem, such as failure to use community resources, is really a function of lack of community institutions.

The aggregate analysis used available measures of neighborhood social conditions such as child maltreatment, violent crime, drug trafficking, juvenile delinquency, teen pregnancy, and low-birth-weight births. While there is general agreement that these are all of societal concern, these outcomes are not ordinarily considered within the same study. Some of the indicators, such as delinquency, violent crime, and drug trafficking, have been associated with the criminal justice field, while child maltreatment, low birth weight, and teen pregnancy have typically been within the purview of public health and social services. The fact that all of these were well explained by the same structural factors implies that they are all embedded within a similar set of forces in the community (Coulton et al. 1995).

The ethnographic study, in addition to expanding our understanding of the factors identified in the aggregate analysis, also reveals the interconnectedness of these problems facing neighborhood residents. Inability to control the behavior of neighborhood children deepens, in part, our understanding of the child-care-burden factor. It is also likely that the presence of more persons over sixty-five years of age and males between the ages of twenty-one and sixty-four serves to keep up the maintenance of properties and streets and promotes greater watchfulness in the community. The presence of elderly persons, who often move out of dangerous areas, may also be a result of lowered levels of drug trafficking and violent crime, rather than a cause of these lowered levels.

The ethnography also enriches the aggregate findings concerning impoverishment and geographic-economic isolation. An important consequence of impoverishment appears to be the lack of community resources, leading residents of high-risk areas to interact with institutions at some distance. Geographic-economic isolation of the neighborhood, defined as a location adjacent to other extreme-poverty areas, makes it even more difficult for residents to seek these external resources. Reliance on institutions outside the neighborhood presumably undermines the neighborhood-based networks that emanate from local institutional support. The absence of resources in the neighborhood is keenly felt by residents.

Interpretation of the instability factor was also aided by the ethnography. Instability produces more strangers in the area and people who are not known by the residents. These are the people over whom residents feel they have no influence or control. However, it seems to matter who is moving in and who is moving out. If, as in the African American areas, the new residents are the returning middle class, some of them are already known. Sometimes they are the adult children of people who still live, or used to live, in the area. Regardless of who they are, they are welcome. In contrast, if the new residents are poorer, and if they are renting homes that used to be owned, the consequences are viewed as negative.

A few cautions are in order in the interpretation of these results. First, these neighborhoods were categorized as high, medium, and low on the basis of reported rates of child maltreatment, which are thought to be an underestimate and to be biased by poverty and race. Second, census tracts do not necessarily represent the neighborhood as it would be defined by residents. Third, the patterns observed in the aggregate analysis and the ethnography could be explained, in whole or in part, by selection processes in neighborhood residence patterns (Tienda 1991). And finally, debate continues about the degree to which socialization processes and maltreating parents are actually influenced by their neighborhood environment (see, for example, Polansky et al. 1985; Darling et al. 1995). This study cannot address that question, but it can point to the need for more research attention to the person-environment relationship, or an ecological perspective, in understanding child maltreatment outcomes for children.

Most importantly, the aggregate analysis and the ethnography complement each other, enhance the conclusions that would be possible with either approach alone, and suggest the processes through which neighborhood conditions affect child and family well-being.

This research was supported by a grant from the National Center on Child Abuse and Neglect, Administration for Children, Youth and Families, Department of Health and Human Services (90-CA1494), and by grants from the Cleveland and Rockefeller Foundations. The authors are grateful to the Cuyahoga County Department of Human Services for their assistance, and to the editors of this volume for their comments. Research support for the aggregate analysis was provided by Julian Chow and Marilyn Su. Ethnographic research assistance was provided by Lynn T. Barone, Latina Brooks, Nichelle Dickerson, Jennifer Furin, Mario Houston, Heather Lindstrom, Candis Platt-Houston, and Lisa Reebals. Assistance in analyzing the data was provided by Sarah Chard, Sarah Colgrove, Carmit Kurn, Jennifer Rutkowski, and Penny Verin.

NOTES

1. In addition to the research described in this chapter, we have recently completed a neighborhood survey to tap perception of neighborhood by caregivers and parents of young children (Coulton, Korbin, and Su 1996). We also are initiating another aggregate and ethnographic study aimed at understanding the relationship among household and neighborhood factors on child well-being.

2. Residents' delineations of neighborhood boundaries are being analyzed as part of another project.

3. All "substantiated" and "indicated" reports in 1991 were included in the calculation of rates. In 9.4 percent of the cases, the same child had multiple reports of maltreatment during the year. In the calculation of rates, these cases were counted only once because we were interested in the proportion of children who experienced maltreatment rather than the number of reports that were made. Child maltreatment report rates were calculated by counting the total number of children living in each census tract who experienced one or more substantiated or indicated case of maltreatment and then dividing by the population of the tract ages zero through seventeen.

4. Resident interviews were not tape recorded. Detailed notes were recorded during the interviews. However, because statements cannot be verified as verbatim, we have elected to present them as paraphrased.

5

Sibling Estimates of Neighborhood Effects

Daniel Aaronson

Despite the large body of cross-disciplinary literature on neighborhood effects that has emerged over the past fifteen years, there is little agreement on the extent to which neighborhoods affect children's outcomes. This debate continues primarily because the empirical findings have not been robust to data issues, outcome measures, and estimation techniques. For example, significant neighborhood effects have been found by, among others, Borjas (1995), Brooks-Gunn et al. (1993), Case and Katz (1991), Crane (1991), Duncan (1994), and Summers and Wolfe (1977). However, other researchers, most notably, Evans, Oates, and Schwab (1992) and Corcoran et al. (1992), have found no evidence that neighborhoods matter. The lack of consistent evidence could stem from a number of factors. Perhaps survey data cannot adequately represent the complex nature of how communities influence children. Another possibility, often discussed in the literature, is the role of bias in the estimating equations.

One source of bias that is particularly difficult to resolve arises because families are not randomly placed in neighborhoods but rather choose their locations based on a variety of factors, including the importance they put on their children's development. Nonrandom allocation of households into neighborhoods is problematic because it becomes difficult to adjust estimates of the effects of neighborhood conditions for the effects of unobservable characteristics of parents that might drive neighborhood selection.

For example, imagine families that emphasize the welfare of their children. These households are likely to move to communities in which the quality of the school, peers, and neighborhood environment is better than what one would expect, given the families income and wealth. As a result, their children might do better in school, have a lower chance of experiencing a teenage pregnancy, or a lower likelihood of involvement in crime. In this case, the neighborhood has indeed benefited the children. However, suppose children in these families are also likely to do better because parents spend more time with them, hire tutors if they fall behind, or generally take more interest in their children's lives. Unfortunately, many of these parental characteristics and behaviors are unobserved by the researcher. As a result, a bias develops because the effects of unobservable family characteristics are mistakenly attributed to observable neighborhood characteristics. Therefore, the influence of neighborhoods is estimated as the sum of two factors: the actual causal effect of neighborhoods plus the spurious effect of unmeasured parental characteristics.[1] In this case, the bias would be positive, since too much of an effect is attributed to the neighborhood coefficients.

However, the bias could work in the other direction. Suppose a household lives in a neighborhood with low school and neighborhood quality. In this scenario, parents might compensate for their unfavorable environment by spending more time with their children. Again, parental time spent with the children is typically not measured in most developmental data sets. As a result, the neighborhood effect includes an additional spurious effect of omitted parental characteristics that, in this case, lessens the impact of neighborhood conditions on children's outcomes.

Consequently, the direction of the bias is related to the way the unobservables associated with neighborhood selection are correlated with the unobservables associated with children's outcomes. It is generally thought that this bias is positive, reflecting the potential of attributing family characteristics (such as parental competence, tastes for education, or time spent with the children) to the neighborhood measures.

What can be done to solve this estimation problem? Several studies have used instrumental variables (IV).[2] The idea behind IV regression is to eliminate the correlation between the unobserved family characteristics and the neighborhood variable. This procedure is typically accomplished in two stages. In the first stage, the neighborhood variable is regressed on a list of variables that are known as instruments. These instruments include all of the independent variables in the final outcome equation plus variables that are determinants of neighborhood choice but not of the outcomes of children. The first-stage regression is used to predict neighborhood values that are based only on these observed characteristics. In the second stage, the outcome regression includes the predicted neighborhood value in place of the actual neighborhood measure. With a predicted neighborhood covariate that is solely a function of observable characteristics, the correlation between the unobservables and the neighborhood variable is eliminated.

Instrumental variables estimation is a clever way to eliminate the selection problem, but it requires assumptions that are often hard to justify. Most importantly, finding a viable instrument that is correlated with neighborhood selection but not with the unobservables associated with children's outcomes is very difficult. Therefore, an alternative approach called fixed effects, which is commonly employed in economics, sociology, and developmental psychology, warrants attention.

The key advantage to fixed-effect models is that the source of variation in neighborhood quality and developmental outcomes used is within-family. In the case of neighborhood background, variation arises between siblings when the family moves or a neighborhood evolves over time. If we assume that the omitted factors associated with neighborhood choice—such as parental competence, interest in the children's welfare, and taste for education—are constant within families, then these unobservables are, by construction, eliminated from the estimating equation. Therefore, sibling differences in neighborhood conditions offer a natural way to eliminate the family-specific heterogeneity biases associated with neighborhood selection. This chapter draws heavily on Aaronson (1996), where a more detailed discussion of such issues can be found.

FAMILY FIXED-EFFECT MODELS

A SIMPLE MODEL

Family fixed-effect models have been used by economists for many studies in which nonrandom allocation posed a problem, as in measuring the rate of return to education (Ashenfelter and Krueger 1994, Griliches 1977), the effect of Head Start (Currie and Thomas 1995), and the consequence of teenage childbearing (Bronars and Grogger 1994, Geronimus and Korenman 1992, Rosenzweig and Wolpin 1995). In the context of neighborhood effects, the primary assumption in these models is that a family's neighborhood-selection process is independent of the characteristics of the individual children in the family. As a result, the omitted parental characteristics (such as concern for or time spent with the children) that may be correlated with neighborhood conditions can be captured in a family-specific error term. These family unobservables are then eliminated by basing the estimation only on variation within families.

The framework is typically a variation of the following. Let Y_{if} be the dependent variable (for example, whether the individual graduated from high school) for the ith individual in family f. Y_{if} is a function of an individual-specific variable X_{if} (for example, neighborhood conditions) and a vector of observed control variables Z_{if} (for example, the child's gender or parental income). There is also an error term that has two components: a family-specific error term ϵ_f that includes omitted characteristics that are constant across members of a family, and a random error term ϵ_{if}. The estimating equation would look like the following:

(5.1) $$Y_{if} = \alpha X_{if} + \beta Z_{if} + \epsilon_f + \epsilon_{if}$$

Estimating equation 5.1 using ordinary least squares regression would yield α—the impact of neighborhood conditions on the likelihood of graduating from high school. However, this estimate of α is biased, due to the correlation between neighborhood conditions (X_{if}) and unobserved family characteristics (ϵ_f) that arises if parents' competence, taste for education, or interest in their children's welfare is not properly measured and explicitly included in the model.[3]

The fixed-effect model works by differencing out this family-specific error component. For simplicity, assume there are two children in each family f.[4] The older child's high school graduation equation is

(5.2) $$Y_{1f} = \alpha X_{1f} + \beta Z_{1f} + \epsilon_f + \epsilon_{1f}$$

The younger child's equation is

(5.3) $$Y_{2f} = \alpha X_{2f} + \beta Z_{2f} + \epsilon_f + \epsilon_{2f}$$

Subtracting equation 6.3 from equation 6.2 eliminates ϵ_f and the potential correlation between the error term and X_{if}. The model to estimate is then a sibling first-difference equation of the form:

(5.4) $$Y_{1f} - Y_{2f} = \alpha\left(X_{1f} - X_{2f}\right) + \beta\left(Z_{1f} - Z_{2f}\right) + \epsilon_{1f} - \epsilon_{2f}$$

In equation 5.4, sibling differences in school attainment are related to sibling differences in neighborhood conditions and time-varying parental characteristics. It should be emphasized that the effects of family background variables that are constant within families, such as parental education, cannot be estimated in this framework; all family-invariant conditions are differenced out. However, for time-varying variables, equation 5.4 gives consistent parameter estimates.

If the dependent variable is continuous, then this first-difference model can be estimated using ordinary least squares (OLS). Since many outcomes of interest (such as high school graduation) are dichotomous, several methods have been developed to estimate logit fixed-effect models (Chamberlain 1980; Mundlak 1978). However, these techniques require special data assumptions and are more difficult to estimate.

PROBLEMS WITH THE FIXED-EFFECT ESTIMATOR

The family fixed-effect estimator offers an attractive, but somewhat problematic, way to eliminate bias from nonrandom neighborhood selection. In particular, four issues may be a concern for estimating neighborhood effects.

The most serious issue arises because siblings are separated by age, and therefore they may experience different family environments due to, say, marital changes, different family income circumstances, or less measurable changes in household characteristics. These between-family differences are particularly worrisome if the neighborhood variable is simply picking up changes in family conditions that preceded or resulted from changes in residential location. For example, suppose a family moves to a worse neighborhood after the parents are divorced. If divorce is not included explicitly as a variable in the sibling model, the effect of the marital change on the children will mistakenly be attributed to the change in neighborhood conditions. As with all heterogeneity problems, some of this bias can be reduced by controlling for demographic changes such as divorce. However, not all possible between-sibling family differences are measured in our data. Therefore, we must cautiously interpret neighborhood coefficients in the sibling model, since they reflect both community influences and latent family conditions.

Similarly, differences may exist between siblings, such as ability, ambition, or parental expectations and treatment, and may be correlated with neighborhood characteristics.[5] Fortunately, this is likely to be a serious concern only if parents choose neighborhoods based on these sibling differentials; sibling differences unconnected with neighborhood differences will not bias the estimates of neighborhood effects. The existing evidence, which is scant, on the impact of siblings' differential ability on neighborhood choice suggests little effect. Altonji and Dunn (1995) estimated the effect of IQ scores on school choice and found little evidence that ability matters to this decision within families. However, to be safe, it is useful to include some measures of sibling differences in the sibling model and to check whether the estimates are sensitive to the addition of more-detailed controls.

A third concern with the fixed-effect neighborhood equations is classical measurement error. For a number of reasons, neighborhood conditions are likely to be measured with error. Unfortunately, differencing across siblings exaggerates this measurement bias, resulting in the elimination of much of the true variance used to identify the parameters. However, unlike the heterogeneity concern, measurement-error bias will likely result in an underestimation of neighborhood effects.

Finally, we must be concerned about whether there is enough between-sibling variation in some of the key measures, in particular the differenced neighborhood conditions $X_{1f} - X_{2f}$. Clearly, most of the variation in neighborhood conditions is across families. However, the sibling model relies on between-sibling variation in neighborhood background to identify the parameters. Therefore, if the older sibling's history of neighborhood conditions (X_{1f}) is nearly identical to the younger sibling's neighborhood history (X_{2f}), the neighborhood effect α cannot be estimated reliably. Sibling differences in neighborhood conditions stem from two possible sources: the changing conditions over time in the same neighborhood (which allows siblings separated in age to experience different neighborhood environments even though the family does not change residences), or a household move (which places siblings in different neighborhoods). I have shown elsewhere (Aaronson 1996) that most within-family variance in neighborhood conditions arises from residential migration. Approximately one-half of the children in the Panel Study of Income Dynamics (PSID) experienced a change in census tract at some point between the ages of ten and eighteen. So while the majority of the variation is clearly across families, a small amount still exists across siblings as well. However, by relying on a small portion of the total variance in the key variables, the precision of the estimated relationship between neighborhood conditions and the outcome measure will decline.

DATA

SAMPLE COMPOSITION

As with several chapters in volume 1, the data used in this study were from the PSID and the accompanying geocode file for 1968 through 1985. Individuals were included in the sample if they had a sibling who was at least three years younger or older than they, had turned eighteen by 1985, were in the PSID for at least two years between the ages of ten and fourteen, and were in the sample for one year after age eighteen so that high school graduation could be ascertained. These constraints resulted in a sample of 2,178 individuals from 742 families.

The requirement of a three-year age difference between siblings was imposed to provide meaningful variation in the residential location of siblings. Most of the difference in neighborhood background between siblings close in age is likely to be composed of measurement noise. Because siblings further apart in age are more likely to experience true differences in neighborhood composition, I could identify real differences in background influences. Choosing the age restriction was an ad hoc approach, with sample-size considerations balanced against the advantages of using more age-separated siblings. I used a cutoff of three years. Experimentation had suggested that using a four- or five-year age difference did not affect parameter estimates but did decrease the precision of the estimates due to the smaller sample sizes.[6]

The sibling sample was constructed by pairing siblings who fit the age criterion for selection into the sample. For example, in a family with three children, aged x, $x + 2$, and $x + 5$, I would include two pairs of siblings in the sample: the oldest with the third child (five years apart in age), and the oldest with the second child (three years apart in age). This procedure produced 1,892 sibling pairs from the 2,178 individuals in the sample. Because a sibling from a multiple-child family could be included in several pairings, the sibling sample had more sibling pairs than one-half of the 2,178 individuals in the sibling sample.

OUTCOME AND CONTROL VARIABLES

Table 5.1 displays descriptive statistics on the main variables used in the analysis. All statistics are weighted using the PSID-constructed probability of selection into the sample.[7] The top of the table shows the outcome variable used in the analysis. Although there are many dimensions in which peer and neighborhoods might be influential, I concentrate on an educational outcome: whether the individual graduated from high school.[8] I chose an education variable because, unlike other outcomes such as teenage pregnancy, the sample was not limited to a single gender. Other variables that are often studied in the neighborhood-effects literature, such as crime rates and drug use, were not available in the PSID.

TABLE 5.1   Mean Characteristics of Main Individual, Neighborhood, and Family Variables,
            Weighted by PSID Sample Weights

	Mean (1)	SD (2)
Outcome variable:		
High school graduate	0.871	0.335
Family and individual controls:		
Whether child is female	0.494	0.500
Whether child is nonwhite	0.186	0.389
Household money income (1982–1984 dollars)	40,046	23,737
Parents married all years[a]	0.740	0.439
Dad high school graduate	0.561	0.496
Mom high school graduate	0.631	0.483
Number of children in household	3.23	1.56
Percentage worked during youth	0.801	0.400
County unskilled wage (1982–1984 dollars)	5.48	1.17
Variance of household income between ages 10 and 18 (1982–1984 dollars)	226	576
Percentage of years that family moved between ages 10 and 14	0.118	0.207
Whether ever moved, ages 10 to 18	0.485	0.500
Whether in own household by age 18	0.097	0.295
Head experienced at least one transition while youth age was 10–18:		
Married → divorced	0.152	0.359
Married → widowed	0.051	0.220
Divorced → married	0.091	0.288
Single → married	0.012	0.110
Widowed → married	0.021	0.145
Employed → unemployed	0.111	0.315
Employed → retired	0.063	0.243
Employed → temp. laid off	0.098	0.298
Unemployed → employed	0.088	0.284
Retired → employed	0.068	0.252
Temp. laid off → employed	0.115	0.320
Neighborhood Characteristics:		
Percentage youth not employed or in school	0.134	0.094
Percentage households in poverty	0.125	0.097
Percentage white	0.852	0.252
Percentage female household heads	0.134	0.088
Average income	40,761	14,051
Number of unique individuals	2,178	
Number of unique families	742	

Note: Sample includes all individuals with (1) one sibling who is three years younger or older, (2) two years of data between ages ten and fourteen, and (3) one year after age eighteen that can distinguish whether the individual graduated from high school. Time-varying variables are averaged for each individual between ages ten and eighteen. Family background variables are averaged over years that the person lived at home.

[a] Equals 1 if the parents stay married while the child is living at home between ages ten and eighteen.

The next group of variables consisted of family and individual covariates. The interest in comparing results from sibling-based and more conventional individual-based models led me to include a range of time-invariant, as well as time-varying, measures—child's gender and race, parents' education, household income, parents' marital status, the number of children living in the household, and whether the child worked during his or her youth. The household income measure included all labor income, transfers, and asset income, net of the teenager's income. To obtain more "permanent" measures of time-varying background variables—such as household income, the number of children in the household, and the county unskilled wage—I averaged these variables over the years that the youth lived at home between ages ten to eighteen. If data were not available for a child for, say, age ten, the averaging was only over ages eleven to eighteen. Parents' marital status was defined as taking a value of 1 if the parents stayed married while the child was between ages ten and eighteen, and 0 otherwise. The "whether child worked" variable was set to 1 if the child worked for wages while living at home with her or his parents between ages ten and eighteen. This measure was included as a control for sibling ability or ambition differences. However, it was possible that the variable would pick up the availability of jobs or itself be a component of other neighborhood influences. If the latter interpretation proved correct, including the "whether worked" variable would bias the neighborhood coefficient downward.

Changes in income, marital status, and geographic location are also likely to affect the likelihood of continuing schooling. Therefore, I also included controls for a number of transition variables that measure instability in the family environment, including the variance of income during the youth's years in the household between ages ten and eighteen, the percentage of years that the household moved between ages ten and fourteen, five detailed marital transitions, and six detailed employment transitions.[9] The employment and marital transition indicator variables were set to 1 if the child was living in the household between ages ten and eighteen when the household head experienced such a transition, and 0 if no such transition occurred. To see if measures of individual heterogeneity changed the estimate of community influences, I also experimented with controls for birth order to control for learning by the parents (see note 5), whether the individual had an older sibling who graduated from high school, the number of moves made by an individual between ages ten and fourteen, and whether the teenager moved into her own household by age eighteen.[10]

THE NEIGHBORHOOD MEASURE

The bottom rows of table 5.1 provide statistics for some neighborhood measures commonly used in neighborhood-effects models. Other researchers have used many different measures, including the fraction of disadvantaged students in the individual's school (Evans, Oates, and Schwab 1992), the percentage of families living in the neighborhood with incomes below ten thousand dollars and above thirty thousand dollars (Brooks-Gunn et al. 1993), the percentage of families on welfare (Corcoran et al. 1992), the percentage of female-headed households (Corcoran et al. 1992), and racial composition (Summers and Wolfe 1977). Duncan (1994) tested many of these measures within the same data set and specification. Case and Katz (1991) aggregated household data to derive neighborhood averages of the numerous outcomes they studied.

I concentrated my analysis on the percentage of young adults in a census tract who were aged sixteen to nineteen in 1980 (or sixteen to twenty-one in 1970) and who had not graduated from high school and were not in school. In an earlier study (Aaronson 1996) I explored alternative neighborhood measures, such as poverty rates, the percentage of female heads, average family income, and percentage of the population that was white. The neighborhood measure was an average of the community conditions that the person lived in from ages ten to eighteen. This averaging technique implicitly weights each age in this range equally and all other ages as zero in the neighborhood-impact estimate. Thus, it does not pick up any additional effect that may occur from neighborhoods lived in prior to age ten.[11]

The data for the neighborhood variables came from the PSID geocode files and the census geographic database. The geocode file is a set of addresses collected from mailings to PSID respondents. From these addresses, identifiers are assigned for various levels of geographic aggregation. The smallest geographic area classified by the Census Bureau is the census tract or block-numbering area (BNA), which is the basis for the neighborhood measure I describe. A census tract is an area of, on average, forty-two hundred people that local authorities deem a "neighborhood." BNAs are the equivalent of census tracts for untracted urban areas. When census tracts are unavailable, enumeration districts (EDs), the rural equivalent of census tracts, are used. When tracts, BNAs, and EDs were unavailable, I employed five-digit zip codes, which tend to encompass a larger area than the other identifiers. These geographic identifiers are matched to 1970 and 1980 census identifiers and data on numerous area dimensions on family structure, income, employment, race, education, housing, and mobility. I linearly interpolated neighborhood variables for 1970 to 1978 and set 1980 to 1985 and 1968 to 1969 values equal to their closest census year.

RESULTS

Table 5.2 displays coefficients and standard errors from OLS estimation of individual-based (equation 5.1) and sibling-based (equation 5.4) high school graduation equations using the 2,178 children in the sample. Each child's high school graduation outcome is regressed on the neighborhood variable, as well as family and individual variables. The top row reports the impact of

TABLE 5.2   Individual-Based and Sibling-Based High School Graduation Regressions

	Individual-Based Model		Sibling-Difference Model	
	(1)	(2)	(3)	(4)
Neighborhood dropout rate	−0.061**	−0.049***	−0.061*	−0.063*
	(0.013)[a]	(0.012)	(0.037)	(0.036)
Intercept	0.320	0.424	0.052*	−0.049*
	(0.279)	(0.273)	(0.028)	(0.027)
Whether female	0.062***	0.081***	0.075***	0.092***
	(0.015)	(0.015)	(0.020)	(0.019)
Log (household income)	0.060**	0.052**	0.011	0.004
	(0.027)	(0.026)	(0.055)	(0.053)
Whether nonwhite	0.079***	0.049**		
	(0.027)	(0.026)		
Parents married	−0.010	−0.019	0.028	0.041
	(0.032)	(0.031)	(0.059)	(0.060)
Dad high school graduate	0.057**	0.055**		
	(0.024)	(0.023)		
Mom high school graduate	0.081***	0.076***		
	(0.023)	(0.021)		
Number children in household	−0.031***	−0.027***	−0.037*	−0.029
	(0.007)	(0.007)	(0.019)	(0.019)
Worked during youth	0.069***	0.056***	0.071***	0.050**
	(0.020)	(0.020)	(0.026)	(0.024)
County unskilled wage	0.017*	0.017*	0.021	0.019
	(0.010)	(0.010)	(0.019)	(0.018)
Variance of household income	−0.021	−0.016	−0.017	0.001
	(0.016)	(0.016)	(0.052)	(0.053)
Parents divorced while youth was aged 10–18	−0.080**	−0.080**	−0.118	0.108
	(0.035)	(0.035)	(0.065)	(0.069)
Percentage of years moved, ages 10–14		−0.194***		0.057
		(0.047)		(0.069)
Own household by 18		−0.218***		−0.222***
		(0.036)		(0.048)
Other transition controls[b]	yes	yes	yes	yes
Year and region controls	yes	yes	yes	yes
Adjusted R^2	0.139	0.175	0.050	0.078

Note: Dependent variable: 1 if high school graduate. Neighborhood measure: log of the dropout rate.

[a] Huber standard errors are in parentheses. Huber standard errors correct for cluster sampling by 1968 neighborhood and arbitrary forms of heteroskedasticity.

[b] All regressions include 8 employment transition variables, 4 other marital status transitions, and region and year-turned-15 dummies.

* $p \leq .10$.   ** $p \leq .05$.   *** $p \leq .01$.

neighborhood conditions on the likelihood of graduating from high school; higher negative coefficients signify a lower probability of graduating from high school. In column 1, the model is estimated using OLS on the sample of individuals. The resulting magnitude of –0.061 has the interpretation that a change from a neighborhood in which all youth graduated from high school to one in which no youth graduated is associated with a 6.1 percentage point decrease in the likelihood of high school graduation. A more useful interpretation for economists comes from converting the coefficient to an elasticity. In this form, the –0.061 coefficient can be interpreted as a 10 percentage point increase in the neighborhood dropout rate reducing the likelihood of graduating from high school by 3.6 percent.[12]

These regressions include controls for race, gender, household income, parents' marital status, whether the father or mother graduated from high school, whether the child worked, the number of children in the household, the county unskilled wage rate, the variance of family income over the youth's data, detailed transitions into employment, detailed transitions into marital status, and year and region dummies. To gauge the effect of events that might have produced sibling differences in ability, I reran the models but added controls for the percentage of years that the household had moved and whether the individual had moved into his or her own household by age eighteen (column 2). Although both measures appeared important, neither affected the size of the neighborhood coefficient. The same was true for other controls that might have been important to high school graduation, such as birth order and whether the individual had an older sibling who had graduated from high school. Many of these characteristics, especially whether the child had formed his own household by age eighteen, may themselves have been a function of other independent variables and may better have been left out of the model. But the robustness of the neighborhood coefficient to their inclusion was encouraging.

In columns 3 and 4, the models are reestimated on a sample of sibling pairs rather than individuals in the hope that a sibling difference approach would correct for family-specific unobservables that affect neighborhood selection. Comparing columns 1 and 3 or 2 and 4 gives an indication of how family-specific omitted variables affect the results. However, the effects of variables that do not vary much within families, such as family income or parental marital status, are not estimated very precisely with the sibling-difference technique.

The effect of the sibling differencing on the neighborhood variables is surprisingly small. In fact, the neighborhood coefficient does not change at all between columns 1 and 3. However, a substantial increase in the standard error produces an increase in the p value to about the .10 significance level. These findings are robust to adding more controls to account for transitions that may differ across siblings. Even the "own household" variable, which is highly significant in the regressions, has little indirect effect on the magnitude of the neighborhood estimates in column 4. These results are also robust to using alternative ways to construct the pairings (such as using only one pair per family) or fixed-effect discrete choice methods. However, they are somewhat sensitive to the outcome measure and the neighborhood measure employed. I explored these and many other issues in much more detail elsewhere (Aaronson 1996).

CONCLUSION

A well-known complication to estimating the influence of neighborhoods on children's outcomes arises because families are not randomly assigned to neighborhoods but rather choose their locations on the basis of many factors, including the importance they place on their children's welfare. As a result, the effects of typically unmeasured family characteristics, such as parental competence, taste for education, and time spent with the children, may be mistakenly attributed to the neighborhood measures. In previous studies, researchers who attempted to correct for this selection bias used questionable instrument variables.

The approach I have described relies on the assumption that the unobservables associated with neighborhood choice do not vary across siblings. Therefore, family residential changes provide a source of neighborhood background variation within families that is free of family-specific heterogeneity biases associated with neighborhood selection. This approach is feasible because of the high levels of residential migration in the United States. Using a sample of multiple-child PSID families in which the children were separated in age by at least three years, I estimated family sibling-difference equations of children's educational outcomes. The fixed-effect results suggest that the impact of neighborhoods may exist even when family-specific unobservables are controlled.

However, our enthusiasm for the sibling-difference approach is tempered to some degree by the larger standard errors in this approach. Both small sample sizes and measurement noise that might arise if there is not enough variation in the differenced neighborhood variables contribute to the larger standard errors. In addition, it is possible that the sibling-based models have not adequately isolated important changes in family background or between-sibling individual differences. Therefore, in future research, these results should be replicated on different data and with more controls for time-varying family heterogeneity.

My thanks to Joe Altonji, Becky Blank, Greg J. Duncan, Bruce Meyer, and Lauren Sinai for helpful suggestions. All errors and omissions are mine. The views expressed in this paper are those of the author and are not necessarily those of the Federal Reserve Bank of Chicago or the Federal Reserve System.

NOTES

1. Furthermore, this bias could be accentuated by unobservables that are associated with clustered households. For example, communities are often sorted by specific characteristics of the population, such as race, ethnicity, income, or taste for public services. If any of these variables is not measured for individual households, it is possible that they also could be part of the estimated neighborhood effect, thus adding further to the spurious correlation between the neighborhood and the outcome variables.

2. Case and Katz (1991), Evans, Oates, and Schwab (1992), and Foster and McLanahan (1996). Foster and McLanahan provide a useful description of the methodology. See Aaronson (1996) for further discussion of these studies.

3. The parameter estimated ($\hat{\alpha}$) is a sum of the actual neighborhood effect (α) and the correlation between X_{if} and ϵ_f

$$\hat{\alpha} = \alpha + cov\left(\tilde{X}_{if}\tilde{\epsilon}_f\right)/var\left(\tilde{X}_{if}\right)$$

where $\tilde{X}_{if}$ and $\tilde{\epsilon}_f$ are the components of X_{if} and ϵ_f that are orthogonal to Z_{if}.

4. This framework is easily extended to families with more than two children.

5. For example, Summers and Wolfe (1977) found that lower-skilled students were more affected by classmates and school quality than their more-able peers. Other omitted differences between siblings, such as parents' expectations or treatment, might have opposing effects. Plomin and Daniels (1987) reviewed the genetics and psychology literature and found a wide range of components—including the closeness to the mother, the friendliness of the siblings, the role of siblings in family decision making, and parental expectations—that might affect the outcomes of siblings, particularly those with differing abilities, in distinct ways.

   The characteristic where sibling differentials might matter most is age. If parents learn how to care for their children over time, it is possible that their younger children will benefit by being placed into better neighborhoods than their older siblings. Fortunately, this age differential is easily observed and can be controlled for in the sibling models.

6. A problem with using the age restriction is that the sample is composed solely of children from larger families. This can bias the results in an unknown direction when fixed effects are excluded. In one scenario, parents invest less per child in large families, resulting in a positive bias in the neighborhood effects measure. However, if there are spillovers from large families that make it easier for children to relate to community externalities, the bias might work in the opposite direction. Fixed-effect specifications sweep out this family-specific heterogeneity, but it remains in the ordinary least squares specifications.

7. This sibling-based sample is not representative of the U.S. population of children. It is a sample of large families. Therefore, a full sample of 4,410 PSID children was constructed that did not impose the three-year age difference requirement. Compared to this full sample, the sibling sample has lower education levels for the parents and children, lower household income, lower mobility, more minorities, and more two-parent families.

8. Aaronson (1996) reported findings using college attendance and grades completed. Using the PSID education variables might cause an attrition problem, because grades completed are not reported until an individual has finished full-time schooling. As a result, a number of individuals over age eighteen leave the sample without ever reporting data on grades completed. The high school graduation variable is coded as 1 if the individual ever reports completing twelve grades or the individual remains in the sample after age twenty but still reports being a student. Individuals who dropped out of the sample before age twenty without reporting grades completed are excluded.

9. The six employment transitions are employment to unemployment, employment to retired, employment to temporarily laid off, unemployment to employment, retired to employment, and temporarily laid off to employment. The five marital transitions are marriage to divorce, marriage to widow, divorce to marriage, single to marriage, and widow to marriage.

10. I include the latter variable only as a test of the robustness of the results. Because of the endogeneity of the measure, it is probably best not included.

11. For evidence of neighborhood effects on younger children, see Brooks-Gunn et al. (1993). No outcome measure currently exists for younger children in the PSID, which makes it difficult to determine neighborhood effects on children prior to age ten.

12. This elasticity computation is calculated as $\alpha*(Y_{if}/X_{if})*10 = -0.061*(1/0.167)*1$. X_{if} is equal to the unweighted average of the neighborhood dropout rate (0.167), and Y_{if} is equal to 1, representing graduation from high school. Unweighted data are used in the regression work, and thus in the elasticity calculation, to avoid heteroskedasticity problems. The elasticity is multiplied by 10 to derive the impact of a 10 percentage point change in neighborhood conditions.

These effects seem fairly large, so I reran the regressions using a sample of 4,410 children that does not require the existence of a three-year age-separated sibling. This sample produces 35 percent smaller point estimates than the three-year sibling sample, but tests of the sample coefficients show that these differences are not statistically significant. The larger sample's results are in line with the small neighborhood effects findings in the literature. Therefore, it should be kept in mind that the estimates presented here are representative of the impact of neighborhood, family, and individual characteristics on the educational attainment of children from *large* families.

6

Capturing Social Process for Testing Mediational Models of Neighborhood Effects

Thomas D. Cook, Shobha C. Shagle, and Serdar M. Değirmencioğlu

Ethnographers have long studied how neighborhoods influence individuals, usually documenting how they constrain and shape behavior (for example, Burton, Allison, and Obeidallah 1995; MacLeod 1995; Williams and Kornblum 1985) but also sometimes emphasizing how individuals and groups shape the environments in which they live (Furstenberg and Hughes 1995). Against this steady backdrop of qualitative research, the past decade has seen an explosion in the amount of quantitative research on neighborhood effects, mostly among economists and sociologists interested in Wilson's (1987) theoretical work on urban poverty (for example, Crane 1991; Jagowsky 1996; Jencks and Mayer 1990) as well as among those developmentalists who have taken to heart Bronfenbrenner's (1979) call to study individual development within the social contexts in which it occurs (for example, Brooks-Gunn et al. 1993).

This quantitative research has been made possible by new theories about neighborhoods' influences on human development (for instance, Furstenberg 1992; Wilson 1987) and by the ability to use individuals' home addresses for attaching neighborhood data from the Census Bureau to other information about individuals' beliefs and behaviors. Most quantitative studies define neighborhoods as census tracts or block groups, assigning to individuals the values corresponding to those neighborhood characteristics central to the theory under test. The variables so obtained are mostly demographic or compositional insofar as they describe neighborhoods in terms of aggregates of individual differences, such as the percentage of local households that are minority or female-headed, or the percentage of households that include an unemployed person or someone working in a professional or managerial capacity. Other census variables cannot be reduced to individual demography, such as the availability of local businesses or the percentage of houses that are uninhabited or boarded up. But even these have a demographic flavor in that they describe a setting's physical attributes rather than any of its internal social dynamics.

A typical example of such quantitative research is the work by Brooks-Gunn and colleagues (1993). Holding constant many demographic background variables at the individual level, they explored how the percentage of tract residents employed in managerial and professional jobs is related to individual cognitive and behavioral changes during childhood (in one data set) and during adolescence (in another). They concluded that living in a setting with a higher density of middle-class neighbors positively influences individual development. To explain this link, they proposed that middle-class neighborhoods provide young people with more models of what conventional success is and of how it can be attained. In this approach, a *neighborhood effect* was defined as an "emergent property" (Jencks and Mayer 1990)—that is, net of neighborhood differences in social composition—although in the real world, neighborhoods do have different types of residents. Also, the form of the argument in this type of research is such that a neighborhood demographic attribute (the percentage managerial and professional) is presumed to influence a social process (the density of role models), which then affects individual behavior.

The same theoretical assumptions are common in other neighborhood effects research. In work on urban ghettos, underclass neighborhoods are usually defined as having 40 percent or more of their households officially classified as poor (Wilson 1987). Living in such a neighborhood is presumed to affect young people's behavior adversely through a number of different social process mechanisms, depending on what a theorist chooses to emphasize from among many related neighborhood processes. One hypothesis is that a high density of urban poverty enhances social disorganization by reducing social control and social cohesion (Elliott et al. forthcoming; Sampson 1992); another is that it stimulates a more vigorous local drug trade (Bound and Freeman 1992); another is that it lowers the availability and quality of institutions serving young people (Carnegie Council on Adolescent Development 1966); and a fourth is that it weakens family connections to formal and informal job networks (Wilson 1996).

Another example of neighborhood research of this same mediational form comes from work in criminology. Ever since Shaw and McKay's (1942) theory, social disorganization has been invoked to explain why a combination of local poverty, ethnic heterogeneity, and residential turnover increases criminal involvement. In the successor theories to Shaw and McKay (such as Elliott et al. forthcoming; Sampson 1992), social disorganization has continued to play this same mediating role, so that a set of neighborhood demographic characteristics is assumed to instantiate social disorganization, which then affects individual outcomes.

Direct tests of theories of this form require measures of individual outcomes, neighborhood demography, and context-dependent social processes. Unless all three types of measures are available, inferences about mediating processes will be indirect, as they are in nearly all the existing literature where social processes are more often assumed than directly measured. The assumptions that are made are rarely without empirical content, however. Researchers typically draw conclusions about mediating processes by citing findings from quantitative and qualitative process studies that other investigators have conducted and by heuristically linking these process discoveries to the relationships they themselves obtained between neighborhood demography and individual outcomes. Nonetheless, a mismatch exists: while the form of the theory is mediational, no measures of mediating processes are entered into the analysis of the relationship between the demographic and the outcome data.

This mismatch is easy to explain, since it is difficult to design research with *both* a measurement plan that has all three types of variable *and* an adequate sampling frame. The Census Bureau routinely samples densely within tracts and blocks in order to estimate aggregate neighborhood characteristics, but perceptions of social processes are typically not among the measures collected. National surveys can also be used to collect neighborhood process information. But the data so resulting can rarely be aggregated to the tract level because such surveys seek to describe the nation at large; thus, the major priority is to achieve a large sample of tracts rather than a large sample of individuals within tracts. Adding to within-tract sample sizes entails significantly larger research budgets, and this may be why even in atypically large national studies like the PSID and the NLSY, the modal number of residents per tract is very small. To describe each census tract in terms of its central tendency (or dispersion) requires either a within-tract sampling design that national studies do not now implement or social process measures that the Census Bureau does not now collect.

A consequence of this conundrum is that studies with the three types of measures that mediating models require are relatively circumscribed in where they take place. Many involve a single city, with families and individuals being sampled from within all (or some) of the city census tracts. Interviews are then used to elicit information about neighborhood processes and resources, with parents typically being the respondents. The data they provide are then linked to interview or questionnaire responses about outcomes that are collected from children or adolescents. Other studies get at neighborhood-process information less directly. Common are school-based samples representing all (or some) of the schools within a district. Knowing each student's address then allows researchers to append census-tract information to school records or questionnaire responses and also to interview adults from each of the neighborhoods where students live in order to learn about social conditions there. (In practice, though, these interviews tend to be with the parents of students in the sample.) A few researchers learn about neighborhood process by interviewing local experts or sending observers into the community. But these methods are less common, perhaps because they entail considerable logistical difficulties if there is a need for large samples of neighborhoods and of families within neighborhoods.

Testing mediational models within circumscribed local settings leads to special problems. We want to concentrate on two of them here. The first concerns *curtailed variation*, since for any neighborhood attribute the range of mean differences will inevitably be less in a local sample than a national one, biasing neighborhood effect estimates downward. Moreover, all neighborhoods have internal variation, whether in demographic attributes, in perceptions of neighborhood resources and social processes, or in individual outcomes. The larger the within-neighborhood variation relative to the between-neighborhood variation, the more difficult it will be to demonstrate reliable effects in tests of neighborhood models. In addition, covariances among neighborhood attributes and outcomes will likely vary from location to location, meaning that neighborhood-effect findings from a single city or school district will be of unknown generalizability and will need replication elsewhere. Researchers using circumscribed local samples to test mediational models need to demonstrate that the range of neighborhood mean differences does not severely distort correlational patterns; that the variation within tracts does not overwhelm the variation between them; and that the neighborhood effects found in one location are replicated in different settings with different patterns of covariation among outcome predictors.

The second issue with circumscribed samples concerns the possibility of limited *discriminant validity between demography and process* (Campbell and Fiske 1959). The ability to test mediational models supposes the ability to differentiate empirically between a neighborhood's demographic and process attributes. Otherwise, the process variables cannot be shown to function in the more causally proximal role that mediational theories assign them. As far as we are aware, this hypothesis has not yet been tested, so we cannot reject the possibility that neighborhood demographic and process measures are all exemplars of a single, latent, higher-order construct—something akin to "neighborhood quality." Indeed, the underclass literature often makes it seem as though a neighborhood's poverty rate is intrinsically bound up with its social dynamics, and it is not easy to find densely poor neighborhoods with commendable social processes (Furstenberg et al. forthcoming; Wilson 1987). In a similar vein, but referring now to affluent neighborhoods, professionals moving to a new community believe that communities with more rich families enjoy better social dynamics, making it difficult to disentangle community demography and process if their impressions are correct (Brett, Stroh, and Reilly 1993; Hormuth 1990). In local studies with a limited sample size of neighborhoods, is it in fact difficult to differentiate empirically between neighborhood demography and neighborhood social process—a distinction that is crucial for testing mediational models of neighborhood effects?

The data we present touch on the two issues just cited. We hope our analysis will stimulate debate, not so much about the utility of testing mediational models—of which we remain convinced—but rather about what it takes to test such models well. We do not elaborate on all the problems inherent in doing

neighborhood-effects studies, but only on those that arise when testing mediational models. Nor do we elaborate on all the problems of causal modeling, but
only on those that arise when aggregate-level causes are at stake. But before
we present data on between-neighborhood variation and on discriminant validity among the neighborhood measures, we need to describe the two study sites
—Philadelphia and Prince George's County—and the demographic, process,
and outcome data. We want to make the case that the sites are very different
and that the neighborhood measures are similar to those specified in current
theories of neighborhood effects. Data were collected in Philadelphia before
Prince George's County, and the lessons learned from the Philadelphia study
were used to modify the later study. Thus, the two data sources involve some
comparable, but not identical, measures.

THE TWO RESEARCH SETTINGS: PHILADELPHIA
AND PRINCE GEORGE'S COUNTY

PHILADELPHIA

Unlike predominantly middle-class Prince George's County, where the population is increasing and more and more jobs are available in the service and
high-technology-manufacturing sectors, today's Philadelphia resembles a
number of older U.S. cities whose economies have been eroded by the disappearance of manufacturing and skilled-labor jobs since the 1970s. Indeed,
the city's population declined from 2.1 million to 1.6 million between 1960
and 1990. Despite a boom in the financial, insurance, real estate, and construction industries, the standard of living has generally not improved, and
many communities still struggle to maintain adequate schools and decent services. There also seems to be a growing separation of rich and poor into spatially segregated neighborhoods, stratifying neighborhoods by the level of
institutional support available and by the frequency of crime, drugs, teenage
childbearing, gangs, and the like.

SAMPLING

Philadelphia has 365 census tracts. A sample of sixty-five of them was drawn
from four large sections of the city, selected because they surround the family planning clinics included in an evaluation study whose sampling design
formed the basis for our research. The areas selected include some of the
less affluent parts of Philadelphia. The western part of the city is home to
mostly poor and near-poor African Americans, though solidly working-class
sections of homeowners survive here. South Philadelphia embraces some
impoverished census tracts with black residents but also retains working-
class white neighborhoods, a few of which have been recently gentrified.
North Philadelphia is mostly Puerto Rican and desperately poor. The north-

western part of Philadelphia is predominantly African American and includes some communities that are mixed socioeconomically, some that are solidly working class, and a few that are primarily middle class. These four sections of the city include a varied collection of smaller neighborhoods, and while they are not formally representative of the entire city, they do contain some of the poorest white sections in the city and a wide range of black neighborhoods.

The sample of sixty-five census tracts resulting from this process involved some restriction in range. Absent were the upscale white tracts from the Center City and the predominantly white, moderate-income sections of the Greater Northeast. Somewhat underrepresented were tracts where 30 percent or more of the families lived in poverty. Of the 350 city tracts with at least 100 families, 27 percent of them had at least 30 percent poverty families, whereas in this study only about 20 percent of tracts (thirteen of sixty-five) met this criterion. Nonetheless, substantial differences existed among the neighborhoods. Census information for 1990 showed that for this sample the mean percentage white was 32.5, with a range from 0 to 99; the mean percentage black was 61.6, with a range of 0 to 99; the average median household income was $20,982, with a range of $9,877 to $36,439; the mean percentage of female-headed households was 18, with a range of 7 to 35; the mean percentage of families in poverty was twenty-one, with a range of 5 to 62; and the mean percentage of college graduates was 9, with a range of 0 to 45. Thus, there seems to have been considerable tract variation, despite the absence of affluent white communities.

Ethnographers have also noted differences in the physical characteristics of the neighborhoods (Furstenberg et al. forthcoming). On one hand, most families are living in attractive single-dwelling or attractive twin and row homes in well-kept neighborhoods with parks and urban amenities close by. Parents are content to have their children play on the streets or in local parks, and a visitor to the neighborhood is likely to get a friendly nod from residents during the day and a careful look at night. Neighbors are used to looking out for one another. They can be seen sharing news and gossip at street corners, parks, or stoops. All but a few of the families living in these neighborhoods have parents employed in middle-class jobs, and many families send their children to parochial schools. At the other extreme are neighborhoods dotted with abandoned and burnt houses, schools and convenience stores covered with graffiti, and corner lots littered with uncollected trash. Relatively few families in such neighborhoods can afford to send their children to parochial or private schools, and parents typically worry about their children's safety outside the home.

Families were sampled within these sixty-five census tracts by a multistage process. First, from one to three block groups were randomly selected per tract, depending on population size. Next, within each of the selected block groups, listed phone numbers were enumerated using a reverse phone directory. The sample of households so identified was then screened by a group of interviewers, yielding 805 potentially eligible families with a child between the ages of ten and fourteen. A letter was sent to all of these families describing the objectives of the research, encouraging parents to participate, and offering them an incentive for participating. (To reduce biases associated with telephone ownership, a small number of families were selected by walking the neighborhoods and asking local residents where families lived that had a child in the target age range.) In all, 482 parent and teen pairs participated in the study. In-person interviews and self-administered questionnaires were used to collect data from both parents and children.

MEASURES

The neighborhood demographic measures used included: (1) the percentage poor, (2) the percentage white, (3) the percentage of college graduates, and (4) the percentage of single-mother households.

The neighborhood-process measures, which were taken from the parents, assessed constructs within three domains. The first concerned institutional resources: the quality of teen programs, the quality of local schools, and the availability of formal and informal neighborhood organizations such as hospitals and scout groups. The second domain, social networks, included measures of the size of networks, of the number of relatives and close friends living in the neighborhood, and of the extent to which residents thought they could count on members of their networks for material and emotional support. The final domain, social climate, assessed general liking for the neighborhood; the extent of social control; the likelihood that local children could succeed in life; the degree of consensus among parents about child-relevant matters; the extent of social cohesion; and the level of social problems stemming from crime, drugs, violence, and the like.

Parents and children also reported on various aspects of their family functioning. Some of the variables assessed parenting style, especially around warmth, monitoring, and autonomy promotion (Baumrind 1978). Others assessed aspects of family management, the way parents dealt with the world outside the home by restricting a child's physical activities outside the home, investing in the child at home through specific activities, linking the child to formal and informal institutions outside of the home, linking the child to positive social networks, or enrolling the child in private or selective schools that were particularly likely to create a positive, all-embracing environment.

Also measured, albeit at a single point in time, were some individual child outcomes. These included measures taken from the parent about the child's mental health, assessments of school performance taken from both the parent and the child, measures of the positive activities in which children took part, and measures of the negative activities in which children were engaged.

PRINCE GEORGE'S COUNTY

Prince George's County, in the southernmost part of Maryland, wraps around the southern, eastern, and, to some extent, northern parts of Washington, D.C. The county is physically large, and in 1990 its kindergarten through twelfth-grade school system was the fifteenth largest school district in the nation. The county (population 729,268) is predominantly African American (51 percent) and white (43 percent), with small but equal percentages of Asian Americans and Latinos. According to the Maryland Office of Planning, the 1989 median black household income in the county was $41,265, while the corresponding white value was $46,822. These values are higher than the U.S. national average (blacks, $18,676; whites, $31,231), and in percentage terms the race difference is smaller in the county than in the nation at large.

Nonetheless, income varies considerably within the county, with the poorest census tract having a median household income of $11,326 in 1989 and the most affluent, $75,200. Moreover, the county is less affluent and more prone to social problems than other counties bordering Washington. Between 1980 and 1991, county murder rates more than doubled (from 8.1 to 19.1 per 100,000 residents), while they remained more or less stable at 4.1 in the neighboring counties. Data on county schools show that from 1960 to 1995 the percentage of white students declined continuously and that overall school achievement was disappointing. Moreover, there is considerable apprehension in the county about more poor blacks from Washington moving in and about affluent blacks and whites leaving the county for more exclusive counties around Washington. In many ways, then, the county is a world between the inner city and the affluent suburbs, incorporating much of the variation that characterizes the United States at large, but not the extremes of poverty associated with the urban underclass and the extremes of wealth associated with the most exclusive suburbs.

SAMPLE SELECTION   There are twenty-five middle schools in the county, twenty-three of which participated in the study. One nonparticipating school exclusively teaches children with special educational needs, and the other was undergoing extensive multiyear restoration. Entering seventh-grade students were sampled in three cohorts at the beginning of the 1990, 1991, and 1992 school years, yielding an eligible population of 22,314 enrolled students. Letters were sent to the parents or guardians inviting them to consent to their children being in the study, and several reminders were later sent home by mail or by hand. Of that group, 17,276 parents (77 percent) gave consent. However, among Latino students ($N = 304$) only 50 percent gave consent, and so they were excluded from the population. Eventually, 12,398 white, black, and Asian students entered the longitudinal sample, so named because they provided data at both the beginning of seventh grade and the end of eighth grade. This was 56 percent of the initially eligible non-Latino population.

As mentioned, students provided information about their beliefs and behaviors at two times, nineteen months apart. Teachers, staff, and students also provided information on the school climate at the end of each academic year. A subsample of fifteen hundred parents from the second cohort volunteered for in-depth interviews and self-administered questionnaires assessing their involvement in school, their parenting practices, and their views of the neighborhood and school. Their neighborhood reports were then aggregated to the tract level to provide details on local social processes. Neighborhood demographic data were also obtained from census reports, and like the process data, they were then attached to individual outcome data obtained from both student questionnaires and school archives.

The county has 172 tracts, but 2 of them had no children in this study. Of the remaining 170 tracts, 7 had no adult interviews; 8 had only a single interview; and 16 had only two. Pilot work with 15, 5, 3, and fewer adults per tract indicated that 3 was the minimum acceptable sample size per tract; 137 tracts met this criterion. The mean number of adults interviewed in these tracts was 10, and the corresponding number of students was 107. To represent the other 33 tracts for which we had considerable student (but less parent) data, "synthetic" tracts were created by adding to each individual adult score from that tract the mean score of each physically contiguous tract. Comparisons of the means, standard deviations, and intercorrelations for the resulting 170 tracts with the 137 tracts with at least three adult respondents showed few differences. So, in most analyses we used 170 tracts, except when the independence of tracts was crucial to the point being made.

MEASURES

Ten multi-item scales were constructed to measure many of the social processes occurring within tracts that have figured prominently in existing neighborhood theories. Most were collected from parents, but some were from students. In all cases, the individual responses were aggregated to the tract level. The Social Control scale focused on informal mechanisms of social control via neighbors (as opposed to more formal means via the police). For example, parents were asked, "How likely is it that someone in the neighborhood would do something if kids were getting into trouble?" The Neighborhood Disorganization scale addressed neighborhood problems and dangers in the neighborhood (for example, parents responded to items such as "How much are delinquent gangs or drug gangs a problem in your neighborhood?"). The Neighborhood Adolescent Acting Out scale assessed more petty neighborhood problems and was obtained by aggregating student reports on problem behavior to the neighborhood tract level (for example, "How often have you damaged public or private property that did not belong to you, just for fun?"). The Availability of Neighborhood Resources scale provided information on the availability of neighborhood resources and services (such as community family health service, after-school recreational programs). The Adult Participation Rates in Neighborhood Activities and Programs scale included aggregated parent reports regarding participation in neighborhood activities such as a community organization or a tenants' council in the past year. The Neighborhood Satisfaction scale combined two pieces of information provided by parents: a rating of how satisfied they were with their neighborhood and of whether they thought they would continue to live in the same neighborhood five years from the interview time. The Cultural Capital scale assessed adolescents' perceptions of the extent to which parents in the neighborhood encouraged them to go to the public library, go to museums, read in their spare time, and go to music concerts, plays, or other performances. The Social Cohesion scale measured the extent to which neighbors could be counted on to provide information about opportunities for children, plus the availability of positive adult role models. The Probability of Success for Children scale dealt with parents' opinions regarding the likelihood that children in the neighborhood would graduate from high school, complete college, and find a stable and well-paying job as adults. The Youth Perceptions of a Positive Neighborhood scale was an aggregate of youths' perceptions of neighborhood (regarding role models, employment opportunities, and so on).

Tract demographic data were obtained from the 1990 census. The mean percentage white was 48, with a range from 0 to 100. The average median household income was $44,177, with a range from $11,326 to $75,200. The mean percentage in professional and managerial occupations was 30, with a range of 10 to 63. The mean percentage black was 48, with the range being 0 to 99. The average percentage of college graduates was 25, and the range was to 0 to 71. The mean percentage of families in poverty was 4, with the range being 0 to 27. The average percentage of female-headed households was 23, with the range being 0 to 58. These ranges led us to conclude that there was considerable tract variation within the county, but there were no tracts that could be labeled as underclass, as there were in Philadelphia.

There were nine child outcomes, though we present only a composite here. Individually, the measures were (1) test scores in English and Mathematics taken from the Maryland State Achievement Test; (2) average grades across math, English, social studies, and science, combined; (3) a multi-item scale of engagement in conventional activities that assesses the proportion of time students spend engaged in various growth-oriented activities that adults tend to value (such as participation in clubs and reading for fun); (4) a scale of engagement in problem behaviors based on the number of times students had engaged in risky and delinquent activities in the past year, such as damaging property just for fun or bringing alcohol or drugs to school; (5) a multi-item scale assessing positive feelings of self that covers self-efficacy in school, satisfaction with self, and future positive outcome expectancies; (6) a similar scale for negative feelings that gets at the frequency of depressed moods, anger, and the use of negative coping strategies; (7) adolescent self-reported drug use; (8) absenteeism, taken from school records; and (9) enrollment in advanced mathematics courses, also taken from records. A composite success index was constructed by defining cutoff points for each of these nine measures and then simply summing the number of times a student scored above the cutoff. The cutoffs were deliberately selected to be modest—for instance, achieving the state standard for achievement and getting a grade-point average of C+ or higher.

VARIATION BETWEEN NEIGHBORHOODS

THE RANGES

Table 6.1 shows the means for some demographic tract characteristics that can be understood intuitively. On all measures except one, the Prince George's County neighborhoods were found to be more socially advantaged. Table 6.1 also shows that, for nearly all measures, the range of tract means was greater in the county than in the city because the county's maxima were almost twice the city's. Thus, median tract income varied from $11,326 to $75,200 in the county and from $9,877 to $36,439 in the city; the proportion of college graduates varied from 0 percent to 71 percent in the county and from 0 percent to 45 percent in the city; the proportion of households with a resident working in a professional or managerial role went from 0 percent to 63 percent in the county and from 0 percent to 51 percent in the city; the proportion of female-headed households ranged from 0 percent to almost 58 percent in the county and from 7 percent to 35 percent in the city; and finally, the average proportion of families in poverty varied from 0 percent to 24 percent in the county, but from 5 percent to 62 percent in the city. Although these ranges are inevitably less than in the nation at large, it still seems warranted to conclude (1) that each location is characterized by reasonable variation in tract demographic attributes, (2) that the county's ranges generally exceed the city's, and (3) that this is more because the city's maxima are curtailed than that the minima differ between sites. These results suggest that the inevitable restriction in mean range occasioned by a local sampling design will not attenuate coefficients by much, particularly in the county where only the percentage poor seems to be noticeably curtailed.

INTRACLASS CORRELATIONS

Table 6.2 presents intraclass correlation values (ICCs) for those neighborhood demographics where we had individual-level measures similar to those of the census, for neighborhood social processes, and for early adolescent outcomes. An ICC is computed as the ratio of the amount of variation between census tracts relative to the amount of variation within them, the latter being

(Text continues on page 107.)

TABLE 6.1 Compositional Factors in Philadelphia and Prince George's County

	Mean		Prince George's County		Philadelphia	
	Phil.	PGC	Minimum	Maximum	Minimum	Maximum
Neighborhood Composition						
From Census						
Median household income	20,983	44,177	11,326	75,200	9,877	36,439
% Family poverty	21.30	3.99	0	27.03	5.00	62.00
% College graduates	9.12	24.60	0	70.80	.00	44.60
% Black	61.15	47.46	0	99.36	.07	99.01
% White	32.53	48.0	0	100.0	.31	99.55
% Female-headed household	18.17	22.77	0	57.50	5.09	35.17
% Prof/managerial	7.75	29.53	0	63.00	0	51.43

Note: Phil. = Philadelphia; PCG = Prince George's County.

105

TABLE 6.2   Intraclass Correlations for Demographic, Process, and Outcome Measures in
Philadelphia and Prince George's County

	Philadelphia	Prince George's County
Family SES resources	.18	.43
Household education	.14	.16
Household income	.13	.34
Household assets	.18	.44
Neighborhood climate	.22	.25
Social control	.11	.06
Probability of child's success	.20	.26
Social cohesion	.10	.13
Lack of problems	.19	.05
Neighborhood organizations		
Availability of organizations	.13	.17
Quality of teen programs	.06	—
Quality of schools	.06	—
Parenting		
Parent–child communication	.04	.03
Discipline effectiveness	.11	.10
Autonomy	.03	.00
Parent psychological resources	.05	.00
Family management		
Institutional connections	.03	.04
Parent investment	.08	.07
Positive social networks	.11	—
Parent restrictiveness	.13	—
Attending private school	.08	—
Child/adolescent outcomes		
Academic		
Academic competence	.07	—
Achievement tests	—	.08
Grades	—	.06
Algebra enrollment	—	.08
Absenteeism	—	.06
Activities		
Activity involvement	.04	.02
Problem behavior	.04	.00
Soft drug use	—	.02
Psychological well-being		
Emotional problems	.00	—
Positive feelings about the self	—	.01
Negative feelings about the self	—	.00
Global success	—	.05

Note: The ICC values reported for Philadelphia differ slightly from Furstenberg et al. (forthcoming)
values because measures were altered slightly to increase comparability between two sites.

the product of genuine individual differences, *plus* measurement error, *plus* any statistical interactions between neighborhood and individual difference attributes. An ICC value greater than .50 indicates that more of the variation is between neighborhoods than within; a lower value indicates the opposite. The results cited in table 7.2 point to three important findings.

1. *ICC values were similar across the two research sites.* Table 6.2 shows a high degree of consistency in ICCs across the two locations, whatever the type of variable under analysis. The only salient exception is that tract differentiation in socioeconomic status (SES) was greater in suburban Prince George's County than in the urban Philadelphia sample—something the data on ranges suggested might occur. All the other ICC values were similar, though, whether for neighborhood process or student outcomes. This suggests that, as different as the two locations are in their central demographic tendencies, they are nonetheless similar in the way process and outcome variation is partitioned within and between tracts.

2. *ICC values differed systematically by domain.* The second finding evident in table 6.2 is that, though none of the ICC values were high, neighborhoods still differed from each other more in some attributes than others. Between-tract variation was about .2 for the local social climate and the socioeconomic standing of neighbors, though the latter was higher in the county; it was about .1 for the size and dependability of social networks and for family management strategies like the institutional connections and restrictiveness that were measured only in Philadelphia; it was about .05 for indicators of the availability and quality of local institutions; and it was close to zero for neighborhood differences in the psychological attributes of caregivers (and children) and for family processes associated with warmth, autonomy promotion, and discipline effectiveness.

   It seems, then, that psychological factors and internal family processes vary between individuals, but not between neighborhoods. This conclusion would probably not change if, instead of self-reports, clinical assessment techniques were used to measure mental health and if observation techniques were used to measure family processes. Such assessment techniques would have to be considerably more valid than self-reports for the very low ICC values to increase by much. As a result, we are prepared to conclude that neighborhoods hardly differ in internal family processes and in the gross psychological health of their average resident. Such conclusions indicate there will not even be a modest causal link between neighborhoods and mental health or between neighborhoods and traditional in-home family parenting practices based on autonomy promotion, discipline effectiveness, and family warmth.

The ICC values for the family management constructs (average about .1) were higher than those for the traditional parenting style measures, perhaps because the family management constructs are meant to reflect how families react to the outside world either by linking their children to resources or by restricting their mobility when the outside world is dangerous. The fact that the family management variables varied more by neighborhood provides an empirical indication that this family domain is different from traditional family-process measures, being more closely related to how families are situated in their local context.

Neighborhoods differ most in their social climate (particularly regarding the prevalence of social problems), in their economic and human capital resources, and in the size and quality of social networks. Fortunately, these are the domains that neighborhood theorists emphasize when they assign a central causal role to community disorganization and local resource levels. Thus, their emphasis is well placed, relative to the other potential causes examined here, though the modest size of the neighborhood variation in these processes might surprise the theorists in question.

3. *In all domains, variation was greater within tracts than between them.* The third finding is perhaps the most important. No ICC value exceeded .5, and were it not for the one high-SES value just mentioned, none would have exceeded .25. This suggests that there is much more variation within census tracts than between them, despite the wide range in neighborhood demographic means presented earlier. Corrections for unreliability of measurement (Raudenbush, Rowan, and Kang 1991) do not change this conclusion. They increase some ICC values by as much as 25 percent, but this is from such low base rates that the corrected correlations are still not very high.

The ICC values in table 6.2 might well have increased if neighborhoods had been measured differently. However, using census blocks and city planners' neighborhood designations, instead of tracts, failed to change the ICC values in Philadelphia, further supporting the conclusion that tracts are more internally heterogeneous than externally differentiable. Had local experts (like real estate agents, politicians, or police officials) been asked to draw local neighborhood boundaries, then the ICC values in table 7.2 would have increased to the extent that such officials have valid expertise about local social dynamics. Unfortunately, we do not have neighborhood data collected this way. Still, we are tentatively prepared to conclude that ICC values are at best modest across a wide range of neighborhood-process attributes and individual outcomes.

Why might this be? Great physical changes have taken place in both Philadelphia and Prince George's County since tracts were first created there about fifty years ago—although the original boundaries have been somewhat revised since then to reflect population-density changes in some areas and new housing developments in others. In any event, new roads and businesses have influenced who lives where, most of the old immigrant groups have moved out, and the newer groups that have moved in have not always respected the older social boundaries. Moreover, with easier means of communication (via cars and telephones, for example), family members may now find it easier than their grandparents to forge and maintain links with family members, work friends, and shared-activities friends who live far away, thereby extending family, school, and work networks across a city and its suburbs and beyond. Psychological and physical mobility are salient attributes of American life, and the media present to young people social worlds and personal possibilities they do not observe locally. Do such things make today's young people less and less dependent on their geographic neighborhood? Is there more need today to study the spatially dispersed communities that individuals and families carve out for themselves without necessarily paying much attention to how physically distant they are from their own homes? These are all intriguing possibilities that the ICC values in table 6.2 hint at but do not directly test.

There is considerably less variation between neighborhoods than within them when it comes to individual outcomes—academic performance, acting out, engagement in conventional activities, and mental health. However, it is important to remember that both samples are of *early* adolescents, aged eleven to fifteen. Some early evidence has suggested that for many of these outcomes ICC values will increase with age (Elliott et al. forthcoming), and some frequently replicated individual relationships imply the same age increase in ICC values. For instance, surveys have shown that crime rates hardly differ by race and social class during early adolescence but vary strongly with each of them by late adolescence. Since race and class are important neighborhood attributes in the United States, the individual relationships between crime, race, and class will inevitably result in larger ICC values for older adolescent samples. But even so, the late-adolescent ICC values in the Denver sample of Elliott and associates did not exceed .50, further supporting the contention that there is nearly always more variability within census tracts than between them.

This does not mean, though, that the neighborhood differentiation described in table 6.2 is trivial. In research on how schools and classrooms influence student performance, it has been traditional to construct theories and empirical tests around ICC outcome values as low as .05—even lower in some cases (Bryk and Raudenbush 1992). Indeed, if we took .20 as the cutoff point for deciding what is worth explaining, there would probably be no literature at all on the determinants of school climate or even of school differences in achievement levels (Bryk and Thum 1989; Raudenbush, Rowan, and Kang 1991). Moreover, analyses of many process and outcome variables (not presented here) showed we were able to use the neighborhood demographics to predict very high percentages of the neighborhood-level variation in social process, even when it was as low as 2 percent in the Prince George's County case. Finally, Rosenthal and Rubin (1982) have shown how small-seeming correlations can imply much larger percentage differences, so that clinical trials have been called off prematurely because the percentage results were so positive, even though they were associated with correlations between treatment and outcome as low as .20. These ICC results are not trivial, therefore. But they should still be a source of discomfort to those theorists of neighborhoods who have lost sight of two facts: (1) that communities vary considerably internally and (2) that dissimilar settings contain some families having similar dynamics and child outcomes. Neighborhoods are not monolithic places.

Although the ICC values in table 6.2 are not trivial and may sometimes increase with age, they nonetheless imply that neighborhood theories about main effects are not likely to have much predictive power. However, the total impact of neighborhoods on development also depends on the ways different types of families and individuals respond to their neighborhood's characteristics, for statistical interactions between neighborhood and individual attributes are sources of individual-level (rather than aggregate-level) variation. Should explanatory neighborhood theories devote more effort to identifying the kinds of individuals who are more or less affected by neighborhood circumstances, given that within-neighborhood variation nearly always exceeds the between-neighborhood variation? Only by building cross-level interactions into neighborhood models can full justice be done to the multiple ways in which neighborhoods influence individuals—through both causal mediation and causal moderation (Kenny and Judd 1984).

DISCRIMINANT VALIDITY

THE ISSUES

To test mediational models, researchers need to demonstrate that measures of the neighborhood social process in their theory are reliably different from the measures of demographic composition. So a relevant question is the classical discriminant validity one: Are the intercorrelations among the relevant demographic or process measures higher than the correlations between process and demographic attributes? If we find a clear empirical distinction between tract demographic and process attributes, then it is easy to test mediational models; if we do not, empirical tests will be more problematic, and we will need to rely heavily on substantive theory to decide among various explanations of the paths through which neighborhoods influence individuals.

Neighborhood theories also differ in the specific demographic or process characteristics considered important. One example of a theory invoking specific neighborhood constructs is the contention that social disorganization (rather than, say, resource availability) is a crucial mediator between neighborhood poverty, criminal behavior, and a composite of ethnic heterogeneity and residential stability. Another is the claim of Brooks-Gunn et al. (1993) that social modeling is a crucial process mediating between how middle class a community is and how individuals behave. Specific theories such as these require discriminant validity, first among a wide range of process measures; second among various demographic measures; and third between process and demographic attributes. If measures in either the compositional or process domains are highly intercorrelated, it will be all the more difficult to test whether a specific neighborhood attribute plays the role theoretically attributed to it.

The available evidence on discriminant validity is sparse but suggests that neighborhood-process attributes are *both* discriminable *and* interrelated. Thus, Skjaeveland, Garling, and Maeland (1996) analyzed communities in Bergen, Norway, on fourteen process attributes and discovered four community-process factors, three of which were correlated at .45 or more. The same picture has emerged in factor-analytic studies of demographic variables. In a study of 325 tracts and nineteen demographic variables, Aber and colleagues discovered "four conceptually unique but interrelated factors" (Gephart 1996), (Sampson 1996) finds something similar. Such findings imply that some discrimination is warranted within both the demographic and process domains, though the factors so resulting are far from independent, making it difficult to distinguish among them if the intercorrelations are very high and the number of neighborhoods is low. The latter will often be true when the need for neighborhood-process data forces a researcher to study a single local site.

THE RESULTS

The Philadelphia data were not amenable to sensitive analyses of discriminant validity, given the relatively small number of tracts and the relatively large number of demographic and process predictors we would have liked to use.

THE PRINCE GEORGE'S COUNTY RESULTS   The relevant neighborhood-level correlations based on 170 tracts are reported in table 6.3. Correlations among the neighborhood composition variables averaged .41; among the process variables, .42; and between the process and demographic measures, .37. The fact that the correlations between demography and process were almost as high as the correlations within either process or demography suggests little discriminant validity. (The Philadelphia correlations show a similar pattern of simple correlational results.)

We then selected three demographic variables a priori for their centrality in neighborhood theories: the percentage white (correlated almost perfectly with the percentage black in this county), the percentage in professional and managerial jobs, and the median household income. These three variables alone produce a multiple R of .77 when predicting variation in a global neighborhood-

TABLE 6.3 Tract-Level Correlations Between Neighborhood Demography and Process Variables in Prince George's County (170 Census Tracts)

	1	2	3	4	5	6	7	8	9	10	11	12	13	14	15	16
1. % White households	1.00															
2. % Professional & managerial	.57**	1.00														
3. % College graduates	.60**	.88**	1.00													
4. Median household income	.47**	.66**	.45**	1.00												
5. % High school graduates	-.46**	-.50**	-.71**	-.10	1.00											
6. % Males ages 16+ unemployed	-.55**	-.49**	-.44**	-.48**	.17*	1.00										
7. % Females ages 16+ unemployed	-.43**	-.57**	-.46**	-.46**	.14	.35**	1.00									
8. % Family below poverty line	-.51**	-.57**	-.41**	-.68**	.01	.48**	.55**	1.00								
9. % on public assistance	-.47**	-.53**	-.53**	-.44**	.08	.42**	.49**	.72**	1.00							
10. % Dropouts	-.16*	-.35**	-.31**	-.43**	.05	.15	.23**	.35**	.31**	1.00						
11. % Female-headed households	-.78**	-.63**	-.61**	-.72**	.39**	.55**	.48**	.66**	.55**	.30**	1.00					
12. % Home owners	.31**	.30**	.11	.76**	-.02	-.25**	-.21**	-.46**	-.12	-.30**	-.57**	1.00				
13. Culture promotion	-.10	.19*	.23**	.08	-.21**	-.03	.02	-.06	-.10	-.16*	-.03	.02	1.00			
14. Neighborhood cohesion	.35**	.42**	.36**	.48**	-.09	-.24**	-.39**	-.41**	-.37**	-.22**	-.51**	.32**	.04	1.00		
15. Participation in organized acts.	.27**	.35**	.39**	.35**	-.25**	-.23**	-.27**	-.30**	-.27**	-.21**	-.37**	.21**	.13	.33**	1.00	
16. Neighborhood social control	.36**	.38**	.31**	.41**	-.08	-.35**	-.33**	-.32**	-.33**	-.07	-.42**	.25**	.01	.60**	.25**	1.00
17. Positive expectations for adols.	.60**	.68**	.65**	.63**	-.32**	-.51**	-.44**	-.48**	-.51**	-.28**	-.66**	.29**	.08	.61**	.33**	.58**
18. Adolescent positive att. toward nbd.	.50**	.57**	.54**	.52**	-.26**	-.38**	-.29**	-.45**	-.43**	-.27**	-.60**	.28**	.13	.52**	.20**	.45**
19. Adolescent problem behavior	.37**	.40**	.43**	.29**	-.32**	-.41**	-.25**	-.32**	-.29**	-.13	-.44**	.20**	.36**	.18*	.20**	.10**
20. Neighborhood stability/satisfaction	.42**	.47**	.44**	.56**	-.27**	-.23**	-.35**	-.43**	-.39**	-.19**	-.59**	.40**	.16*	.65**	.31**	.38**
21. Availability of resources	.60**	.52**	.53**	.37**	-.36**	-.31**	-.36**	-.37**	-.37**	-.14	-.55**	.19**	-.08	.39**	.38**	.38**
22. Neighborhood problems/dangers	.45**	.55**	.49**	.42**	-.19**	-.39**	-.38**	-.41**	-.44**	-.24**	-.48**	.19**	.06	.45**	.23**	.38**

quality measure created by standardizing and summing the ten intercorrelated neighborhood-process attributes. Taking account of unreliability in this index raised the multiple R value as high as .86. Had we used any other combination of three demographic predictors, the results would have been generally similar, since the three predictors just cited did not have especially high correlations with the neighborhood-process index. A principal components analysis was also conducted. Although it resulted in three factors, one was very dominant, and ten of the thirteen tract attributes, including all three demographic attributes, loaded on it. There is not much evidence of discriminant validity here.

It might be argued that selecting only three demographic and ten process variables biased the analysis, as did the use of 170 tracts when 33 of them were constituted from information about the tract itself *and* contiguous tracts. So, we conducted a second principal components analysis, with oblique rotation, using all ten demographic attributes, all ten process attributes, and eigenvalues only the 137 manifestly independent tracts. The eigen-values in table 6.4 show that one factor dominated in the analysis and that the variables with loadings on it over .40 included both process and demographic attributes, though the former were more numerous and tended to have the higher loadings. Of the four much-less-potent multi-item factors with eigen-values greater than one, two were homogeneous. The first had its highest loadings on "social disorganization" processes; and the fourth was composed almost exclusively of demographic poverty attributes. However, the other two factors were more mixed. The second had both demographic variables that tapped into race and education and process variables that tapped into how available and frequently used neighborhood organizations were. The fifth factor was composed of both demographic items about income and process details about perceived neighborhood stability and satisfaction. So, we do not find clear demarcation into process and demographic factors. The dominant factor had both process and demographic components (with the former predominating), while the smaller factors were as often heterogeneous as homogeneous.

Many scholars are willing to invoke theory alone to justify a distinction between demography and process and to claim that demography has temporal precedence. Accepting these assumptions makes it easier to test mediating models of neighborhood effects. This can be seen in figure 6.1, in which a model was tested of global success at the end of eighth grade, understanding this as the nine-item index assessing the number of life domains in which a young person is getting by. The model makes success dependent on many individual difference factors (of which only the strongest are presented in the figure), on the three Prince George's County demographic attributes mentioned earlier, on the global ten-item neighborhood-quality index also mentioned earlier, and on success measured nineteen months earlier at the beginning of seventh grade. Individual difference variables are in the model because, like other scholars, we have chosen to define *neighborhood effects* as "emergent properties" rather than compositional effects. The model assumes that both the

(Text continues on page 116.)

TABLE 6.4   Mean, Standard Deviation, and Factor Loadings of Neighborhood Demography and Process Variables for 137 Census Tracts

	Mean	SD	Factor 1	Factor 2	Factor 3	Factor 4	Factor 5
Eigen value			9.50	1.81	1.62	1.30	1.19
Neighborhood cohesion	3.38	.33	.83	−.17	.00	−.38	−.43
Neighborhood social control	3.28	.28	.77	−.19	−.15	−.35	−.25
Neighborhood positive expectations for adolescents	3.58	.47	.68	−.53	−.06	−.67	−.49
% High school graduate/ some college	58.07	7.86	−.03	.87	−.05	.09	.19
% College graduate or higher	24.07	12.23	.37	−.86	.16	−.64	−.33
% White households	48.38	29.63	.28	−.67	−.41	−.56	−.53
Neighborhood availability of services	3.77	.91	.51	−.65	−.17	−.42	−.28
Neighborhood participation in organized activities	3.69	.79	.40	−.43	.35	−.26	−.26
Neighborhood culture promotion	2.84	.13	−.14	−.13	.82	.06	−.14
% Receiving public assistance	4.05	3.45	−.30	.32	−.02	.88	.34
% Families below poverty line	3.83	4.17	−.38	.23	−.02	.82	.63
% Managerial & professional	29.77	9.15	.52	−.68	.17	−.73	−.42
% Males ages 16+ unemployed	4.64	2.82	−.43	.26	.16	.68	.23
% Females ages 16+ unemployed	4.09	2.30	−.16	.38	.25	.62	.43
Neighborhood problems & dangers	2.44	.27	.49	−.33	−.05	−.61	−.32
% ages 16–19 not in school/ not HS graduate	9.25	8.62	−.15	.04	−.55	.56	.22
% Home owners	57.94	25.15	.35	−.09	.11	−.24	−.86
Median household income	44578	11522	.55	−.28	.16	−.63	−.79
% Female-headed families	22.92	12.61	−.44	.53	.15	.65	.78
Neighborhood stability/ satisfaction	−.02	.74	.66	−.38	.08	−.35	−.66
Neighborhood adolescent problem behavior	6.91	.38	−.11	−.50	.13	−.32	−.63
Adolescent positive attitude toward nbh.	3.64	.26	.50	−.43	−.01	−.52	−.60

	Factor 1	Factor 2	Factor 3	Factor 4	Factor 5
Factor 1	1.00				
Factor 2	−.20	1.00			
Factor 3	−.03	.00	1.00		
Factor 4	−.36	.33	.01	1.00	
Factor 5	−.28	.30	−.06	.39	1.00

FIGURE 6.1   Effects of Neighborhood Demography and Quality of Neighborhood Processes on Overall Success at Early Seventh and Late Eighth Grades.

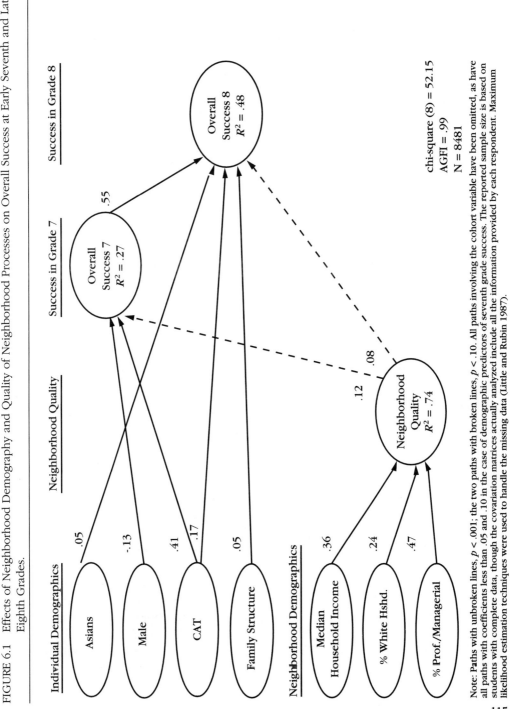

Note: Paths with unbroken lines, $p < .001$; the two paths with broken lines, $p < .10$. All paths involving the cohort variable have been omitted, as have all paths with coefficients less than .05 and .10 in the case of demographic predictors of seventh grade success. The reported sample size is based on students with complete data, though the covariation matrices actually analyzed include all the information provided by each respondent. Maximum likelihood estimation techniques were used to handle the missing data (Little and Rubin 1987).

individual differences and the neighborhood demographic measures affect global neighborhood quality and seventh-grade success, while neighborhood quality is assumed to influence both initial seventh-grade standing and eighth-grade performance. The analysis was done in LISREL with corrections for unreliability of measurement.

Figure 6.1 shows that the model fit the data well; that the three demographic variables almost completely determined neighborhood process; that the outcome was stable over nineteen months; that the direct path between neighborhood process and the eighth-grade outcome was positive, but only marginally reliable; and that the indirect path from neighborhood process to eighth-grade outcomes via seventh-grade outcomes was reliable, though the part from neighborhood quality to seventh-grade success was once again only marginal. Nonetheless, there was a total effect of global neighborhood process, implying that it is indeed possible to test simple and plausible mediational models of global neighborhood effects.

However, the high relationship between demography and process in the model means that we would have achieved similar results if the temporal ordering of demography and process had been reversed. Such a model would have quite different substantive implications, though. Neighborhood process would then be treated as a cause of community composition—perhaps through its influence on migration—and a neighborhood's social composition would there be a more proximal cause of adolescent outcomes than process. Given the strong empirical link between neighborhood demography and process found in the data reported here, making the case for independent causation or temporal precedence has to depend on theory alone.

The lack of clear discriminant validity within the process and demographic domains also has implications for testing neighborhood theories, the vast majority of which are couched in terms of specific, rather than global, neighborhood attributes. The preference for such theory implies that some neighborhood processes produce different consequences than do others. Let us consider, for example, Shaw and McKay's (1942) theory of social disorganization. It is not enough with such a theory merely to demonstrate that the specified neighborhood demographic variables relate in the predicted way to social disorganization (understood as social control and social cohesion) and that social disorganization then directly or indirectly influences criminal behavior or its precursors. If process variables in this theory cannot be clearly differentiated from other neighborhood-process measures, then an obvious alternative interpretation arises. Would a different set of process variables from those specified in social disorganization theory—even a randomly chosen set—produce a similar result? Instead of probing a single specific model using only measures from that model, it seems preferable to us to pit different models against each other, including models predicated on other process variables highly correlated with, but conceptually distinct from, those in the neighborhood effects theory under test.

A second strategy for testing specific neighborhood theories seeks to hold constant all other theoretically irrelevant process characteristics so that conclusions can then be drawn about the characteristics specified in a particular theory. We explored this strategy at an early stage with the Prince George's County data, but as might be expected by now from the limited discriminant validity among the process measures and our only modest sample size of tracts, the results varied considerably from one early adolescent outcome to another and did not always make theoretical sense. So we reluctantly concluded that analyses of some neighborhood processes, holding others constant, will not always permit easy answers about the unique influence of the (particular-process attributes specified in a theory. Instead, such analyses capitalize on sampling variability in relationships among process attributes and between these attributes and individual outcomes. The same general point is also likely to be true when it comes to differentiating among theories of neighborhood demography and their unique influences on individuals.

The foregoing conclusions are based on a single study with the type of circumscribed sampling design that is usually required for testing mediational models of neighborhood effects. Other studies might show a different pattern of results. But for now we are prepared to suggest that it will often be difficult to test mediational models unless theories explicitly try to minimize tract-level interdependencies among process and demography, unless there are very large samples of neighborhoods, and unless care is taken in data collection to minimize sources of irrelevant shared variance influencing the process measures. Under conditions such as these (see Duncan 1994), it might well be possible to obtain credible results from analyses of process and demographic variables studied together, despite high levels of intercorrelation.

Researchers could also look for settings where neighborhood attributes are not so highly interrelated, though this would have external validity costs, given that the neighborhood variables in question are highly correlated in most other locations. Researchers could also seek to minimize interdependencies among process variables or between demography and process by collecting data on many attributes and then selecting out for analysis only those that are less highly correlated with each other. The tables presented here show that we could have selected neighborhood attributes according to this criterion and could thereby have reduced the interdependencies noted in table 6.4 and figure 6.1. But there is an obvious cost to this, too, since the process and demography constructs so resulting are likely to lose their correspondence with theory and to capitalize on fluctuations in measurement error.

Finally, the empirical reality is that social processes tend to covary considerably, as do most process and demographic characteristics. Since most neighborhood theories postulate models of neighborhood effects that include specific mediational components and specific demographic components (or both), it will not be easy to meet the data requirements for strong tests of theories of this form in studies where the need to measure process results in circumscribed local sampling plans. Instead, heavy reliance will have to be placed on theoretical distinctions between constructs that have limited independent empirical justification.

SUMMARY

Two major substantive findings were described in this chapter. First, the intraclass correlations in table 6.2 were generally low across a wide range of neighborhood attributes, despite ranges on these variables that seemed large. These generally low ICC values suggest that neighborhoods are not monolithic and are instead internally heterogenous.

Second, it is difficult to make a clean empirical distinction between neighborhood demographic and process attributes, as well as between different demographic attributes and different process ones. We do not want to be too dogmatic here, for there was evidence of some partial independence among factors that were otherwise correlated. Even so, in all the relevant analyses a single factor was dominant that included both demographic and process measures, and three demographic variables were enough to account for nearly all of the global neighborhood-process variance in Prince George's County.

These major findings have implications for testing mediating models of neighborhood effects. The low ICC values set a limit on what can be achieved by the neighborhood main effect models so prevalent today. Although a few demographic characteristics usually permit predicting most of the neighborhood variance in almost any attribute, the sad fact is that there is not very much neighborhood variance in process or outcomes to explain in the first place. Given the larger-than-expected heterogeneity within neighborhoods, neighborhood theorists might profitably spend more time considering individual-difference factors that interact with neighborhood characteristics to predict individual behavior. But such a moderator-variable approach to neighborhood effects should complement, not replace, a mediating-variable approach.

The finding about unclear discriminant validity suggests that in studies with circumscribed sampling designs, it will be very difficult to decide on empirical grounds alone whether neighborhood demography is independent enough of process to justify the distinction made in conventional mediational theories. If decisions about conceptual independence and temporal precedence have to be made, then our guess is that they will usually have to be made exclusively on theoretical grounds, as in figure 6.1. Moreover, the difficulties inherent in discriminating among various process (and demographic) attributes suggest that testing specific models of neighborhood effects will be most convincing when researchers can also show that (1) a model derived from a specific theory is *reliably* different in its neighborhood outcome relationships from other models using different (but equally reliable) neighborhood social process measures or (2) the results obtained from theory-specified neighborhood variables are net of the effects of other theoretically irrelevant neighborhood variables. It will not be easy to meet either of these requirements, and researchers should therefore consider developing neighborhood theories based on conceptions of neighborhood demography and process that are more global and holistic than is the preference today.

This paper has been supported by the MacArthur Foundation Research Network on Successful Adolescent Development among Youth in High-Risk Settings. It has benefited from the comments of Greg Duncan and Rob Sampson. Jeong-Ran Kim, Meredith Phillips, and Richard Settersten provided helpful comments on an earlier draft.

7

Community Influences on Adolescent Achievement and Deviance

Nancy Darling and Laurence Steinberg

The original motivation for research into the influence of communities on child and adolescent development was based on a simple observation— some neighborhoods are better than others. Large, stable differences in rates of delinquency, school dropout, crime, alcoholism, and unemployment across neighborhoods led investigators at the University of Chicago to explore the predictors and processes underlying neighborhood decay (see chapter 1; Gephart vol. 1; Shaw and McKay 1969; Shaw et al. 1929). Although family influences were often implicated in the etiology of delinquency and other problems, the stability of neighborhood differences in rates of problem behavior in the face of relatively rapid turnover in the particular families and individuals living in the neighborhoods suggested that characteristics of the community itself, rather than individual families in the community, contributed to and maintained neighborhood differences (although selection biases also could have played a role; see Duncan, Connell, and Klebanov, vol. 1). More recently, developmental psychologists, sociologists, and demographers have focused on community differences in child and adolescent outcomes (for reviews, see Bronfenbrenner, Moen, and Garbarino 1984; Garbarino et al. 1992; Gephart vol. 1; Sampson 1992; Steinberg 1989; Tienda 1991). This work includes investigations of the defining characteristics of neighborhood ecologies characterized by high levels of developmental problems and the influence these neighborhoods have on the children living in them.

This chapter explores several processes through which communities may influence child and adolescent development. We focus on the influence of neighborhoods on individuals' developmental outcomes, rather than on predicting neighborhood or community differences in the aggregate, as do the six studies analyzed in volume 1. Because of this focus, we build on the extensive literature on processes known to affect child and adolescent development—specifically, the socialization influences of parents and peers—and explore how these processes both mediate and are moderated by characteristics of the communities in which they take place. As will become clear, a focus on child and adolescent outcomes at the individual, rather than aggregate, level alters the types of processes examined in the community. This particular focus has important implications for both the types of theoretical models developed and the conclusions drawn from empirical research designed to test them.

COMMUNITY DIFFERENCES AND DEFINITIONS

The term *community* has been defined by different researchers to mean different things. In this chapter, we use it to describe an aggregation of individuals who share resources and a common sense of identity, whether or not those individuals actually know one another. In this spirit, for example, Coleman and Hoffer (1987) described the parents of children attending the same school as belonging to a common community. Many parents in that community have never met, yet they are connected through the shared resource of the school, through shared communication in the form of school bulletins and mailings, and through their own and their children's identification with the school. Our conceptualization of community differs from, among others, Hillery's (1955, 111) classic definition of *community* as consisting of "persons in social interaction within a geographic area and having one or more common ties," in that we neither use geography as a defining feature nor assume that individual community members have direct contact with one another.

Although our conceptualization of community represents a departure from much previous, geographically influenced research, our view may be especially useful for studying the effects of variability in social interaction or residential propinquity on community processes and for studying nonurban environments. The residential neighborhood or block group may be a salient unit of analysis in an urban environment (but see chapter 2), but these units may be less salient in suburban or rural areas. Automobile transportation may change the "boundedness" of community definitions, and communities centered around automobile transportation may be geographically larger than other communities. Sometimes a whole town may be perceived as a community and sometimes a more limited residential areas may be perceived as a community, depending on the extent to which resources are distributed throughout the community and residents perceive their area of residence as distinct from other areas within the town. In some rural areas, catchment school districts may form the primary identification through which families come to define their community. Appropriate community definition is further complicated by developmental changes in the extent to which peer group and school are tied to residential location. Differences in the extent to which residential neighborhoods define selection of friendship groups in rural, suburban, and urban areas, and how this varies as a function of transportation patterns, are important areas of research that have been only tentatively explored.

Our work on community influences also departs from previous, geographically influenced research in its emphasis on interpersonal transactions, rather than demographic characteristics, to characterize community quality (see chapter 2). Educational and income levels, crime rates, residential mobility, ethnic heterogeneity, and other demographic indicators of community resources presumably influence individual families and adolescents through proximal processes such as parenting beliefs and practices and links to resources outside of the community. As discussed later, consideration of interpersonal, as well as tangible, resources available in the community is a prerequisite to an understanding of how community structural characteristics thought to facilitate the exchange and development of resources influence child outcomes.

Also critical to keep in mind is that observed community differences in child or adolescent outcomes do not necessarily imply developmental processes operating at the community level. For example, communities characterized by high parental monitoring will also probably be populated by adolescents who exhibit high academic performance, low dropout rates, and low rates of deviance. Although this appears to be a "community" effect, the correlation between community monitoring and desirable adolescent behavior can be explained without resorting to community-level processes. When parents influence their own, and only their own, children and many high-monitoring parents live in the same community, the aggregated family influences will result in community-level differences in child outcomes. These community-level differences would result entirely from processes operating within the family, however (Bronfenbrenner, Moen, and Garbarino 1984; Darling et al. 1995; Garbarino et al. 1992; Steinberg 1989). At the level of the individual child, community processes may be said to be operating to the extent that child outcomes would differ if the child's family moved from one community to another (Steinberg 1989). Proof that such a process is operating requires, at the least, documenting that the putative community process operates over and above that of the family, or documenting that the community changes the influence of processes operating within the family (see Klebanov et al. vol. 1).

In this chapter we examine community influences on adolescent achievement and delinquency and ask whether such influences are independent of those operating at the level of the family or peer group, similar to the chapters in volume 1. However, in contrast to the work presented by our colleagues, we have made a distinction between family and community parenting, community peer characteristics, and community structural characteristics. The analyses focus on (1) the association of community parenting and peer characteristics with individual adolescent outcomes and (2) the association of an important community variable—social integration—with individual adolescent outcomes.

Although communities can be defined at many different levels of analysis, these analyses parallel the chapters in volume 1 as they rely on the census tract. In our sample, the population of the census tracts studied ranges from under a thousand to almost ten thousand occupants. Census tracts, often used as proxies for neighborhoods, are defined by geographic boundaries rather than by social ties and are designed to reflect meaningful neighborhood, demographic, and physical boundaries. The census tract (or neighborhood) provides one potential pool of friends from whom adolescents can choose, and neighborhood adults are one group of adults who may act to control the public behavior of community youth.

This chapter has two specific emphases that differentiate it from several other studies of community effects. First, processes operating among community youth are examined, in contrast to the longstanding emphasis on the importance of adults and adult-controlled social institutions as the dominant mechanisms of influence on adolescents' socialization in the community. Second, a distinction is drawn between the structure and content of community socialization processes. Most community research emphasizes structural characteristics of communities that are assumed to influence child development— characteristics such as the extent of social integration in a community. Although we believe that variations in these structural features of communities may be important, we believe as well that these structural aspects of community socialization (namely, the mechanisms through which community processes transmit information between members) cannot be examined independent of the content of community socialization (that is, the nature of the information being transmitted).

METHOD

SAMPLE

Our sample is drawn from the student bodies of six high schools in northern California. The schools were selected to yield a sample of students from different socioeconomic brackets, a variety of ethnic backgrounds (African American, Asian, Hispanic American, and white), different family structures, and different types of communities (urban and suburban). None of the high schools were magnet schools, nor did the communities allow school choice. Data for our analyses were collected during the 1988–1989 school year via self-report surveys filled out by the students on two days of survey administration each school year. Approximately 85 percent of students agreed to participate in the study and were in school on each of the two days the questionnaires were administered. About half (57 percent) of the participating students lived in neighborhoods with twenty-five or more other respondents and completed both questionnaires. These students form the sample for the following analyses (the exact number for each analysis varies, depending on the variables used, and is reported in the relevant tables). For a detailed description of the sample, refer to Steinberg and colleagues (1992).

MEASURES

Three sets of measures are of interest in our analysis: measures of parenting practices, measures of adolescent outcomes, and measures of community processes.

PARENTING PRACTICES   Two parenting practices were measured. *Parents' involvement in education* was used as a predictor of educational outcomes. Students reported on the frequency with which their parents were involved in their high school education in five respects: helping with homework when asked, attending school programs, watching the student in sports or other extracurricular activities, helping the student select courses, and knowing how the student is doing in school. Response categories were *never, sometimes,* and *usually.* A composite index of involvement was formed by averaging across items. *Parental monitoring* was used as a predictor of problem behavior and was assessed using a five-question monitoring scale (Patterson and Stouthamer-Loeber 1984). A sample item was "How much do your parents REALLY know . . . where you are most afternoons after school?" Adolescents responded on a three-point scale, with 1 representing *don't know* and 3 representing *know a lot.*

ADOLESCENT OUTCOMES   Students reported their own *grade-point averages* (GPA), scored on a conventional four-point scale. Previous work indicates that self-reported grades and actual grades taken from official school records are highly correlated (r = .80; Donovan and Jessor 1985; Dornbusch et al. 1987). Our index of *classroom engagement* (Newmann 1981) was based on students' reports of their effort, concentration, and attention, as well as their frequency of mind wandering (reverse coded) during class in the four main subject areas. Responses were on a five-point scale for each item, ranging from 1 = *never* to 5 = *always* or *almost every day. Bonding to teachers* and *school orientation* were two scales derived by factor analyzing a set of items that assessed the students' feelings of attachment to school (Wehlage et al. 1989). Responses to these items were on a scale from 1 (*strongly agree*) to 4 (*strongly disagree*). Bonding to teachers assessed the student's attachment to his or her teachers (sample item: "I care what most of my teachers think of me"). A measure of school orientation assessed students' valuing of and commitment to school (sample item: "I feel satisfied with school because I'm learning a lot"). *Work orientation* was measured using a subscale of Greenberger's Psychosocial Maturity Inventory (Form D; Greenberger et al. 1974) that assessed the adolescent's pride in the successful completion of tasks.

Two types of adolescent deviance were measured: substance use and delinquency. Both frequency and seriousness of deviance were used in the assessment. Adolescent *substance use* was assessed using three questions that asked respondents to report how often they had used alcohol, smoked marijuana, or used a drug other than marijuana since the beginning of the school year, and they responded on a scale from 1 (*never*) to 4 (*often*). A measure of substance use was derived from this information, in which adolescents were classed on a five-point scale 1 = *nonusers of either drugs or alcohol*, 2 = *experimenters with alcohol only*, 3 = *experimenters with marijuana and/or alcohol*, 4 = *regular alcohol or marijuana users*, or 5 = *experimenters with drugs other than alcohol or marijuana*). These five categories were used as a linear variable of substance use. The measure of *delinquency* was based on both frequency of delinquent acts and seriousness of the offense. Acts at three levels of seriousness were tapped: status offenses (false identification use), property offenses (vandalism and petty theft), and violent or potentially violent offenses (carrying weapons to school or fighting in school). Students rated their involvement with each act since the beginning of the school year on a scale from 1 (*never*) to 4 (*often*). Using this information, we built a five-category measure of student involvement. Students were rated as 1 if they reported no delinquency other than use of a false identification; 2 if they had been involved in property crimes once or twice, but not involved in fighting or carrying weapons; 3 if they either had been involved in property crimes at least several times *or* had been fighting or had carried weapons to school at least once; 4 if they had either carried weapons to school several times or had both been involved in fighting and had carried weapons to school; or 5 if they reported having fought several times.

COMMUNITY VARIABLES   Individuals' scores on the measures of parenting practices and the adolescent outcomes were used to generate aggregate indices of these variables at the community level. Census tracts were used as units of analysis, and parenting and peer characteristics were computed using the mean score of all respondents identified as living in that tract.

Family social integration was measured using a twelve-item scale tapping the extent to which adolescents had had an opportunity for nonteacher adult contact and parents had had the opportunity to meet the friends of their adolescents and the families of those friends (α = .67). Each item was coded dichotomously as the adolescent reported the contact as either existing or not. Sample items included "How many of the parents of these school friends know you?" and "How many of the parents of these school friends know your parents?" Items were coded dichotomously as 0 (*none*) or 1 (*some, most, or all*). The average social integration of all families in a census tract was used as a measure of community social integration.

Community income was measured using the median household income taken from the 1988 census.

RESULTS

THE INFLUENCE OF COMMUNITY ADULTS AND PEERS

Theories of communities that emphasize the socializing role of adults rely on two assumptions: (1) an underlying tension exists between adults in a community acting as control agents and community youths in need of control, and (2) neighborhoods are places where nonfamilial adults occasionally act as surrogate parents for other parents' children. Indeed, the decline of community adults' willingness to scold or otherwise control unrelated youths has been used to explain neighborhood decline and neighborhood differences in delinquency (chapters 1 and 3; Coleman and Hoffer 1987; Kornhauser 1978; Sampson and Groves 1989; Shaw and McKay 1969). The emphasis on such "community adult" models in theories of community effects is surprising, however, given what we know about the influence (or, more precisely, lack of influence) of unrelated adults on children and adolescents. There is little evidence to suggest that adolescents' relationships with even those unrelated adults named as significant others are strong predictors of adolescent outcomes (for a review, see Darling, Hamilton, and Niego 1994), and, more importantly, few youths report extensive contact with unrelated adults outside of school (Blyth, Hill, and Thiel 1982).

In the first set of analyses, we examined whether the benefits adolescents recieved from living in neighborhoods characterized by good parenting derived directly from neighborhood adults or, instead, whether they were mediated through the behavior of neighborhood peers. Multiple regression analyses were conducted to assess the independent association of community parenting and community peer characteristics with individual adolescent outcomes after controlling for the parenting that the adolescents experienced in their own families. The results are reported in table 7.1.

TABLE 7.1   Individual Adolescent Outcomes Predicted by Community Parenting and Characteristics of Community Youth

| | Standardized Betas | | | | | |
	Family Parenting	Parenting	Community Peers	Income	Multiple R	N
GPA	.19**	−.04	.31**	−.00	.37	3516
Classroom engagement	.23**	−.07*	.16**	−.02	.27	2511
Work orientation	.18**	−.14	.90**	−.01	.28	2452
School orientation	.18**	−.04	.17**	−.01	.24	2595
Teacher bonding	.22**	−.04	.14**	−.01	.26	2596
Substance use	−.23**	.03	.26**	.01	.35	2582
Delinquency	−.23**	.03	.26**	.01	.35	2582

Note: Analyses control for parenting of the adolescents' own parents and median family income.
*p < .05. **p < .01.

As expected, parenting experienced within the family predicted adolescent outcomes at the individual level (that is, parental monitoring predicted adolescent deviance; parental school involvement predicted adolescent achievement). Characteristics of community adolescents also predicted individual adolescent outcomes ($p < .01$), over and above family parenting, suggesting that contact with well-functioning peers is associated with better adolescent adjustment. As the table indicates, however, the quality of parenting in the community did not predict adolescent behavior once the quality of the individual adolescent's home environment and community peers were taken into account.

The results of these analyses are consistent with a model of community influence emphasizing the significance of socialization within individual families and the benefits to adolescents of contact with well-socialized peers. Thus, adolescents may benefit from the presence of many well-functioning families not, as many theoretical models suggest, because of the direct contact they have with unrelated adults from these households but through their contact with the peers who are raised in them. This finding does not negate the significance of living in a neighborhood characterized by strong families, however. Children in a community characterized by a high proportion of involved, high-monitoring parents will be more likely to experience good parenting within their own families and, as a consequence, will be less likely to engage in deviance and more likely to achieve in school (this is not necessarily an effect of living in that community, but simply a probabilistic statement). The predominance of good parents in the community, however, increases the likelihood that all adolescents in the community will be exposed to well-socialized peers, and the availability of a pool of well-socialized peers does benefit individual adolescents above and beyond the benefits they derive from living in well-functioning families. These results suggest that models of community influences on the development of youth should focus on processes operating within the peer community, and not solely on mechanisms believed to link adolescents with nonfamilial adults.

THE EFFECTS OF SOCIAL INTEGRATION

Community parenting, the characteristics of community youth, and the number, quality, and vitality of community institutions are all resources—either capital resources or social capital (Coleman 1988). Like others who have emphasized social networks and the distribution of capital, Coleman and Hoffer (1987) have stressed the importance of community structural characteristics in allowing the exchange and development of social and capital resources and in changing the processes through which communities can socialize their children. For example, they have emphasized the importance of two structural characteristics in particular—social integration and value consensus—and have referred to communities characterized by high social integration and high value consensus as "functional communities." *Social integration* is defined as the extent to which the social networks of neighborhood adults and youth overlap. Coleman and Hoffer (1987) have argued that social integration increases the ability of communities to socialize adolescents in three ways: by increasing social support, by increasing value consensus, and by strengthening the community's ability to condemn norm violations.

An underlying assumption of the functional community model is that social integration will inevitably lead to well-socialized youths, where *well-socialized* is defined as optimal developmental outcomes as judged by the larger society. To the extent that communities differ in the goals toward which youths are socialized, however, it might be predicted that social integration will result in different developmental outcomes. In particular, rather than inevitably leading to good school performance and lack of deviance, social integration might intensify the influence of community characteristics—whether these characteristics bode well or ill. For example, social integration into a community with widespread alienation from school and deviance may increase, rather than decrease, deviance and diminish, rather than enhance, achievement. Indeed, beliefs about the "dangers" of integration into "bad" communities underlie the behavior of many residents in areas of concentrated poverty: A sensible response to living amidst dysfunctional neighborhoods may be to isolate oneself from, rather than integrate oneself into, the community (see chapter 2). To assess whether structural characteristics such as social integration are associated with better socialization, researchers must take into account the characteristics of community parents and youths (Darling and Gringlas 1994; Darling, Steinberg, and Gringlas 1993; Steinberg, Darling, and Fletcher 1993).

A second set of issues raised by the social integration hypothesis leads us back to the distinction between family-level and community-level processes. Social integration can exist between an individual family and the community or within the community as whole. Thus, an individual family may be integrated into the community, but the community as a whole may or may not be characterized by social integration. A full understanding of the role of social integration as a community socialization process requires that both family-community and within-community integration be examined simultaneously. To date, research has not clearly differentiated between integration operating at the family-community level (that is, whether or not an individual family is integrated into the community) and integration operating at the within-community level (that is, the extent to which the community as a whole is characterized by social integration).

In the next set of analyses, multiple regression was used to examine the association of family social integration and community social integration with adolescent academic outcomes and deviance. Again, *community* was defined at the census-tract level.

As illustrated in table 7.2, adolescents from families who were integrated into their communities performed better in school. Interestingly, this is not because integration made it more likely that parents would have become involved in academic affairs (had that been the case, the introduction of the integration variable would have reduced the family parenting variables to nonsignificance). Instead, it may be that adolescents benefit from the increased exchange of resources facilitated by their families' social integration into a formal community institution, such as the school. This interpretation is consistent with the finding that social integration predicts educational outcomes, but not adolescent deviance.

Although the functional community hypothesis advanced by Coleman and Hoffer (1987) suggests that the benefits of social integration cut across communities, we hypothesized that integration would predict positive adolescent outcomes only in "good" neighborhoods (see Brooks-Gunn et al. 1993; Chase-Lansdale et al. vol. 1). To test this hypothesis, we used multiple regression to predict adolescent outcomes from family parenting, family integration, community adolescent characteristics, and the interaction of family integration and community characteristics. We found that family social integration was associated with adolescent school engagement and lower levels of substance use *only* in communities where other adolescents were engaged in school and were not involved in substance use. In contrast, social integration was associated with *lower* engagement and *more* substance use when community adolescents were more deviant or less involved in school. In other words, social integration exaggerated the potentially negative influence of living in a community with poorly adjusted peers.

Thus far, social integration has been used vis-à-vis the extent to which the adolescent's family is integrated into the community. This variable also may be examined at the aggregate level, by looking at the effects of living in a community in which many, versus few, families are socially integrated. We

TABLE 7.2   Individual Adolescent Outcomes Predicted by Integration of the Family into the Community and Characteristics of Community Youth

		Standardized Betas				
	Family Parenting	Community			Multiple	
		Integration	Peers	Income	R	N
GPA	.15**	.04	.28**	−.03	.35	2188
Classroom engagement	.21**	.06**	.15**	−.09**	.28	2159
Work orientation	.19**	.09**	.14**	−.06**	.29	2138
School orientation	.14**	.09**	.18**	−.05*	.26	2207
Teacher bonding	.16**	.12**	.13**	−.07**	.27	2207
Substance use	−.23**	.01	.25**	.02	.35	2211
Delinquency	−.21**	.03	.17**	−.01	.28	2227

Note: Analyses control for parenting of the adolescents' own parents and median family income.
*$p < .05$. **$p < .01$.

refer to this construct as community social integration. Regression analyses revealed that once family parenting and family social integration were controlled, community social integration neither predicted adolescent academic outcomes or deviance nor moderated the association between community characteristics and adolescent outcomes.

Taken together, the results suggest that adolescents benefit from the social integration of their own families into the community, but they do not benefit directly from living in a socially integrated community. Further, the results suggest that family social integration increases the influence of the community—both for better and for worse—at least in terms of classroom engagement and substance use. Thus, in some communities, the social integration of the family may actually increase adolescents' risk, rather than buffer adolescents from the potentially deleterious effects of poor neighborhoods.

CONCLUSION

The functional community hypothesis is appealing in that a well-functioning community provides a buffer for youth whose parents are not able to socialize them adequately to dominant cultural values. Qualitative descriptions of coping mechanisms used by families in resource-poor environments (chapters 2 and 3; Stack 1974), however, demonstrate that structural links facilitating the transfer of resources allow resources to flow in both directions. Like an osmotic gradient, resource-poor families in relatively rich environments may benefit from community ties (see Klebanov et al. vol. 1). Conversely, however, in resource-poor environments, children in relatively well functioning families may suffer when their families maintain strong ties to the neighborhood. Thus, the benefits of community structural characteristics may be context-specific and may depend on the relative resources of families and the communities in which they live.

In attempting to understand the processes through which communities influence children's development, we have emphasized three major points. First, mean differences in outcomes between communities can result from processes operating at the community level, the family level, or both. Before drawing conclusions about the processes through which communities influence development, researchers must consider proximal influences that are not genuine "community" processes. Our results indicate that the major benefit received from living in a neighborhood where there are many well-functioning families is that children are much more likely to become friends with well-functioning peers. In contrast, little direct advantage seems to be gained from living in a community with a high proportion of well-functioning families over and above the impact of having well-functioning parents of one's own and well-socialized peers.

Second, community socialization processes specific to youth—such as mutual influence, availability of potential friends, school climate, and availability of contexts for adult sanctioned activities—are important. In our view, current theorizing about community effects on adolescent development may overestimate the roles played by nonfamilial adults and underestimate the significance of other adolescents as the primary agents of community socialization. Theoretical models of how community characteristics change how youth cultures develop and function will differ in focus from those emphasizing adult socialization and should be further developed.

Finally, although structural characteristics of communities may covary with resources, it is critical to recognize the potential for contextual variation in the correlates of structural linkages as a function of community resources. We illustrated this point by showing that under certain conditions, children fare better when their families are not well integrated into the community. Thus, rather than asking whether social integration in a community is beneficial (or worse yet, just assuming that integration is always beneficial), researchers must differentiate between the conditions under which social integration is a positive force in youngsters' lives and those under which it places children at risk.

———————————

Preparation of this manuscript was supported by grants from the Lilly Endowment and the William T. Grant Foundation. The study on which this report is based was supported by grants to Laurence Steinberg and B. Bradford Brown from the U.S. Department of Education, through the National Center on Effective Secondary Schools at the University of Wisconsin–Madison; and to Sanford M. Dornbusch and P. Herbert Leiderman from the Spencer Foundation.

8

On Ways of Thinking About Measuring Neighborhoods: Implications for Studying Context and Developmental Outcomes for Children

Linda M. Burton, Townsand Price-Spratlen, and Margaret Beale Spencer

As noted in earlier chapters, renewed scholarly interest in urban ecology, poverty, and developmental outcomes has spawned a lively scholarly discourse on the relationship between neighborhood context and child development (Berg and Medrich 1980; Coulton and Padney 1992; Garbarino and Crouter 1978; Garbarino, Kostelny, and Dubrow 1991; Jencks and Mayer 1990; Lewin-Epstein 1985; Proctor, Volser, and Sirles 1993; Wilson 1987). Although this discourse has generated a rich, yet inconclusive, knowledge base on neighborhood effects and child outcomes, a systematic examination of the impact that particular conceptual and methodological frameworks have on the study of neighborhoods and children has yet to appear in the literature (Brewster, Billy, and Grady 1993; Brooks-Gunn et al. 1994; Crane 1991; Price-Spratlen and Burton 1995; Sampson 1992). Specifically, social scientists have not addressed the following questions: How do particular paradigms and measurement strategies affect the insights generated about neighborhood context and developmental outcomes for children? Do existing conceptual and methodological frameworks accurately capture the relationship between neighborhood context and child development?

Given the growing interest in the study of context and children, and the concomitant need for social scientists to examine conceptual and methodological models that guide the empirical research in this area, it seems particularly timely to assess how "ways of thinking about" and "ways of measuring" neighborhood influence our understanding of child development (Bennett 1993; Bronfenbrenner, Moen, and Garbarino 1985; Garbarino et al. 1992; Olson 1982; Wohlwill and Heft 1987). Thus, in this chapter we present an overview of the various ways in which neighborhoods have been conceptualized and measured, and discuss the implications of these frameworks for the study of context and developmental outcomes for children. First, we discuss issues that should be considered in selecting conceptual frameworks and measures for studying neighborhoods and child development. Second, we outline four categories of "ways of thinking about" and "ways of measuring" neighborhoods and the implications of their use in generating knowledge on community context and developmental outcomes for children. The four categories include (1) neighborhood as site (Bennett 1993; Downs and Liben 1993), (2) neighborhood as perception (Haney and Knowles 1978; Hyson and Bollin 1990; Jessor and Jessor 1973), (3) neighborhood as social network (Emirbayer and Goodwin 1994; Keller 1968; Oliver 1988), and (4) neighborhood as culture (Super and Harkness 1986; Swidler 1986). Third, we discuss the implications of these conceptual and measurement categories for future research on neighborhoods and children.

CONCEPTUAL AND METHODOLOGICAL CONSIDERATIONS IN THE STUDY OF NEIGHBORHOOD AND DEVELOPMENTAL OUTCOMES FOR CHILDREN

In reviewing the existing literature on context and children, we have identified four key issues that should be considered in the selection of conceptual and methodological frameworks for studying the relationship between neighborhoods and developmental outcomes for children. The first concerns the conceptual definition of *neighborhood* (Tienda 1991). As indicated by Gephart (vol. 1), Sampson and Morenoff (chapter 1), and Furstenberg and Hughes (chapter 2), there are a variety of conceptual and operational definitions of *neighborhood* currently used in the study of context and child outcomes. The most frequently used definition is one in which neighborhoods are defined as specific territorial or geographic sites (Bennett 1993; Chaskin 1994; Keller 1968; Tepperman and Richardson 1986). This definition, often considered to be an objective delimiter of *neighborhood*, does not typically incorporate the subjective meaning experienced by a neighborhood's residents (Allen, Bentler, and Gutek 1985; Bronfenbrenner 1993; Guest and Lee 1984; Haney and Knowles 1978; Hunter 1974; Lewin 1935).

Lee, Oropesa, and Kanan (1994) noted that neighborhoods are not merely "demarcated territorial units, but rather, they are social constructions named and bounded differently by different individuals" (250). This conceptualization underscores the importance of considering subjective appraisals of neighborhood (chapter 2). Subjective neighborhood appraisals are particularly critical in the study of context and developmental outcomes for children. Children's cultural experiences and social constructions of neighborhood boundaries and experiences are often vastly different from the objective neighborhood delimiters imposed by social scientists and other adults (Berg and Medrich 1980; Bryant 1985; Garbarino et al. 1992; von Andel 1990). Consequently, researchers' lack of attention to the subjective nature of neighborhoods may result in both the collection and interpretation of data that do not accurately represent the relationship between neighborhood influences and developmental outcomes as experienced by the child (Elliott and Huizinga 1990; Super and Harkness 1986).

The second issue that social scientists should consider in the study of neighborhoods and child development concerns Bronfenbrenner's (1986) discussion of individual development and the "social address." The social address paradigm is limited to the comparison of developmental outcomes for children living in contrasting environments, as defined by the socio-demographic features (for example, racial or ethnic composition, or percentage of families living in poverty) of the geographic area they reside in (Bronfenbrenner 1986). Individuals are typically ascribed certain contextual experiences based on the "social address" of their current geographic residence. Bronfenbrenner and Crouter (1983) noted that this paradigm has a number of limitations:

> [Within this paradigm] no explicit consideration is given . . . to intervening structures or processes through which the environment might affect the course of development. One looks only at the social address— that is, the environmental label—with no attention to what the environment is like, what people are living there, what they are doing, or how the activities taking place could affect the child. (361–62)

In addition to the limitations outlined by Bronfenbrenner and Crouter (1983), assigning social address labels to children using the children's current geographic residences as the "locators" of contextual experiences is particularly problematic in studying the lives of ethnic or racial minority children. In general, research on ethnic or racial minority families, particularly African Americans, suggests that family living arrangements are flexible and fluid. Families live coresidentially or extraresidentially, both within and across neighborhoods (Burton and Jarrett 1991; Martin and Martin 1978; Stack 1974; Valentine 1978). Holloman and Lewis (1978), in an ethnographic account of urban African American families, clearly illustrated this point in a profile of the residential dispersion of a family referred to as the "clan":

> At present, nine households of the clan are located within a maximum of seven blocks of each other in the Uptown area. . . . Before the move Uptown by those now in the central cluster, the entire clan was located on the West Side of Chicago. Six households remain in three general locations, but are not in the same building. . . . Members of the core group who live away from the central cluster are still within walking distance of one other household. (230–31)

The work of Holloman and Lewis (1978), as well as others, suggests that using *one* designated residential address as an identifier of the primary neighborhood in which a child or youth develops may not provide an accurate view of the impact of neighborhood on developmental outcomes for children (Aschenbrenner 1975; Clark 1983; Furstenberg 1993; Jarrett forthcoming; Silverstein and Krate 1975; Stack and Burton 1993; Williams and Kornblum 1994; Zollar 1985). Some children experience a multiplicity of "neighborhoods of residence." The developmental effects of the multiplicity of neighborhood residences are not captured in research that ascribes social address characteristics to a child using a child's single, currently reported address as an indicator of neighborhood membership.

Moreover, the recent ethnographic work of Allison and colleagues (1994), Burton and Duncan (1993), and Merriwether–de Vries (1994) indicates that particularly in the case of adolescents, considering the multiplicity of neighborhoods of residence is not sufficient for understanding the impact of context on development (Allison and Takei 1993; Bell-Scott and Taylor 1989). Their longitudinal community-based studies of urban African American teens suggest that adolescents engaged in the developmental process of individuation venture beyond the confines of their neighborhoods of residence and experience the influence of other neighborhoods through "hanging out" in these environments. These authors argue that these "other neighborhoods," termed "neighborhoods of sociability," are as, if not more, important to consider in the study of context and adolescent development than are neighborhoods of residence. Comparable perspectives have been indicated in the neighborhood and adolescent development research of others (Noack and Silbereisen 1988). The research of Stokols and Shumaker (1981) suggests that the adolescents are less place-dependent with respect to their neighborhood of residence than young children, since their desired activities can be satisfied in alternative settings. Schiavo (1988), in a neighborhood study of suburban youths, indicated that, for adolescents, the neighborhood of residence diminishes in its role in daily life because of outside-neighborhood relationships, mobility, and independence. It is plausible then, that the effect on development of neighborhood of sociability is a critical factor to consider as children become mobile adolescents. Alternative perspectives, however, have argued that it is within neighborhoods of residence that children and adolescents develop "attachments to place." Such attachments are hypothesized to have long-term, lasting effects on individuals' developmental outcomes (Proshansky and Fabian 1987; Rivlin 1982).

A third consideration concerns the notion of child and neighborhood as interdependent systems, as neighborhoods and children reciprocally influence one another (Wynn et al. 1988). Overton and Reese (1977) argued that

> man and environment reciprocally interact and exert formative influences on each other. The assumptive base of this relation is opposed to both static material reality and a static reality of inherent forms. . . . Man in this relation is an active system which transforms or assimilates other

active systems (i.e., environmental systems), and on the basis of the activity accommodates or changes itself in conformance with the earlier transformation. Human behavior and its development can be described as a "shaping" process only to the extent that it is accepted that man actively shapes the environment so transformed.(15–16)

In contrast to the interdependent systems approach, most of the existing research on causal links between neighborhoods and child outcomes has involved unidirectional models (for example, neighborhood child outcome). However, Overton and Reese (1977) suggested children and neighborhoods are engaged in constant interaction to produce developmental outcomes. Although these interactions are invariably mediated by family (see chapter 4), it seems equally important to consider the effects that children have on neighborhoods. Several ethnographic researchers have highlighted the impact of adolescents on their environment (MacLeod 1987; Ogbu 1974; Sullivan 1988). Reporting findings from a five-year community-based study of context, family development, and teenage pregnancy, Burton, Allison, and Obeidallah (1995) described the role of Anthony, a nineteen-year-old high school dropout, in his neighborhood:

> Anthony may not have finished high school, and he may not have a job, but he is the treasure of our community. He helps the young mothers around the neighborhood with their kids. He does the grocery shopping for some of the old folks around here who can't get out. And he keeps the peace between rival street gangs in the community.

The fourth consideration involves the notion of neighborhood as a "contextual moment" (Burton 1991). With the exception of several ethnographic accounts of the lives of children in urban neighborhoods (Furstenberg 1993; Gans 1962; Hagedorn and Macon 1988; Hippler 1971; Howell 1973; Kotlowitz 1991; Moore 1969; Newman 1992; Williams and Kornblum 1994), most of the existing studies of neighborhoods and developmental outcomes for children present static, demographic profiles of neighborhood characteristics as they influence children's lives. Neighborhoods, however, are not static. They have temporal rhythms and dynamic "life cycles" of their own (Guest 1974). Merry (1981), in an ethnographic study of neighborhoods and crime, highlighted the differential temporal use of public spaces in neighborhoods by varying ethnic groups. In another ethnographic study, Burton (1991) found that variations in the temporal organization of activities (such as drug trafficking) in neighborhoods was directly related to the type of care and monitoring children received.

Although difficult to measure using standard survey research strategies, the dynamic, fluid nature of neighborhoods must be considered in conceptualizing and designing studies of context and child development. At the same time, neighborhood constructs and measures should reflect more than an assessment of "contextual moments." Indeed, neighborhoods have a developmental trajectory of their own, and the processes involved in that trajectory probably are what have the greatest impact on developmental outcomes for children (chapter 4; Tienda 1991).

CONCEPTUALIZING AND MEASURING NEIGHBORHOODS

Given (1) the objective and subjective definitions of *neighborhood*, (2) neighborhoods as the "social address," (3) the interdependent relationship between neighborhoods and children, and (4) the "contextual moment" perspective of neighborhoods, it is clearly important that conceptual and methodological assessment strategies have different utilities, depending on the neighborhood and developmental phenomena of interest. In our review of the literature, we have identified four categories of paradigms and measures that have been used in the study of neighborhoods and child development: neighborhoods as sites, perceptions, networks, and cultures.

NEIGHBORHOODS AS SITES

Neighborhood as physical site is the most commonly used conceptualization in studies of neighborhood context and child development (Bennett 1993; Downs 1981). Studies in which neighborhood is conceptually defined as site are concerned with the social milieu (for instance, racial mix, poverty levels, crime rates, rates of high school completion, and unemployment) and the physical quality (for example, quality of housing, density, and street maintenance) of a designated geographic area. The designated boundaries of the geographic area are typically defined by the researcher.

The conceptualization of neighborhood as physical site is frequently used in studies that explore the unidirectional influence of neighborhood on child outcomes. Large survey data sets are used in these studies to provide information on the social milieu and physical quality of neighborhoods. Reported at the level of zip code or tract, census data are frequently a source of information on neighborhood as site.

The use of census-tract-level data to profile the social milieu and physical quality of neighborhoods has several limitations (see also chapter 2). First, census-tract data comprise geographic units that are much larger than the developmental neighborhood niches of children. Second, the focus on census tracts as the unit of analysis for neighborhoods does not facilitate the exploration of the range of heterogeneous outcomes evident in the smaller geographic units in which children live. Third, analyses based on census-tract delineations of neighborhoods often are based on a social address approach—that is, the assessments of neighborhood effects are restricted to neighborhoods of residence rather than also including assessments of the neighborhoods of sociability. Fourth, census data, unless analyzed across time periods, can provide only profiles of the "contextual moment" of a neighborhood. Fifth, the representativeness of census data, particularly for ethnic or racial minorities, has consistently been challenged by social scientists. Thus, questions exist concerning its generalizability in studying context and the lives of ethnic or racial minority children.

Although census-tract-level assessments of neighborhoods have many limitations, recent developments both in the conceptualization and measurement of neighborhoods as sites have enhanced this approach's scientific utility. One development has been the use of census data at the block and block-group levels. The use of block- and block-group-level census data allows social scientists to generate "finer-grained" profiles of the developmental niches of children and adolescents. In Burton and Duncan's (1993) work, for example, adolescent respondents defined the geographic boundaries of their neighborhoods of residence and sociability. Then, Burton used block-group-level census data to create profiles of the social milieu and physical quality of the neighborhoods in which her respondents lived and "hung out." A distinct difference between the block-group-level profiles of the neighborhoods, and the census-tract-level assessments was found. For instance, at the tract level, 50 percent of the children under age eighteen lived in poverty. However, the application of block-group-level data within the respondent-defined neighborhood boundaries indicated that in at least two neighborhoods within that same census tract, the proportions of children under the age of eighteen living in poverty were 86.6 percent and 1 percent, respectively. Clearly, this finer-grained distinction provided by the block-group neighborhood assessments offered a more accurate profile of the contextual experiences of poverty in the developmental niches that the respondents formed.

Another methodological advance in the assessment of neighborhood as site includes "windshield surveys" (see chapter 9). This method involves researchers who directly observe various social-milieu and physical-quality dimensions of the neighborhood (for example, housing stock, upkeep of neighborhood gathering places, and the temporal organization of neighborhoods) by systematically driving through the neighborhoods of interests and recording the characteristics on a structured checklist. This method of neighborhood assessment has a high degree of reliability in terms of capturing the existing social milieu and physical quality of neighborhoods and, when used in concert with census-block and block-group data, provides a much more accurate profile of neighborhood environments.

Assessing neighborhood as site can provide useful baseline data on context. However, to generate the most comprehensive assessment of the neighborhood environments of children, this "way of thinking about" and "way of measuring" neighborhoods should be used in concert with assessments based on viewing neighborhoods as perceptions, networks, or cultures.

NEIGHBORHOODS AS PERCEPTIONS

A perspective useful in assessing the relationship between neighborhood effects and developmental outcomes for children involves a subjective treatment of context—neighborhood perceptions. Neighborhood perceptions comprise individuals' personal evaluations of the social milieu and quality of the geographic area they define as neighborhood.

An important issue to consider in the study of neighborhood perceptions as they relate to child development outcomes concerns variability in the subjective evaluations of neighborhoods. Adults, adolescents, and children perceive risks in neighborhoods differently (Burton 1991; Hart 1979; Huckfeldt 1983; Jessor and Jessor 1973; van Vliet, 1981). However, perceptions of neighborhoods, as typically explored in child development research, have focused on aspects of the adult contextual experience with which children and teenagers may have limited direct contact (Huckfeldt 1983). For example, these perceptions may reflect adult assessments of the economic viability of the neighborhood and the availability of an adult child-monitoring network (Furstenberg 1993; Sampson 1992; Tienda 1991). It is not clear whether children and adolescents perceive these dimensions of neighborhood quality as important (see chapter 2). Moreover, it is not clear whether children and adolescents use adult information in these areas to formulate opinions concerning overall neighborhood quality.

An area of neighborhood research that reflects greater attention to variability in perceptions across adult, adolescent, and child generations has to do with subjective appraisals of environmental risks. Hyson and Bollin (1990; 51) defined *environmental risks* as "a subjective, personal evaluation of the possibility of harm" in a particular environment. Examples of harm within the physical environment include accidents on the street or playground (such as traffic accidents or random injury from street violence). Theories of cognitive appraisals suggest that developmental outcomes may not necessarily be the product of whether the potential for harm (such as gang warfare) actually exists in the environment (Hyson and Bollin 1990). Rather, it is the perceived probability that an environment is harmful that affects developmental outcomes.

Increasingly, social scientists have recognized that children's perceptions of risks in their environment, as compared to their parents' perceptions, are uniquely important predictors of behavioral outcomes (Garbarino, Kostelny, and Dubrow 1991; van Andel 1990). Children's appraisals of risks in neighborhood environments are a function of their developmental stages and understanding of physical space (Hart 1979). As children experience developmental changes, their appraisals of space and risks change. Changes in appraisal of space and risks over the life course of a child have been hypothesized to have a direct influence on behavioral outcomes (Lynch 1977; Schiavo 1988; Torrell and Biel 1985).

Hyson and Bollin (1990) have suggested a variety of methodological strategies for assessing children's perceptions of neighborhoods' risks. Field observations of how children use neighborhood environments have provided richly detailed data on how children appraise risks (Lynch 1977). Interviewing children about their environment during a concrete physical task such as a walk around the neighborhood is another useful strategy (Bryant 1985). Asking children to draw maps or create models of their neighborhoods and then analyzing these products for content and style is a third strategy (Hyson and Bollin 1990). Risk appraisals also may be studied by asking children to comment on videotapes, pictures, or hypothetical situations about their neighborhoods. Structured rating scales, such as the Environmental Rating Scale and the Semantic Differential Measure of Environmental Hazards can be administered to older children and adolescents (Bunting and Cousins 1985).

In brief, children's appraisals of their environments, as distinct from adults' appraisals, are an important factor to address in studying the relationship between neighborhood context and child development. Specifically studying neighborhood as a perception allows for attention to three concerns: (1) the assessment of neighborhood is "developmentally anchored"; (2) the subjective meaning of neighborhoods in assessing developmental outcomes is addressed; and (3) the interdependent relationship between neighborhood context and child behaviors can be readily assessed.

NEIGHBORHOODS AS NETWORKS

The network approach to neighborhood research complements the other two approaches by its emphasis on the primacy of interpersonal linkages in context, rather than an exclusive focus on the classification of neighborhoods according to their spatial, demographic, or perceived physical characteristics (Craven and Wellman 1973). Downs (1981) noted that neighborhoods can be defined as geographic units within which particular social relationships and networks exist. Since most children are embedded in a network of friends and acquaintances that considerably affects their attitudes and behavior (Campbell and Lee 1992), network analysis is well suited to improve our understanding of neighborhood structure, processes of change, and the developmental consequences such structure and processes can have for children.

Networks, or patterns of interaction among residents of an area, shape the understanding of a neighborhood's form and function. A *social network* can be defined as "a specific set of linkages among a defined set of persons, with the . . . property that the characteristics of these linkages as a whole may be used to interpret the social behavior of the persons involved" (Mitchell 1969, 4). The network approach is "essentially a perspective which focuses on structured relationships between individuals and collectives. . . [and] it gives attention to structured patterns of relationships and not the aggregated characteristics of individual units, analyzed without reference to their interrelationships" (Wellman and Leighton 1979).

The development of children takes place "in networks of supportive relations with intimate others" (Lee, Campbell, and Miller 1991). Viewing neighborhoods as networks allows researchers to operationalize the mechanics of neighborhood attachment and the dynamics of neighborhood aggregation in the creation of urban context. The quality of development is in large part a product of the character and quality of the people and setting that make up children's networks, suggesting a major role for network analysis.

The personal networks of children within geographic units are most commonly produced in survey research with the use of name generators. The respondent is asked to name a group of individuals with whom he or she has social ties of one form or another. The open-ended question that instigates the generation of names may involve persons (1) who would likely provide some form of assistance in a time of need (see, for example, Fischer 1982), (2) with whom the respondents have discussed matters important to them (Marsden 1987), or (3) who do not live in the respondents' homes but to whom the respondents feel closest (Wellman 1979). The individuals named likely relate to the respondent in many potentially overlapping ways—as kin, comember (for instance, fellow church member), neighbor, or friend (Oliver 1988).

Two dimensions of personal networks—types and traits—form the framework for network analysis in neighborhood research. There are five types of name generators, depending on the parameters or boundaries placed on network relationships, and three primary traits, which condition the links within a given network and the effects that each parameter can have on any existing interactions. According to Campbell and Lee (1991), the types include (1) content or role variation, (2) the feelings attached to a network member, (3) geographic accessibility, (4) time limitations, and (5) the size of the network. Building on earlier work evaluating the texture of social and neighborhood networks (for example, Craven and Wellman 1973; Fischer 1982; Wellman and Leighton 1979), Lee, Campbell, and Miller (1991) also identified three primary traits of neighborhood networks, which can be evaluated using any one of the name-generator strategies previously identified. The three primary traits conditioning a child's developmental network are (1) the frequency of contact; (2) the degree of investment placed on a given tie, and (3) the manner and diversity of uses. Specification of both types and traits from children themselves at various developmental stages could assess the local and extralocal dimensions of their networks of influence.

The "neighborhood walk" strategy employed by Bryant (1985) is among the clearest specifications of the role of networks and network analysis in children's developmental process. The neighborhood walk is a methodology in which the physical environment of children and the forms of support available to them within it are identified. Using the neighborhood walk, Bryant (1985) identified three forms of support networks for children: others as resources, intrapersonal sources, and environmental sources. The support that networks provide children has been shown to decrease the likelihood of poor social adjustment in negotiating stressful environments, improve psychological functioning, and enhance other dimensions in children's social-emotional development (Garbarino, Galambos, Plantz, and Kostelny 1993).

Although Bryant's work provided valuable insights into children's geographic networks, her analysis was restricted to the immediate neighborhood of the child, and thus did not directly address extralocal members of a child's network. As noted in our earlier discussion of neighborhoods of residence and neighborhoods of sociability, networks outside of the immediate environment often are important. Researchers need to identify how developmental outcomes are associated with each network trait and type combination across both local and extralocal networks. Such efforts can effectively build on the earlier developmental work of Bryant (1985) and others (Hill 1989; Sudman 1988).

NEIGHBORHOODS AS CULTURES

The fourth "way of thinking about" and "way of measuring" neighborhoods involves an assessment of culture within a defined geographic unit. Culture, or the "social processes of sharing modes of behavior and outlook within [a] community" (Hannerz 1969, 184) is the expression of the way of life among children and adults in a specific neighborhood. The developmental process of children is likely influenced by "symbolic vehicles of meaning, including beliefs (e.g., perceptions of opportunity) . . . language, gossip, . . . and rituals of daily life" (Swidler 1986, 276) that make up the character of a given neighborhood. Because of its potential impact on the formative perceptions of children, viewing neighborhood as culture is an important conceptual starting point in the study of neighborhoods and child development (Super and Harkness 1986).

In her evaluation of childhood sources of social support, Bryant (1985) illustrated the overlap between neighborhood networks and the cultural context (that is, informal systems) of neighborhoods, as well as measured their links to sources of support in middle childhood. Allowing the children to speak for themselves, Bryant walked around children's neighborhoods in order to explicate different types of social support. By doing so, Bryant provided a uniquely person-centered assessment of developmental outcomes. These forms of support were essential elements of the rituals of daily life that define the cultural context of neighborhood child development (Swidler 1986).

A cultural approach emphasizes the assessment of the "style or set of skills or habits, [not the] set of preferences or wants" (Swidler 1986, 277) of a child, which allows for a focus on skill variations across developmental processes. First, partnered with the site, perception, or network perspective, a cultural approach can contribute to a specification of the relative impact of popular

culture by clarifying local-area influences on the formation of action strategies across (and within) the development process. Second, it can help us
move beyond the debate about the "culture of poverty," to the specification
and quantification of the behavioral links in children's developmental
choices. Third, viewing neighborhoods from a cultural perspective can allow
for the empirical comparison of developmental chains of action, potentially
(both) across the developmental process and between (and within) ethnic or
racial groups.

Future research on neighborhood as culture can contribute to the clarifica-
tion of existing ambiguities in the context of child development by specifying
and measuring the mechanics of neighborhood culture borne of the social
construction of communities (Suttles 1972), as well as evaluating the manner
in which developmental outcomes interact with children's rituals of daily life
(Swidler 1986). Supplementing the focus on individual outcomes, what is the
manner in which childhood choice-making influences the cultural context of
urban setting (that is, developmental reciprocity)? What developmental skills
are formed at what point in the growth process? Which skills are most
amenable to change, and what is their malleability a product of? Answering
these and other similar questions can help us better understand the complex
relationship between context and childhood development.

DISCUSSION AND CONCLUSION

The goal of this chapter was to examine existing "ways of thinking about"
and "ways of measuring" neighborhoods as they relate to the study of developmental outcomes for children. Four issues that should be considered in
selecting particular paradigms and methodological strategies for the study of
neighborhoods and child development were outlined: (1) the objective and
subjective nature of definitions of neighborhoods, (2) the limitations of studying neighborhoods using the social address perspective, (3) the utility of
viewing neighborhoods and children as interdependent systems, and (4) the
importance of assessing neighborhood processes beyond the contextual
moment. These issues were subsequently highlighted in the discussion of
four conceptual and methodological frameworks used in the study of context and child development—neighborhoods as sites, perceptions, networks,
and cultures.

Our point is that the conceptual and methodological approaches outlined
cannot by themselves provide an adequate assessment of neighborhood for
studying children's outcomes. The strengths of each approach, however, can
be used simultaneously to form a useful set of research approaches in order
to address contextual effects on children.

The critical strength of the site framework is its specification of both physical quality and social milieu in geographically bounded terms. However, this
emphasis limits its ability to analyze social processes within neighborhoods,

thus emphasizing a contextual moment effect on child outcomes. Neighborhood as perception addresses issues concerning the subjective meaning of context, but in the past it has not been appropriately developmentally anchored (for example, adult perceptions have been used to understand the world of children) in the study of neighborhoods and children. The network approach is especially strong in evaluating the relational character of neighborhoods, but all too often it overlooks place-specific characteristics that can condition relational outcomes. The cultural view effectively accounts for neighborhood norms, beliefs, and values, but among the four approaches specified, it has the least-developed pool of measurement strategies (see chapters 3 and 7).

The fusion of these approaches poses extraordinary conceptual and methodological challenges. More robust conceptual and methodological frameworks may be developed in order to provide a more advanced look at neighborhoods. We believe that explicating "ways of thinking about" and "ways of measuring" neighborhoods is necessary to address the links between neighborhoods, families, and children.

This research was supported by grants to Linda Burton from the William T. Grant Foundation and a FIRST Award from the National Institute of Mental Health (No. R29MH 4605-01); by a National Institute on Aging Postdoctoral Fellowship (T32AG 00208) to Townsand Price-Spratlen and support services provided by the Population Research Institute, Pennsylvania State University, which has core support from National Institute for Child Health and Human Development Grant 1-HD28263; and by grants to Margaret Spencer from the Spencer Foundation, the William T. Grant Foundation, the Russell Sage Foundation, the Ford Foundation, the Commonwealth Foundation, and the Annenberg Foundation.

9

An Alternative Approach to Assessing Neighborhood Effects on Early Adolescent Achievement and Problem Behavior

Margaret Beale Spencer, Paul A. McDermott,
Linda M. Burton, and Tedd J. Kochman

I t is within the physical environments of neighborhoods that the effects of economic inequalities may be most apparent (Kochman 1992). The physical environment and its stressors have an immense impact on the development and functioning of humans (Hambrick-Dixon 1990). Environmental stressors such as overcrowdedness, toxic pollution, and lack of greenspace can have severe negative effects on the physical development and psychological responses of families and their youths (Kochman 1992). The idea that development does not occur within a vacuum, but rather in a context of environmental influence, is gaining increased attention (see Bronfenbrenner 1979; Markstrom-Adams and Spencer 1994; Spencer 1985; Washington and LaPointe 1989). Exposure to physical environmental stressors poses risks for all humans. However, of particular concern is the fact that lower-income African Americans, whose options are restricted by status and race, are more likely to be disproportionately exposed to environmental stressors, with little chance of escaping (Bullard and Wright 1987).

As Jacob (1990) suggested, the gap between blacks and whites apparently extends well beyond simply examining poverty and unemployment rates to include the significant effects of environmental constraints. From infant mortality rates that are at Third World levels in some resource-poor neighborhoods, to high levels of crime due in part to the lack of police visibility, to problems with housing where residents experience overcrowding and segregation, blacks' development and opportunities are often hampered by the physical environment (see Jacob 1990). Hambrick-Dixon (1990) speculated that the prevalence of environmental stressors within the communities of black America serves as a harsh reminder that racial inequity still thrives. Economists, sociologists, designers, and planners have documented the positive and negative attributes of different patterns of neighborhood spacing. However, rarely have the consequences of these varying community designs and general environmental confounds been examined in terms of their impact on behavioral development and psychological growth (Wohlwill 1985). Cognitive processes may be particularly vulnerable. Attention span, memory, language, and cognition, along with physiological functions, can be compromised for individuals confronted with spacing problems and environmental stressors (Heckler 1985). Evidence suggests that both neighborhood spacing schemes and the overall physical environment affect developmental processes (Wohlwill and Van Vliet 1985).

An important spacing issue is overcrowdedness and high density levels within neighborhoods. McHenry (1990) noted the particular sensitivity of black American communities to space limitations. Altman (1975) suggested that research on crowding has shown a relationship to psychological stress (and a need to cope), due mainly to sensory overload and a lack of privacy. Numerous studies have linked overcrowding and spacing problems to increased aggressiveness, delinquency, and ill health (Ruffins 1989; Spencer and Glymph 1993). The fact of crowded conditions, then, in many minority communities may be linked to the fact that blacks account for 14 percent of the population, but for 46.5 percent of all arrests for violent crimes. Further, black youths accounted for 55 percent of those under eighteen who were arrested for violent and aggressive crimes, and for 30 percent of all index crimes (Brown 1988). In addition, Powell (1990) found that high-density living among black Americans may contribute to learned helplessness and subsequent poor performance in mathematics and science. Comer (1990) observed that, in general, the disproportionate social and environmental stressors experienced by black youths greatly affect their school performance. He demonstrated that as the limitations of social and economic opportunity become more apparent, the importance of education is disregarded and is not dissimilar to Fordham and Ogbu's (1986) observation of academic oppositional behavior among African American youths.

Research has suggested that the duration of exposure to environmental constraints is a mediator of environmental stress (Kochman 1992). Cohen and colleagues (1980) suggested that the longer one is exposed to an intense stressor, the more likely are negative effects. Further, Baum, Singer, and Baum (1982) concluded that the social and psychological consequences of stress and strain contributed to by environmental racism in black communities remain enormous, relative to individual developmental outcomes.

In the project reported, we explored an alternative strategy for assessing neighborhood characteristics that is more proximal than most single-source, traditional, census-based neighborhood assessment methods. We tested the efficacy of an alternative neighborhood assessment procedure with census composites, family-level measures, and developmental outcome variables.

METHOD

The research findings reported are from a cross-sectional longitudinal study which addresses the developmental effects of persistent poverty among African American youth. The data represent a subsample of adolescents assessed during the first year of study.

SAMPLE

Analyses for 293 adolescent males and 123 adolescent females are reported (see chapter 8 in volume 1 for a more complete description of the sample from which this sample is drawn). All subjects were African Americans in the sixth, seventh, or eighth grades and were randomly selected from the public middle schools in Atlanta, Georgia. For the four schools, signed consent rates for participation by school ranged between 55 percent and 80 percent. For three of the four schools, 80 percent to 90 percent of the students attending the respective schools received free or reduced-price lunch support. For the fourth school, approximately 70 percent of the students qualified for free or reduced-price lunches. From self-reported family income information, it was determined that 58 percent of the subjects' families met federal poverty guidelines (that is, for a family of four, the criterion for poverty was an annual family income of $13,950 or less). Neighborhood poverty was also extensive: the sample was 2.5 standard deviation units below the national average for neighborhood-level poverty.

PROCEDURES AND MEASURES

Because the participants were involved in a larger longitudinal study concerned with the development of competence and resiliency of African American boys (Spencer 1988), two (generally school-based) administration formats were used. For survey-completion tasks, subjects were seen in small groups at their respective schools, and they completed the survey instruments during three sessions. Adolescents were also seen one-on-one to complete more-sensitive or open-ended questions. As part of an extensive in-home interview, parents completed the adult version of the same rating instrument as their children.

All of the in-home parental interviewers were same-race examiners. The majority of the small-group testers were the same race as the adolescent participants. All testers were well-trained graduate, undergraduate, or older-adult interviewers who were hired specifically as adolescent interviewers. The in-home parental interviewers were local mental health professionals who had earned at least one degree in mental health (including pastoral counseling) or, in fact, were practicing ministers. All parental interviewers were familiar and comfortable with working in African American lower-income homes and communities.

NEIGHBORHOOD RISK COMPOSITE   Neighborhood-background measures were assessed using 1980 census-tract data. A principal components analysis of thirty-five census-tract variables revealed five factors: (1) poverty, female headship, and race (African American); (2) high socioeconomic status (SES) families in neighborhood; (3) ethnic diversity; (4) crowding and age structure; and (5) joblessness (Duncan and Aber vol. 1). Factors were transformed to indices that represented standard deviation units away from the average of a nationally representative sample of neighborhoods developed by Duncan and his colleagues on the Panel Study of Income Dynamics (PSID) data set (Duncan and Aber vol. 1). In addition, three of the five factors were aggregated to form one neighborhood risk composite: (a) low SES; (b) low concentration of high-SES residents, and (c) high level of joblessness. A high score on this neighborhood risk measure indicates increased preexisting risk. Means and standard deviations for the neighborhood census measures are presented in table 9.1.

NEIGHBORHOOD ASSESSMENT OF COMMUNITY CHARACTERISTICS (NACC)   Trained observers conducted "windshield surveys" of the participants' neighborhoods. Thirty-one census tracts were surveyed, with the number of subjects per tract ranging from 1 to 66 ($M = 15.5$, $SD = 16.2$). Two central streets were surveyed in each tract that represented the major cross streets for the subjects representing the tract. Specifically, one street running north–south and one street running east–west were included per tract. All surveys were completed on weekdays between 8:00 A.M. and 8:00 P.M. Observers used a 145-item protocol developed specifically as a windshield method for assessing neighborhood characteristics (see Spencer et al. forthcoming). However, of the 145, 72 Neighborhood Assessment of Community Characteristics (NACC) instrument items actually produced full data sets and were included in the analyses presented. The actual protocol was used to record observations during the field runs. Protocol items addressed housing (for example, condition, proximity to major thoroughfares, upkeep of

TABLE 9.1   Means and Standard Deviations for Neighborhood Census Measures

Neighborhood Measure	Males (N = 394)		Females (N = 168)	
	M	SD	M	SD
Poverty/female headship/race	2.35***	0.81	2.12	1.01
High socioeconomic status	−1.13	0.57	−1.06	0.64
Ethnic diversity	−0.42	0.38	−0.36	0.43
Crowding	0.59	1.03	0.45	1.10
Joblessness	1.79	1.16	1.70	1.29
Composite neighborhood risk	1.76	0.44	1.63	0.54

***$p < .01$.

yards), neighborhood (for example, condition of streets, degree of trash accumulation, noise levels, billboard advertisements), recreational areas, type and number of stores and businesses, gathering places (hangouts), transportation, and security. The items assessing neighborhood character-istics were rated for several possible responses (for instance, for recre-ational areas): 1 (*poor*), 2 (*fair*), 3 (*good*), or 4 (*excellent*). For each of the items, means of the values from two runs were calculated and used for the analysis. Interrater reliability for the measure was assessed by computing the percentage agreement on protocol items for four pairs of observers who made two field runs each. The percentage agreement ranged from 90.4 to 95.8 (M = 93.3). As noted, for this set of analyses, 72 of the 145 items were selected for scaling and analysis purposes, based on conceptual grounds.

The crime statistics by census tracts and police zones were obtained from the police authorities and corresponded to the specific counties that encom-passed the subjects' neighborhood. Homicide, robbery, burglary, rape, auto theft, and assaults were selected as categories to reflect the level of crime occurring in the youths' neighborhoods. One county categorized crime data by census tract, and the other categorized crime data by zone. To compare the two groups of data effectively, we divided a crime category for each geo-graphic area by the number of persons in that area.

FAMILY ECONOMY   Mother's education was assessed using highest level of completed education and was coded as number of years of schooling (for example, *high school diploma* was coded as 12, *college degree* was coded as 16). Female headship was included as a dichotomous measure (respondents who reported *living with mother and without a male caregiver* [female head-ship] were coded as 1, and those who reported *living with mother and a male caregiver* or *living with father but without mother* coded as 0). Family income was assessed using parents' self-reported family income; these figures were then transformed into an index based on family size and federal poverty guidelines. The reported family income was divided by the criterion income for poverty for that family size. An index of 1.0 indicated that the family was living at poverty level; an index of less than 1.0 indicated that the family was living below poverty level.

ACADEMIC PERFORMANCE   School records were used to obtain students' national percentile rankings (NPRs) for the spring administration of the Iowa Test of Basic Skills (ITBS). These included reading, vocabulary, language, mathematics total, and complete composite.

BEHAVIOR PROBLEMS   Participants completed the Youth Self-Report (YSR; Achenbach 1991a). The YSR is a 118-item self-report instrument designed to assess eleven- to eighteen-year-olds' reports of behavior problems. A parent or guardian completed the Child Behavior Checklist (CBCL; Achenbach 1991b). As the parent companion to the YSR, it was used for assessing parents' perceptions of their children's behavior problems. Higher scores indicate a greater number of behavior problems.

RESULTS

Findings are reported in three sections. First, scaling results for first-stage item analysis are presented. Second, several significant intercorrelations between NACC dimensions are presented. Third, a typology of neighborhoods based on hierarchical clustering of census tracts by NACC dimensions is presented.

Seventy-two NACC items produced full data sets and requisite variability across the twenty-nine census tracts. Thus, these items were preserved for first-stage item analyses. Since the phenomena associated with each item were observed twice per tract (the bidirectional rating procedure) and item-scales ranged from binary types to multipoint Likert measures, the final score for each item was derived by averaging the rating for the two directional observation passes and thereafter converting the average to a unit-normal z score based on the distribution across census tracts. Items were initially assigned to nine mutually exclusive groups, based on a rational-inductive Q-sort according to apparent similarity of content meaning and domain. The groupings included items expressing specific dimensions: (1) housing characteristics, (2) housing quality, (3) presence of security devices, (4) support services, (5) food services, (6) retail services, (7) industrial presence, (8) neighborhood meeting places, and (9) information sources (signs, notices, and so on).

Coefficient alpha was computed independently for each item grouping, as well as conditional alphas, item-total correlations, and skewness and kurtosis indices for each component item. Unit weighting (Wainer 1976) was applied, to yield total scores for each grouping, and item valence was reversed as necessary to enhance internal consistency and parsimonious content meaning of total scores. In general, items that reduced internal consistency were discarded, and items having within-grouping item-total correlations below .20 were deleted unless their removal appreciably diminished internal consistency. The procedure preserved forty-eight items comprising eight groupings (or neighborhood dimensions), with respective internal consistency indices ranging from .86 to .67. (See Widaman [1993] on the propriety of regarding such dimensions as suitably reliable.) The discarded twenty-four items included all seven initially assigned to the grouping of information items, with the best combination of those items achieving internal consistency values no greater than .45.

Table 9.2 displays the eight surviving NACC dimensions and component items, associated internal consistency, and item-total correlations. Table 9.3 presents zero-order correlations of the resultant NACC dimensions with the

TABLE 9.2   NACC Dimensions, Component Items, and Internal Consistency

Dimensions and Components	Item Total r	Dimensions and Components	Item Total r
Housing characteristics		Food services	
Space between houses	.69	Fast-food places	.64
Distance from thoroughfare	.65	Grocery stores	.48
Amount of greenery	.57	Lounges/bars	.40
Sparcity of housing	.53	Traditional restaurants	.39
Number of greenspaces	.30		
		alpha = .69	
alpha = .77			
Housing quality		Retail services	
Condition/upkeep of yards	.87	Pharmacy/drug stores	.72
Condition of housing	.84	Furniture/appliance	.70
Absence of trash accumulation	.74	Hardware stores	.66
Absence of vacant lots	.70	Pawn shops	.63
Overall neighborhood rating	.62	Clothing stores	.60
Absence of abandoned structures	.57	All-purpose stores	.59
Absence of noise	.48		
Condition of streets	.41	alpha =.86	
Absence of dysfunctional cars	.08		
alpha = .86			
Security devices		Industrial presence	
Fences/gates	.67	Industrial plants/warehouse	.54
Bars on doors/windows	.67	Nontraditional land use	.54
alpha = .80		alpha = .70	
Support services		Teenage meeting places	
Cleaners/launderettes	.83	Residence-related area	.80
Gas station	.83	Percentage blacks seen	.43
Pay phones	.67	Traditional recreation centers	.33
Movie/video rental	.65	Percentage teens seen	.31
Barbershop/beauty shop	.57	Convenience stores/liquor stores	.29
Medical/dental offices	.56	Street corners	.28
Day-care center	.54		
Auto-repair shop	.46	alpha = .67	
Religious structures	.41		
Mailboxes	.37		
Check-cashing stores	.34		
Visible taxi service	.24		
Post office	.19		
Newspaper-vending machines	.08		
alpha = .84			

Note: Component items are listed by descending item-total correlations.

TABLE 9.3 Correlations of NACC Dimensions with Census Factors, Family Economy Variables, and Crime Rates

| | NACC Dimension | | | | | | | |
Variable	Housing Characteristics	Housing Quality	Security Devices	Support Services	Food Services	Retail Services	Industrial Presence	Teenage Meeting Places
Census factors								
Poverty/fem. head/race	-.49**	-.45*	.01	.02	-.02	-.01	-.06	.54**
High SES	-.58***	-.62***	.18	-.08	.05	-.00	.20	.44*
Ethnic diversity	.02	.17	-.05	-.19	-.14	-.12	.22	-.28
Crowding/age structure	-.23	-.06	.16	-.04	-.02	.16	-.21	.28
Joblessness	-.67****	-.61***	-.11	-.13	-.05	-.18	.06	.50**
Neighborhood risk	-.57	-.49**	-.16	-.06	-.07	-.14	-.06	.53**
Family economy								
Family income	.28	.11	.18	-.12	-.04	-.00	-.18	-.13
Mother's education	.29	.16	.08	-.16	-.02	-.01	-.20	.08
Female headship	-.17	-.04	-.03	.18	.14	.24	-.15	.01
Crime rate								
Rape	-.51**	-.59***	-.10	.08	.21	.06	.21	.30
Homicide	-.48**	-.54**	-.08	.02	.16	.03	.18	.32
Robbery	-.49**	-.60***	-.05	.04	.17	.02	.23	.35
Assault	-.49**	-.61***	-.09	.09	.25	.11	.22	.28
Car theft	-.49**	-.56**	-.08	.00	.10	-.04	.21	.34
Burglary	-.46*	-.56**	-.03	.04	.16	.02	.21	.36

Note: N = 29 U.S. Census tracts.

*p < .05. **p < .01. ***p < .001. ****p < .0001.

152

census factor scores, family economy variables, and crime rates as they varied across the twenty-nine census tracts.

The significant and negative correlations of high SES with the NACC dimensions were unexpected, but consistent for the sample. As described earlier, the sample was unusually impoverished and included few families who qualified as high SES. The unexpected finding that the high-SES factor correlated to NACC as did the low-SES factor suggests that there are small pockets of higher-SES families within highly impoverished communities. The assumption is consistent with descriptive knowledge of the neighborhoods.

The utility of the NACC dimensions can be addressed from several perspectives. One useful approach is the development of a neighborhood typology that might be applied to describe meaningful subsets of tracts (neighborhoods). To this end, the raw total score for each NACC dimension was converted to a standard T score ($M = 50$, $SD = 10$) in order to equate the relative meaning of score elevations across the eight dimensions. Thus, each census tract was described by its profile of T scores across the eight dimensions (a sort of neighborhood profile). Thereafter, the twenty-nine profiles associated with the corresponding twenty-nine tracts were submitted to multistage hierarchical cluster analysis with replications and relocation. The primary goal was to determine whether the neighborhood profile types would resolve a reliable and meaningful typology of distinct neighborhood types.

Having evaluated numerous clustering algorithms, we decided that Ward's (1963) minimum variance procedure would best satisfy the research goals. Monte Carlo studies of competing clustering methods have shown consistently that when full coverage is required, Ward's method recovers known typological structure better (Kuiper and Fisher 1975; Mojena 1977) and outperforms other methods in reducing overlap (Bayne et al. 1980). It is also the most accurate under mixture model testing, where objects must be classified to diversify known populations (Blashfield 1976; Overall, Gibson, and Novy 1993). In contrast, average-linkage clustering (the best alternative to Ward's approach) does comparatively poorly in reducing overlap (Bayne et al. 1980; Milligan 1980). Recent results using community size versus census tracts have demonstrated the case well (see McDermott 1995).

For the NACC data, a three-stage clustering process was applied. First, the twenty-nine profiles were randomly assigned to two mutually exclusive blocks, and Ward's method was applied independently for the profiles composing each block. For each block, the ideal number of clusters was determined through multiple criteria—specifically, (1) atypical decrease in overall between-cluster variance (R^2) and increase in within-cluster variance (Ward 1963), with no reverse trend at subsequent steps and (2) simultaneous elevation of the pseudo-F statistic (Calinski and Harabasz 1974) over the pseudo-t^2 statistic (Duda and Hart 1973) as demonstrated by Cooper and

Milligan (1988). (Note that pseudo F indicates separation among all clusters at the current step, whereas pseudo t^2 indicates separation of the two clusters immediately joined at the current step.)

Clusters derived from the two independent first-stage analyses were pooled and subjected to second-stage clustering. Specifically, a similarity matrix was constructed to impart full first-stage history (cluster mean-profiles, radial and dispersion statistics, and within-cluster profile frequency), and Ward's method was reapplied. In this fashion, first-stage clusters provided independent replications of the final cluster solution. In addition, since agglomerative clustering provides no natural mechanism to relocate retrospectively profiles found to be misplaced, third-stage clustering applied divisive k-means iteration (as advised by Scheibler and Schneider 1985) to relocate misplaced profiles.

Selection criteria for second- and third-stage clustering were identical to those in first-stage clustering, and several more conservative stopping rules were applied: (1) the average within-cluster homogeneity coefficient, H (Tryon and Bailey 1970), had to be >.60 (as per McDermott 1980; McDermott et al. 1989); (2) the average between-clusters similarity coefficient, rp (Cattell 1949), had to be <.40 (see also McDermott et al. 1989); (3) each final cluster had to have a 100 percent replication rate as verified by absorption of the first-stage cluster into the same second- and third-stage cluster (as per Overall and Magee 1992) and a corresponding $rp > .90$ for the cluster under consideration; and (4) the solution had to make psychological sense in terms of parsimonious coverage of the data and compatibility with other empirical research.

Analyses produced six distinct neighborhood types that replicated 100 percent over first- through third-stage clustering, with typical homogeneity averaging .88 and ranging from 1.0 to .76 over types and .93 to .76 over NACC dimensions. Table 9.4 shows the characteristic mean T-score profile for each type. To assist with interpretation, higher T scores are underlined, and the table footnote suggests a corresponding descriptive name for each type. The percentages cited in table 9.4 reflect the proportion of neighborhoods (tracts) that are associated with each type.

A second perspective on NACC utility is afforded by comparisons of the relative contributions of NACC dimensions, census factors, and the family economy variables to prediction of individual youth scholastic achievement and behavioral adjustment and to the prediction of neighborhood crime rates. Such assessment is a delicate undertaking inasmuch as it necessarily covaries data that are essentially group level (census factors, family economy variables, crime rates, and NACC dimensions) and variables that are individual-level youth characteristics (age, sex, grade level, standardized academic achievement, and behavioral adjustment ratings and self-reports). The dangers and limitations of confounding group- and individual-level data are well documented (Burstein, Linn, and Capell 1978; Pedhazur 1982; Roberts and

TABLE 9.4 Typology of Neighborhoods Based on Hierarchical Clustering of Census Tracts by NACC Dimensions

Type[a]	%	NACC Dimension _T_ Score									
		Housing Characteristics	Housing Quality	Security Devices	Support Services	Food Services	Retail Services	Industrial Presence	Teenage Meeting Places	Homogeneity
1	26.7	_60.5_	_62.0_	49.1	44.1	44.3	45.8	46.6	42.7	0.83
2	16.7	50.3	48.4	51.4	_62.3_	_60.1_	_66.7_	46.2	49.5	0.82
3	13.3	55.5	55.2	55.3	43.7	42.0	45.0	44.3	_62.4_	0.84
4	36.7	43.4	43.2	53.6	48.7	49.0	45.3	_58.3_	48.3	0.76
5	3.3	49.0	39.0	49.0	_80.0_	_86.0_	_82.0_	55.0	40.0	1.00
6	3.3	23.0	32.0	24.0	48.0	49.0	45.0	46.0	_77.0_	1.00
		0.89	0.93	0.76	0.91	0.93	0.96	0.82	0.82	0.88

Note: T scores ≥ 58 are considered appreciable and are italicized.

[a] 1 = good housing with little business; 2 = average housing with considerable business and support services; 3 = average housing with many teenage meeting places; 4 = below-average housing with some industrial presence; 5 = average housing with many business and support services; 6 = poor housing with many teenage meeting places.

155

Burstein 1980; Robinson 1950; Thorndike 1939) and, notwithstanding several rare exceptions, generally preclude analyses that would contrast the relative efficiency of group- and individual-level variables. Nonetheless, under certain very restricted conditions, the two levels of measurement can be simultaneously and parsimoniously treated.

Within this context, several cautionary measures were applied. Because differential within-group frequencies can distort the magnitude of correlations, all analyses were carried out on the same set of complete data for all pertinent group- and individual-level variables. Thus, all comparable inferential tests were based on the same degrees of freedom. The sample (N = 232) included 162 males and 70 females ranging in age from 11.0 to 15.3 years (M = 13.0, SD = 1.1) and attending grades six through eight (M = 6.9, SD = 0.9) across four schools. The subjects represented all those for whom a complete data set existed for the complement of group- and individual-level variables. They included youth from twenty-four of the twenty-nine census tracts (neighborhoods).

No contrast was made between group- and individual-level variables. That is, comparisons were made of the relative predictive efficiency of the group-level census factors and NACC dimensions and of the group-level family economy variables and NACC dimensions (all sharing the common group-level origin and variance constraints), but no comparisons were attempted between group-level variables and individual-level variables such as age or sex. In addition, spurious effects associated with redundant univariate multiple regression analyses were checked through application of accompanying canonical regression and associated multivariate tests.

The attendant analyses can be broken down by several distinctive features. Analyses were performed for each of three distinct outcome domains—academic achievement, neighborhood crime rates, and reported behavior problems. Within each of the outcome domains, several variables were used as independent and simultaneous criteria. The academic achievement domain included national percentile performance in reading, vocabulary, language, and mathematics. Neighborhood crime outcomes included rates for homicide, assault, female rape, robbery, burglary, and car theft. Problem-behavior criteria included parent report of youth externalizing (conduct-problem) behavior, youth self-reported externalizing behavior, parent-reported youth internalizing (anxious, withdrawn, depressed) behavior, and youth report of internalizing behavior.

The general strategy was to assess initially and control by partialing the criterion variance that could be accounted for by extraneous variables. That is, certain variables, including age, sex, grade level, and their second- and third-order interactions, could conceivably explain appreciable amounts of criterion variance. These sources of variation, although important, were dually theoretically irrelevant and of incompatible measurement level (individual versus group level) to remain in the theoretical network—requiring that their potential effects be removed before we contrasted the target variable sets (census factors, NACC dimensions, and so on). Therefore, youth age, sex, grade level, and all such pertinent high-order interactions were held as control variables to be first tested and thereafter partialed from regression models. Subsequently, within each outcome domain, hierarchical regression models were constructed to enter one of the competing predictor sets (either census factors or family economy variables), followed by the NACC dimensions. The unique contribution of NACC dimensions was tested by sequential F for the partial R^2 rendered by NACC (having been controlled for age, gender, grade level, related interactions, and the overlap with either the census factors or family economy variables). Having tested the univariate regression model for each criterion within an outcome domain (such as reading or vocabulary), we applied canonical variance analysis for the full set of criterion areas within a domain and calculated multivariate F and canonical redundancy (van den Wollenberg 1977). The entire process was next repeated, reversing the entry order of NACC and other target predictor sets, and predictive efficiency was assessed for the census or family economy variables, with control for age, sex, grade level, their interactions, and the NACC dimensions.

Tables 9.5 through 9.7 present the results of contrasting predictive efficiency for the census factors and NACC dimensions, and tables 9.8 through 9.10 contain the results contrasting the family economy and NACC dimensions. Considering the census factors versus NACC comparisons, table 9.5 pertains to academic achievement outcomes, table 9.6 to crime outcomes, and table 9.7 to behavior-problem outcomes. Similarly, viewing the latter three tables, table 9.8 pertains to achievement outcomes, table 9.9 to crime outcomes, and table 9.10 to problem-behavior outcomes.

DISCUSSION

Several of the findings suggest unexpected themes. Of the eight NACC dimensions, three were consistently linked with four census factors (refer to table 9.3). On the other hand, individual-level family economic characteristics (that is, family income, mother's education, and female headship) were totally unrelated to NACC dimensions, although two of the eight NACC dimensions (housing characteristics and housing quality) were consistently linked to the six crime-rating categories. In sum, the three sources of data (NACC dimensions, census factors, and crime-rating statistics) suggest that housing character and quality are linked to poverty-relevant census statistics and to crime-rating statistics. Importantly, NACC dimensions are not associated with individual-level family economic characteristics (namely, family income, mother's education, and female headship). The findings suggest that individual or family-level characteristics have less to do with crime statistics

TABLE 9.5   Percentage Contribution of Census Factors and NACC Dimensions to Prediction of Academic Achievement

| Achievement Area | Control Variables[b] | Unique[a] | | Combined Census & NACC Variables |
		Census Factors	NACC Dimensions	
Reading	7.7* (nonspecific)	6.0** (–joblessness)	3.8	11.1** (+joblessness)
Vocabulary	7.6* (nonspecific)	9.2**** (+ethnic diversity +joblessness)	5.9	13.5*** (+ethnic diversity, +joblessness, +support services, +security devices)
Language	20.7**** (nonspecific)	2.7	2.3	6.6
Mathematics	8.0** (nonspecific)	7.7*** (+ethnic diversity, +joblessness)	4.7	13.5*** (+ethnic diversity, +poverty, +joblessness)
All achievement	11.0**** (as above)	6.4*** (as above)	4.2	11.2** (as above)

Note: $N = 232$. Row entries for each achievement area equal R^2 (100) derived from regression models applying the respective achievement areas as dependent variable and census factors and NACC dimensions as independent variable sets. Row entries for "All achievement" are standardized canonical redundancy estimates [Rd (100)] where redundancy is based on the full model for prediction of all achievement variation. Parenthetical entries indicate the component variable(s) that contribute significantly to achievement prediction; (–) refers to low contribution and (+) refers to significant contribution.

[a] Relative contribution of census and NACC variable sets is based on R^2 partialed for overlap with the alternate set.

[b] Achievement variability associated with youth age, sex, and grade level, and all of their higher-order interactions is partialed prior to regression of other predictors.

*$p < .05$. **$p < .01$. ***$p < .001$. ****$p < .0001$.

than with the aggregating of families who represent specific census-level characteristics of communities with specific housing characteristics, housing quality, and patterns of teenage meeting places.

Table 9.4 suggests that the organization of neighborhoods based on hierarchical clustering of census tracts by NACC dimensions further substantiated the importance of housing characteristics. The typology indicated that the most typical living arrangement (36.7 percent) for the sample was below-average housing with some industrial presence. This profile, representing over a third of the entire sample, could be linked with feelings of marginalization by local residents. The significant industrial presence, given the table

TABLE 9.6   Percentage Contribution of Census Factors and NACC Dimensions to Prediction of Crime Rates

| Type of Crime | Control Variables[b] | Unique[a] | | Combined Census & NACC Variables |
		Census Factors	NACC Dimensions	
Homicide	2.6	11.4	16.3	56.6
Assault	2.8	10.0	15.8	57.6
Female rape	2.8	11.2	19.1	55.2
Robbery	3.2	16.6	20.6	59.4
Burglary	3.9	21.5	24.3	62.5
Car theft	2.9	15.5	21.1	56.9
All crime	3.0	14.4	19.5	58.0

Note. $N = 232$. Row entries for each type of crime equal R^2 (100) derived from regression models applying the respective type of crime as dependent variable and census factors and NACC dimensions as independent variable sets. Row entries for "All crime" are standardized canonical redundancy estimates [Rd (100)] where redundancy is based on the full model for prediction of all crime variation. Parenthetical entries indicate the component variable(s) that contribute significantly to neighborhood crime prediction.

[a] Relative contribution of census and NACC variable sets is based on R^2 partialed for overlap with the alternate set.

[b] Neighborhood crime variability associated with youth age, sex, and grade level, and all of their higher-order interactions is partialed prior to regression of other predictors.

9.1 statistics and the unusually impoverished nature of the sample, did *not* appear to benefit local residents.

Tables 9.5 and 9.8 make the case that when we were predicting academic achievement from either family economy and NACC dimensions or from census factors and NACC dimensions, the control variables (age, sex, and grade) were always significant and the NACC dimensions alone were not predictors of academic achievement. Similarly, the family economy variables alone (or when combined with NACC dimensions) were not linked to achievement subscale scores. However, as indicated by table 9.5, the census factors served as the single set of significant predictors of achievement. Children's immediate community had no effect. It was the more distal (aggregated) census factors that consistently predicted subscales and overall achievement (except for the language subscale). Do the findings suggest that larger census-tract factors, perhaps through school-linked funding practices, have a greater linkage to competent performance? The query appears critical, since assumptions about neighborhood effects usually link the local quality of neighborhoods with educational practices, learning opportunities, and competence-linked outcomes.

Tables 9.7 and 9.10 suggest different sets of predictors for parent and adolescent-identified behavior problems. As noted, although census factors, and not NACC dimensions, were more associated with achievement outcomes, in general, neither set of predictors were relevant for the prediction of

TABLE 9.7   Percentage Contribution of Census Factors and NACC Dimensions to Prediction
of Youth Behavior Problems

Youth Behavior Problem	Control Variables[b]	Unique[a]		Combined Census & NACC Variables
		Census Factors	NACC Dimensions	
Parent-reported externalizing	3.8	1.1	1.8	3.7
Self-reported externalizing	6.5* (nonspecific)	1.3	4.0	6.5
Parent-reported internalizing	2.5	0.7	3.5	7.8
Self-reported internalizing	6.4* (nonspecific)	1.1	1.6	3.0
All problems	4.8*	1.1	2.7	5.3

Note: $N = 232$. Row entries for each problem behavior area equal R^2 (100) derived from regression models applying the respective problem area as dependent variable and census factors and NACC dimensions as independent variable sets. Row entries for "All problems" are standardized canonical redundancy estimates [Rd (100)] where redundancy is based on the full model for prediction of all problem behavior variation. Parenthetical entries indicate the component variable(s) that contribute significantly to problem behavior prediction.

[a] Relative contribution of census and NACC variable sets is based on R^2 partialed for overlap with the alternate set.

[b] Problem behavior variability associated with youth age, sex, and grade level, and all of their higher-order interactions is partialed prior to regression of other predictors.

* $p < .05$. ** $p < .01$. *** $p < .001$. **** $p < .0001$.

youth behavioral problems, with two exceptions. Table 9.10 indicates that family economy variables (that is, higher mother's education) marginally predicted the parent report of youth externalizing behavior. Similarly, nonspecific NACC dimensions together served as a marginal predictor of parent-reported adolescent internalizing behavior. Inferable, perhaps, is that parental rating of youth mental health is more sensitive to either family economic variables or NACC dimensions. Not surprising was the finding that census factors were in no way linked to youths' mental health as either self- or parent-reported (see table 9.7).

The most surprising finding was the unexpected robustness of crime prediction from census factors, NACC dimensions, and family economic variables as single and combined predictors (see tables 9.6 and 9.9). On the other hand, the control variables were consistently nonsignificant for crime when examined in equations with family economy variables and NACC dimensions or when present in a regression equation with only census factors and NACC dimensions. As indicated in table 9.6, when the census factors and NACC dimensions were entered together, the unique variance accounted for by

TABLE 9.8   Percentage Contribution of Family Economy Variables and NACC Dimensions to Prediction of Academic Achievement

Achievement Area	Control Variables[b]	Unique[a]		Combined Fam. Econ. & NACC Variables
		Family Economy Variables	NACC Dimensions	
Reading	7.7* (nonspecific)	1.4	4.0	6.6
Vocabulary	7.6* (nonspecific)	0.5	4.4	4.9
Language	20.7**** (nonspecific)	0.3	3.7	4.2
Mathematics	8.0** (nonspecific)	1.5	5.7	7.3
All achievement	11.0****	0.9	4.5	5.8

Note: $N = 232$. Row entries for each achievement area equal R^2 (100) derived from regression models applying the respective achievement area as dependent variable and family economy variables and NACC dimensions as independent variable sets. Row entries for "All achievement" are standardized canonical redundancy estimates [Rd (100)] where redundancy is based on the full model for prediction of all achievement variation. Parenthetical entries indicate the component variables(s) that contribute significantly to achievement prediction.

[a] Relative contribution of family economy and NACC variable sets is based on R^2 partialed for overlap with the alternate set.

[b] Achievement variability associated with youth age, sex, grade level, and all of their higher-order interactions is partialed prior to regression of other predictors.

*$p < .05$. **$p < .01$. ***$p < .001$. ****$p < .0001$.

each was impressive and highly significant, and these dimensions together accounted for over 50 percent on the variance for each of the six crime types. The crime data were group-level data, but given the restricted degrees of freedom, we cautiously interpreted them when entered together. Since the results are based on disaggregated data, the sampling error was underestimated. However, the rank order did not change, even though it is not possible to address the magnitude of the significance level.

Generally, the unique variance of the NACC dimensions accounted for significantly more of the variance for crime type than did the census factors. The pattern was particularly evident for female rape. For the NACC dimensions, the dimensions of security devices and black teens' meeting places appeared to be the critical characteristics for predicting the crime category of female rape.

Similarly, table 9.9 suggests a significant role of the NACC dimensions when compared with the family economy variables for crime rates prediction. For each of the six crime categories, the unique variance for the NACC dimensions alone accounted for 40 percent to 50 percent of the variance. As also noted in table 9.9, family economy variables were extremely significant, although they accounted for less unique variance for crime types. Of course,

TABLE 9.9   Percentage Contribution of Family Economy Variables and NACC Dimensions
to Prediction of Crime Rates

| Type of Crime | Control Variables[b] | Unique[a] | | Combined Fam. Econ. & NACC Variables |
		Family Economy Variables	NACC Dimensions	
Homicide	2.6	5.4	47.4	50.6
Assault	2.8	4.0	50.0	51.6
Female rape	2.8	5.1	45.9	49.2
Robbery	3.2	7.7	47.9	50.5
Burglary	3.9	10.7	47.3	51.7
Car theft	2.9	7.8	43.4	49.1
All crime	3.0	6.8	47.0	50.5

Note: $N = 232$. Row entries for each type of crime equal R^2 (100) derived from regression models applying the respective type of crime as dependent variable and family economy variable and NACC dimensions as independent variable sets. Row entries for "All crime" are standardized canonical redundancy estimates [Rd (100)] where redundancy is based on the full model for prediction of all crime variation. Parenthetical entries indicate the component variable(s) that contribute significantly to neighborhood crime prediction.

[a] Relative contribution of family economy and NACC variable sets is based on R^2 partialed for overlap with the alternate set. For the Family Economy Variables, NACC Dimensions, and Combined (Fam Econ. and NACC Variables) variables, percentage contribution is significant at $p < .0001$. The same significance ($p < .0001$) was obtained for all three sets.

[b] Neighborhood crime variability associated with youth age, sex, and grade level, and all of their higher-order interactions is partialed prior to regression of other predictors.

when family economy variables were noted in combination with NACC dimensions, in general, virtually 50 percent of the variance in crime type was accounted for.

Relative to policy implications, it is important to note that the specific NACC dimensions that contributed significantly to overall crime prediction were neighborhood characteristics sensitive to interventions, given the appropriate resources. For example, findings for homicide (see table 9.9) suggest that alternative ways for teens to meet or gather (such as midnight basketball and other available programs and services) would be facilitative; another reasonable security intervention is the installing of security devices and is not a challenging task. In general, the preventive strategy suggested represents a standard feature in most "upscale" communities, and it is also an important deterrent. Further, enhancing neighborhood supports and providing better food services are manageable community-level improvements that should also serve "protective" functions. Finally, housing quality suggests an enhanced role for community-building programs such as Habitat for Humanity.

In sum, the empirical findings presented specify interesting dynamics between aggregate-level (census-tract) neighborhood influences when compared with more objectively obtained neighborhood assessments (that is, NACC dimensions) with specific types of individual and group outcomes

TABLE 9.10   Percentage Contribution of Family Economy Variables and NACC Dimensions to Prediction of Youth Behavior Problems

| Youth Behavior Problem | Control Variables[a] | Unique[b] | | Combined Economy & NACC Variables |
		Family Economy Variables	NACC Dimensions	
Parent-reporting externalizing	3.8	3.5* (+mother's education)	3.0	6.0
Self-report externalizing	6.5* (nonspecific)	0.6	4.4	5.7
Parent-report internalizing	2.5	1.4	7.0* (nonspecific)	8.4* (nonspecific)
Self-report internalizing	6.4* (nonspecific)	0.1	2.3	2.5
All problems	4.8* (as above)	1.4	4.2	5.7

Note: N = 232. Row entries for each problem behavior equal R^2 (100) derived from regression models applying the respective problem area as dependent variable and Census factors and NACC dimensions as independent variable sets. Row entries for "All problems" are standardized canonical redundancy estimates [Rd (100)] where redundancy is based on the full model for prediction of all problem behavior variation. Parenthetical entries indicate the component variable(s) that contribute significantly to problem behavior prediction.

[a] Problem behavior variability associated with youth age, sex, and grade level, and all of their higher-order interactions is partialed prior to regression of other predictors.

[b] Relative contribution of Census and NACC variable sets is based on R^2 partialed for overlap with the alternate set.

*p < .05. **p < .01. ***p < .001. ****p < .0001.

(that is, achievement, behavioral problems, and crime statistics). Most importantly, the findings suggest more specific and clearly proactive ways of supporting improved life outcomes for low-resource American youths.

Research reported was made possible through funding to the first author from the Spencer, W. T. Grant, and Ford Foundations, the Commonwealth Fund, and the Social Science Research Council.

10

Neighborhood Effects and State and Local Policy

Prudence Brown and Harold A. Richman

Where children and families live—specifically, the characteristics of the physical, economic, and social space that they occupy over the life cycle—has important consequences for child and family development. There is much to learn, however, about the nature of this complex, multilevel relationship before we can recommend with substantial confidence new policies and practices that would promote a neighborhood's ability to support the healthy growth and development of its children and families.

The goal of this chapter is to draw on the research presented in these two volumes and elsewhere to speculate about such policies and practices as they operate at the state and local levels. While federal policies in such areas as income maintenance, housing, and health care clearly have significant effects as they play out in local neighborhoods, much of the impetus for neighborhood and family development comes from the public and private sectors locally, with states playing a facilitating role. The focus here is on neighborhood factors that are likely to be important to the well-being of children and families, and the potentially manipulable policy options that exist at the state and local levels that could strengthen these factors (see also Lehman and Smeeding vol. 1).

Before exploring these policy options and the degree to which they can be informed by existing research, there are two related issues concerning poverty and its concentration effects that set a context for the subsequent discussion. The first, as identified in the literature and confirmed by the findings described in this book, is the central role of family and neighborhood socioeconomic status (SES) in child and family development. Poverty's detrimental effects on a whole range of child and family outcomes, directly and as mediated through family and neighborhood settings, have been clearly established. In 1992, more than 20 percent of the children in this country were living in poverty, a rate that climbed sharply for younger children and for those living in minority households. Clearly, any strategy that could reduce child poverty rates, independent of neighborhood context, would have powerful effects on child and family development (Duncan and Brooks-

Gunn 1997). Creating a stronger labor market and more diversified economy, building a more robust safety net, or applying other macroeconomic or social welfare non-place-based approaches to poverty alleviation would help in the long run to build stronger neighborhoods that support children and families. However, such approaches are not, for the most part, within the domain of state and local policies, let alone feasible practically or politically on any significant scale in the short or medium term. Rather, this chapter's focus is on state and local policies that can strengthen the neighborhood characteristics that research suggests could improve child and family outcomes.

A second related issue involves policy responses that are primarily devoted to changing the composition of a neighborhood, more specifically, dispersing the poor. Findings about the concentration effects of poverty (Wilson 1987) have led some policy makers to focus on dispersal of the poor through such avenues as scattered-site public housing or housing vouchers. Although affected by various federal housing and welfare regulations, these policies are often shaped and implemented locally and therefore could fall within the purview of this chapter. Furthermore, some of the findings discussed in the preceding chapters suggest that an economically integrated neighborhood could have positive effects on child outcomes for at least some groups of families. The Gautreaux Assisted Housing Program provides the most robust evidence for such a conclusion. The Gautreaux participants are residents of, or on the waiting list for, public housing in Chicago who are placed in private sector apartments in other areas of the city in predominantly middle-class suburbs.

Certainly, the structural and racial barriers to achieving neighborhood economic integration should be eliminated, both to be fair and to mitigate the concentration effects of persistent poverty. A variety of policy options to achieve economic integration exist, none of which has been implemented and studied on a scale that provides definitive support for the feasibility and advantages of one option over the other. For example, policy can promote economic integration through dispersal of the poor, through stabilizing currently mixed but deteriorating or gentrifying neighborhoods, or through improving the quality of life in distressed neighborhoods and attracting a more economically mixed group of residents. We are assuming that large-scale dispersal of the poor is not a feasible policy objective at this time: even if all public housing residents received housing vouchers and could locate and maintain residences in mixed neighborhoods, only a minority of the urban poor would be affected. Moreover, we see enough promise in existing neighborhood-development strategies to warrant increased attention to rebuilding poor neighborhoods rather than dispersing their residents. When neighborhood factors are conceptualized as primarily structural-compositional, there is a temptation to frame policy implications largely in these terms. But the evidence presented to date has been neither compelling enough nor informed from sufficiently rich sources of data about neighborhood life to warrant dismissing policies that aim to improve child and family outcomes by strengthening the existing assets and addressing the unmet needs of neighborhoods where the persistently poor now reside.

Successful neighborhood development should both strengthen neighborhood factors and processes that mediate some of poverty's effects on children and families and, ultimately, attract a more economically integrated group of residents. Unfortunately, there are so few documented examples of successful neighborhood revitalization that we do not know how often these successes end up pushing out people who can no longer afford to live in the revitalized area. In many cases, the history and stability of the neighborhood, the amount of vacant land, rates of home ownership, and racial factors play a role in the long-term viability of the neighborhood as an economically integrated place.

CURRENT POLICY ENVIRONMENT

The contrast between life for the urban poor in the Great Society period as compared to the 1990s is both encouraging and discouraging. On the one hand, a great deal has been learned in the past thirty years about how to finance and build affordable housing, plan welfare reform and work programs, use the tax system to subsidize low-wage work and provide incentives for economic investment, provide quality child-care and social services, and so forth. Putting neighborhood context and the availability of resources and political will aside, we now know a lot about how to improve the quality of life for many low-income urban families. The discouraging counterpoint is that thirty years later, a significant number of neighborhoods are so depleted economically and socially that simply constructing new housing or adding more Head Start programs is unlikely to have a substantial payoff for many children and families. Even good programs with proven track records will not flourish in neighborhoods whose social fabric and institutional infrastructure are so weak and overwhelmed by social disorder and decline (Skogan 1990). Putnam (1993, 41) concluded that "in any comprehensive strategy for improving the plight of America's communities, rebuilding social capital is as important as investing in human and physical capital. . . . Investments in jobs and education, for example, will be more effective if they are coupled with reinvigoration of community associations."

Such a conclusion presents policy makers with some real dilemmas. Essentially, building social capital and promoting community capacity and participation require intensive community organizing, an activity that is rarely built-in and funded in most publicly, as well as privately, funded social programs. Community organizing encompasses a wide range of strategies to bring people together, help them plan, and take some action in the service of a common interest. But the results of community organizing are "soft" and difficult to measure, require sustained investment, and may create uncomfortable challenges to the "ways things are done" both inside the neighborhood and between the neighborhood and city and state officials. Evaluation is another barrier: little is known about the actual conduct of community organizing or about what works under which conditions and over what time period—let alone how to measure success. To make a successful investment in community organizing, policy makers need to support training as well; by the early 1970s, most of the professional training programs for organizers had been phased out. So funders are understandably wary, even if they appreciate that support for such organizing may be necessary to create the conditions under which already tested interventions could make a difference.

As with social capital, the concepts of participation and empowerment have profound implications for public policy. New governance arrangements may require shifts in the power relations within the neighborhood; between the neighborhood and the larger community; and between the local, state, and federal governing authorities: the political failure of the Model Cities Program and the often paralyzing struggles between mayors and federal program officials in the 1960s exemplifies the many challenges of such power shifts. Building capacity to assume new governance roles within a highly depleted neighborhood can take a sustained and intensive organizing effort. Again, little knowledge exists on which to base alternative policy options for funders and legislators who would want to know with some confidence what the payoff might be for every dollar invested in organizing or leadership development, either in the short or long term. There is also little to offer policy makers in terms of the advantages and disadvantages of various mechanisms for structuring, communicating, and responding to the community voice. One encouraging source of state and local experimentation is in the field of financing: recognizing the constraints imposed on comprehensive approaches by allocating resources within very narrow funding categories, a number of demonstrations now give local authorities, and occasionally neighborhoods, discretion concerning the deployment and concentration of funding and services at the local level.

While policy makers may face dilemmas about supporting community-building initiatives, the most pressing local policy issues are clearly related to how well neighborhoods are functioning: crime and safety, schools, racial and ethnic relations, housing and public infrastructure, and delivery of social and health services. We can speculate, and bring some modest evidence to bear, on the hypothesis that the more a poor neighborhood is organized and has a strong voice (social capital and participation, as discussed later), the more successful will be the implementation of policies in any of these areas. Community policing, parental involvement in the schools, tenants' groups and block clubs, and integrated neighborhood-based services could all function more effectively in and contribute to further development of neighborhoods with high degrees of social capital and participation.[1] Organized neighborhoods with legitimate voice are also more likely to attract resources because they offer state and local policy makers intermediary mechanisms through which to disperse resources and avoid getting overly involved in the local political fray. Many federal and state policies do not get implemented effectively without a strong community voice to demand and monitor such implementation. State legislatures and the formal policies they generate are notoriously buffeted by confounding factors such as urban and suburban divisions and racial divisions that have little to do with the policy implementation needs in local neighborhoods. The success of the Community Reinvestment Act (CRA) in bringing credit into poor neighborhoods depends in part on the "demand" side of the equation, which must be a local function. Other "instabilities" created by disinvestment, redlining, and real estate and code enforcement are less likely to flourish in neighborhoods that have an organized voice.

The one big area yet to be mentioned is economic development and jobs. Family income has powerful consequences for child and family development, but there is considerable disagreement in the field about the role of "place-based" economic development strategies. While Empowerment Zones (and the Enterprise Zones that preceded them) are federally driven comprehensive strategies to stimulate economic revitalization in poor neighborhoods, many states and localities are experimenting with similar, if less concentrated, efforts to link the goals of economic opportunity and sustainable community development in distressed areas. The evidence to date, however, has not been very encouraging and has led some economists and urban policy experts to look toward regional and sectoral approaches, and various transportation and other linkage strategies. While Wilson (1991a) and others have underlined the secondary consequences for the neighborhood of having large numbers of people unemployed or unemployable with little access to job networks and quality job training, the neighborhood may not be the most effective point of entry to address these problems on any scale. Problems of urban and suburban inequality and the economy must be addressed more broadly than at the neighborhood level, even if that is where they play out in day-to-day life. However, community-building initiatives cannot ignore this central feature of neighborhood life, suggesting that much more work is required to understand and recommend to state and local policy makers options for economic development that will maximally benefit poor neighborhoods and their residents.

COMPREHENSIVE NEIGHBORHOOD-BASED INITIATIVES

What neighborhood-development strategies are likely to yield the most positive effects for families and children, and what implications do these strategies have for state and local policies? If this question is posed to social service practitioners working with urban families in low-income neighborhoods, in fields such as early childhood education, youth development, health, and family support, the responses tend to focus on more, higher-quality, better-coordinated and -integrated services, both primary and specialized. Community and economic development practitioners more often identify such strategies as housing, commercial revitalization, and small business development as likely to yield positive family effects.

It is in this context that a new generation of comprehensive local initiatives has emerged. Largely supported by foundations, sometimes in partnership with state or local governments, these initiatives may lead with a housing, economic development, or human service reform strategy but seek from the beginning to implement their approach within a broad, holistic understanding of neighborhood development. Some focus primarily on children and families but acknowledge the need to rebuild the social and economic fabric of the community to support family life. Others begin from a community development framework but do not limit the scope of their work to housing production or economic revitalization. What they all share conceptually is an assumption about the interdependence of physical, economic, and social development strategies and a desire to seek opportunities to create synergy among them. This *as yet empirically untested* perspective has emerged from a sense that too often in the past, narrowly defined interventions did not produce long-term change because they failed to recognize the interaction among physical, economic, and social factors that create the context in which the intervention may thrive or flounder. Policies tended to support interventions aimed at improving people or at improving place. New housing was built without much attention to the social problems facing its occupants. Social services were carried out as if in a vacuum, separate from the violence and physical decay on the clients' block. Children's services aimed to assist troubled children without attention to their family and school environments. Job-training programs had no functional relationship with the local economic development strategy. Each intervention was governed by a separate bureaucracy, funded from a separate budget source, and carried out by separate groups of experts. Few viewed the neighborhood as a whole or tried to coordinate, let alone create synergy among, the different development strategies.

The current call for comprehensive, integrated approaches to urban change comes from a clear recognition of the constraints created by categorical approaches, especially in neighborhoods with concentrated poverty and limited development resources. In one way or another, they attend to the following interrelated conditions of neighborhood life that are seen to have a role in promoting the healthy development of children and families:

- economic opportunity and security
- affordable housing and functional public infrastructure
- safety and security
- well-functioning institutions and services
- opportunities for personal development and training
- opportunities for prosocial interactions and social support
- opportunities for participation, service, and leadership
- opportunities for a sense of belonging, identity, and pride

Each of these areas has been the subject of various program efforts and policy debates; some have been studied. But the specific impact of these factors, alone and in combination, on individual behavior and development and on family functioning are for the most part undetermined empirically and likely to be complex and nonuniform in their effects. So their direct link to policy objectives and policy instruments is difficult to establish. Rather than review the evidence in each area and try to link it to particular implications for policy, we have decided to focus here on two principles for policy development that we propose should be considered as policy implementation takes place in building social capital and promoting community participation.

These two areas were selected for several reasons. First, social scientists have renewed their attention to the concepts of social organization and community participation. For example, in chapter 1 Sampson and Morenoff state that "variations in community social organization—especially informal social control—appear to mediate the effect of structural disadvantage (such as concentration of poverty or family disruption) on crime and delinquency" (p.17). The work of Furstenberg (1990) and Furstenberg and Hughes (chapter 2), Crane (1991), Brooks-Gunn and colleagues (1993), and others provides suggestive evidence that this mediating effect could be extended to a range of child and family outcomes. Second, questions about how to "rebuild the social fabric of the neighborhood" and mobilize community leadership and ownership are evident in many current community initiatives and policy discussions. There is increasing recognition that strategies to strengthen families and the distressed neighborhoods in which they live must attend to the structure and texture of social life in the neighborhood and must draw on the energy, talent, and leadership of its residents. Third, these two concepts represent special challenges in the already challenging field of evaluation: they present both analytic and measurement problems that need to be addressed before their utility to the field can be fairly assessed. So both researchers and practitioners have a current interest in the processes of community social organization and participation. Translating this interest into policies and programs, however, presents funders, legislators, program architects, and program evaluators with many unresolved questions. What are the policy and program instruments available, and which ones are likely to be effective?

For the purposes of this discussion, *neighborhood* is defined as a bounded geographic space that circumscribes an ongoing, meaningful pattern of social behavior and generates some symbolic value for its residents. As the authors of these volumes suggest, viewing the neighborhood from a dynamic ecological perspective that recognizes the embeddedness of people in place requires a multilevel assessment of the implications of a development perspective for state and local policies. For example, housing policies governing the location of subsidized housing may have significant effects on a neighborhood's pattern of social relations, which in turn may promote or undermine young people's development in that neighborhood in different ways at different ages. Similarly, local school, policing, and social service delivery policies may affect in different ways the ability of parents to provide consistent and effective support and supervision of their children. Community social capital and participation can operate at a variety of levels with far-reaching effects within an ecological framework.

BUILDING SOCIAL CAPITAL AND PROMOTING COMMUNITY PARTICIPATION

Social capital refers to characteristics of the social organization of a community, such as networks, norms, and trust, that facilitate coordination and cooperation for mutual benefit. In many persistently poor neighborhoods, social relations have broken down, leading to anger, demoralization, fear, diminished prosocial interaction and informal cooperation, and diminution of individual responsibility and commitment. Parents raising children in such communities tend to be isolated from informal social networks that could help them provide the support, socialization, and social control that children need in order to learn the skills and internalize the values required for success in the larger society. Sampson (1993, 6) wrote that communities "characterized by i) anonymity and sparse acquaintanceship networks among residents, ii) unsupervised teenage peer groups and attenuated control of public space, and iii) a weak organizational base and low social participation in local activities" are vulnerable to increased fear and risk of crime and violence (see chapters 1, 2, and 4).

Participation and empowerment are related to the concept of social capital. A community characterized by strong social cohesion and stability is more likely to be able to develop an effective voice to represent its interests than one that is depleted socially. Gardner (1991, 8) wrote that community breakdown often causes people to lose the conviction that they can improve the quality of their lives through their own efforts. They experience such a breakdown as a "loss of meaning, a sense of powerlessness," one of the most deleterious outcomes of this loss of efficacy is a "diminution of individual responsibility and commitment". Furstenberg (1990) reported that in declining neighborhoods, families are likely to experience a breakdown of social ties and a loss of community consensus, which leads to a decline in participation in community institutions and informal networks and increasing despair about the possibility that they can reverse the downward spiral (see also chapter 4).

The concept of empowerment can have meaning at the individual, group, or community level as a psychological, social psychological, economic, or political phenomenon. Kieffer (in Saegert 1993) described empowerment as "a long-term process of adult development of participatory competence." The Center for Population and Family Health (CPFH 1991, 15) called the essence of empowerment a "process of growth and development leading to deliberate efforts to bring about change." CPFH has developed a framework consisting of nine interrelated components of empowerment, comprising ways of feeling (competence, esteem, and control), ways of thinking (knowledge of environment, critical consciousness, aspirations, and problem solving) and ways of behaving (autonomy and determination). Patton (1993, 8) referred to it as "increased intentionality." Taub (1990, 8) prefers to use the term efficacy, "the capacity of individuals to believe that they can change the course of their own lives by their own efforts. . . . The most effective development efforts may alter the way people think about their world and their capacity to alter it." His research in Chicago demonstrated that people can significantly change how they look at the future of their neighborhoods. The assumption is that this change in attitude can lead to change in behavior, which in turn can induce a communitywide "mood of activism." Empowerment in this light can be seen as both a valuable end in itself and as a force behind profound social and behavior change, as a process and an outcome.

While there is some research basis for interest in the concepts of social capital and participation, there is almost no existing empirical knowledge about how to increase these potential neighborhood assets. Looking to program initiatives under way and the policies guiding them, rather than to the research literature, however, we can see a number of strategies in which such goals are being sought, implicitly or explicitly. The initiatives can be grouped by the following overlapping strategies that they aim to create:

- *Opportunities for increasing overall social interaction and communication that help develop, transmit, and reinforce shared community values and norms.* Here the possibilities are broad and depend on the particular culture and needs of the community. Examples include after-school networks and clubs, baby-sitting co-ops, "friendly visiting" patrols for the housebound, celebrations of community histories and rituals that recognize exemplary community figures, community forums, and cleanup campaigns. These are all mechanisms for decreasing family isolation and alienation and building a sense of shared purpose and identity.
- *Opportunities for intergenerational relationships.* Many initiatives subscribe to the importance of children having the chance to interact with a range of adults, both within formal organizations such as schools and churches and informally in such settings as sports teams, choral groups, and community improvement efforts. Adults, individually and collectively, can serve as mentors, models, and sources of informal social control and socialization. The notion is that a network of caring adults who share a sense of community commitment and responsibility can help even marginal families raise children successfully.
- *Opportunities for residents to work with community-based organizations to address significant social problems in the community.* Such approaches can solve discrete problems and help to reknit the web of social and institutional

networks that support families. The assumption here is that the very act of a community coalescing to address its problems generates hope and contributes to community investment, stimulating neighborhood residents to become community stakeholders and, in so doing, increasing the neighborhood's collective support for family life.

• *Opportunities for residents to have a significant voice in neighborhood affairs and decisions.* Many initiatives devote considerable attention to engaging neighborhood residents in their governance structures and in increasing the neighborhood's ability to have a voice in decisions affecting the neighborhood.

The following list contains descriptions of five initiatives that illustrate in different ways efforts at building neighborhood social capital and participation in the service of child and family development.[2] We did not select these initiatives as exemplary models to be replicated; indeed, most are in their early stages of implementation and may or may not turn out to yield positive results. Rather, they were selected to illustrate the range of the thirty to forty such efforts that are under way currently and that share the same straightforward operating assumption: attempts to improve the lives of children and families will be maximally effective when they alter the neighborhood conditions in which these families live. While they are all characterized by attempts to build the neighborhood's social capital and civic participation, they take different program approaches with differing emphases on targeting the role of professional service providers, community organizing, and policy change. Thus, either explicitly or implicitly, each initiative is testing a hypothesis about neighborhood effects.

1. Children, Youth and Families Initiative (CYF), sponsored by the Chicago Community Trust, is a social service reform designed to build an infrastructure of services in communities to support children and their families. The initiative broadens the existing definition of social services to include both developmentally oriented primary services—day-care and after-school programs, sports teams, youth volunteer opportunities, parent support and education programs, and the resources of parks, libraries, settlement houses, and community centers, plus the traditional specialized services—including child welfare, mental health, and juvenile justice—that respond to problems. An aim of the initiative is that both primary and specialized services should function as part of a coherent, organized service system to support children and parents in the communities in which they live. As the first step in forging separate services into a coherent infrastructure, the initiative is supporting creation of a local collaborative planning anddecision-making mechanism in each of the eight targeted communities in Chicago. Through this planning process, citizens and civic interests can come together to set goals they jointly hold and hope to achieve for their children and families, to define

priorities and develop plans for the provision of services to meet these goals, and to monitor their progress. Initial planning has taken place, and the first round of implementation grants were made in 1993. The Chicago Community Trust has committed $30 million through the end of the decade to test these reforms in eight Chicago communities.

2. The Children, Families, and Community Initiative (CFC) is a partnership between the F. R. Bigelow Foundation (a support organization of the St. Paul Foundation) and the Frogtown and Summit-University neighborhoods of St. Paul. It addresses the needs of children in these two neighborhoods by targeting over five years $1.5 million in grants of up to $25,000 each to resident-controlled groups and organizations that work to strengthen family units and build healthy communities. These organizations must exhibit community ownership as defined by community control, self-determination and empowerment, and leadership development and capacity building. The initiative is governed by a multicultural steering committee, a subcommittee of which is responsible for the evaluation. The initiative has completed three years of operation—two years of developing the philosophy and operations of the approach and one year of actual grantmaking. Some of the lessons reported to date include the importance of paying attention to issues of race and culture, the value of moving away from exclusive reliance on professionals and established social service agencies toward greater reliance on residents doing things for themselves and organizing with others to solve a problem, and the need to approach children's issues in the context of family and community, rather than in isolation.

3. The Rebuilding Communities Initiative (RCI) is a seven-year, $18 million initiative designed to contribute to the transformation of five troubled, economically distressed neighborhoods. The Annie E. Casey Foundation has identified five critical elements of neighborhood revitalization that are key to the overall strategy: (1) maximizing the capacity and impact of neighborhood resources and institutions, (2) developing an effective neighborhood-based human service delivery system for children and youth, (3) reforming existing investment streams to maximize positive neighborhood economic development, (4) developing and maintaining housing and infrastructure, and (5) attracting capital investment. The unifying element of the initiative is a focus upon families, and a commitment to reverse the social isolation and disenfranchisement of families in these communities. Planning grants have been made to a community-based organization in each site to form a representative collaborative governance structure that will ensure the broad participation of residents, community organizations, and key public sector stakeholders in the community and to oversee subsequent development of the initiative.

4. The Community-Building Initiative (CBI) is sponsored by the Local Initiatives Support Corporation (LISC), which recently undertook a study of community development corporations that had promising strategies for providing services to the residents of the properties they owned or managed and for integrating these services with property management activities. This study provided the basis on which LISC developed CBI, whose goal is to help community development corporations (CDCs) rebuild their neighborhoods socially and physically. CBI seeks to help CDCs extend their roles as mediating institutions within poor communities—organizing residents to set the agenda, and then catalyzing broader institutional responses to community priorities. Concentrating on building the foundations of social organization and networks that advance community stability, CBI has established the following broad substantive areas upon which the community-building activities may focus: children and youth; drugs, guns, and crime; employment; housing resident participation; and public services. In eight cities, CBI will provide $145,000 per year for three years to a group of CDCs to create citywide programs. In three cities, CBI will make planning and implementation grants to individual CDCs with especially promising initiatives. All funds will be matched locally two to one; short-term loans, predevelopment loans, and recoverable grants for investments related to CBI projects will also be available. All planning grants should begin no later than June 1994.

5. Community Building in Partnership (CBP) is a partnership between the city of Baltimore, the Enterprise Foundation, and the Sandtown-Winchester neighborhood, whose vision is to build a viable working community in which neighborhood residents are empowered to direct and sustain the physical, social, and economic development of their community. Now formally incorporated, CBP is directed by an individual on loan from the mayor's office, and it has a staff of thirty-nine, the majority of whom are residents, including sixteen VISTA volunteers. CBP's efforts have been focused in three broad areas: strategic planning and program design; immediate projects, including the construction of new townhouses for home ownership and a community center with a range of family services; and community building, including grassroots organizing, leadership development, and other strategies to develop community ownership of CBP. Residents put out a community newspaper, run a food and clothing bank, supervise gardening projects, and volunteer in a variety of community events. Significant new funds from HUD are expected to supplement existing foundation and corporate support.

As in these five examples, most of the comprehensive neighborhood-based initiatives around the country have emerged only in the past several years, many do not yet have substantial evaluations in place, and it is too early for those that do to have more than descriptive findings about start-up and initial implementation.[3] As a group, however, they represent a remarkable confluence of local initiative and like-minded thinking about the general relationship of neighborhood conditions and child and family development. But because the theories behind this relationship are generally not articulated sufficiently and the evaluation problems (discussed in a moment) are so great, translating the experience of these initiatives into lessons for policy becomes a major challenge. As Lehman and Smeeding (vol. 1) pointed out, mediators matter: knowing how the neighborhood changes generated by these initiatives affect the well-being of children and families would make the policy-translation process and the deployment of resources more precise and effective. Such progress would require significantly more work on the development of theories of change by initiative architects, funders, and evaluators, plus stronger efforts as the initiatives are launched and evaluated to interpret the results in light of these theories. Until the mediating processes become less ambiguous, it will be difficult to identify with much confidence the policy implications generated by the results.

RESEARCH, EVALUATION, AND POLICY DEVELOPMENT

The research presented in these volumes, as well as research reported elsewhere on such topics as social organization, participation, and efficacy, underlines the need for and potential payoff of work to establish and test the links between theory, practice, and policy aimed at improving outcomes for children and families in poor urban neighborhoods. It also underlines the many challenges to making those links effectively. One of these challenges is created by the limits of the quantitative data from which these volumes' findings about neighborhood effects have been generated. Chapter 3 contains a detailed discussion of the strengths and limitations of the six quantitative data sets. When current neighborhood-development initiatives are reviewed, however, it is clear that their (usually implicit) hypotheses about the process of neighborhood change and its desired effects on child and family development call for a much richer, more textured description of neighborhood conditions than can be captured by primarily structural-compositional factors. Aggregations of individual demographic characteristics do little to help us understand the meaning of the relationships between the child and the family and the neighborhood settings in which the child is embedded, as well as all the mediating processes that intervene in those relationships (chapters 2 and 3). The more the characteristics of a neighborhood's social organization and social relations—significant targets of neighborhood-development interventions—can be identified, measured, and integrated with the neighborhood's demographic characteristics, the clearer will be the implications for policies and programs. Chapter 3, for example, tries to illuminate earlier quantitative findings with ethnographic data about a parent's embeddedness in social networks. While integrating such different kinds of data into a coherent whole presents its own special challenges, it is clear that the neighborhood's culture, history, controls, and supports must be taken into account, along with the characteristics of its residents, if policies and programs are to be most effective (see chapter 4).

Thus, we come back to the broader questions: How can current urban-change initiatives benefit most from researchers' thoughts? How can researchers inform their theory and knowledge development with the results of actual practice in the field? How can policy makers encourage and learn from both research and practice? Before addressing these questions directly, we briefly review evaluations of the kinds of initiatives discussed earlier.

Because the territory is new, the investments often high, and the consequences of success or failure profound, evaluating comprehensive neighborhood-based initiatives presents daunting methodological and political challenges. Funders issue "requests for proposals" asking evaluators to determine whether the intervention they are funding "works," but the evaluators often have difficulty determining what *it* is, let alone whether and how it affects children and families and the distressed neighborhoods in which they live. Left up to local adaptations that yield different looks in different sites, the *it* is often in development and changes over time. There may be assumptions about the synergy or interaction effects intended among different programmatic strategies, but these are not spelled out in any detail and are difficult to assess, given the nonexperimental structure of the test. For example, the real payoff for RCI's strategy to attract capital investment may come only when the capacity of the neighborhood's nonprofits has been developed sufficiently to achieve measurable impact on the neighborhood's particular social problems. A home-ownership strategy may succeed only when it is accompanied by substantial school improvement that attracts new residents into a neighborhood. A typical comprehensive initiative recognizes the embeddedness of people in place and aims to find strategic points of entry that can leverage change at various levels. For example, in addition to building the neighborhood's housing stock, a housing-rehabilitation program can train youth in the construction trades, be the basis for organizing a block club, or stimulate demand for better public services in the area. Each program intervention need not serve multiple functions, but each must be developed with a comprehensive lens and an appreciation for how the community operates as an ecological system. This premise is one of the explicit core operating guidelines for the initiatives previously described, but it is not easy to operationalize in an evaluation design.

Similarly challenging evaluation dilemmas are presented by nonlinearities that are likely to exist within different program components. Illustratively, CBI may need to deliver a certain critical mass of new housing or involve a particular percentage of community youth in programs before any neighborhood effects are detected. The "transformative" effects of community participation in CBP may depend in part on involving a certain proportion of neighborhood residents as volunteers in the initiative.

The long-term process of improving the quality of life in distressed neighborhoods is clearly another evaluation challenge. Evaluations are rarely funded over a long enough time period to capture this process, but short- and medium-term markers of change are difficult to establish with significant levels of confidence. Traditional evaluation methods are not designed to capture the breadth and complexity of factors operating at a neighborhood level, let alone relate cause and effect to the dynamics of system change over time. Indeed, the problems of attribution are staggering, given the larger economic and social context in which the initiatives are embedded. Even the traditional language of evaluation does not seem to do justice to the new relationships that are being forged between the evaluator and the different constituencies who have a stake in learning from the initiative.

Adding further complexity to the evaluation enterprise is the increased focus on community participation and new governance arrangements that has led to debate about who should be involved in designing, implementing, and overseeing evaluations and who should be the intended audiences for the findings. As Lehman and Smeeding (vol. 1) suggested, the ideal evaluation approach should be shaped by theory and structured to explore "between-neighborhood variations in program effects, as well as within-neighborhood variation between control and intervention subjects, in order to provide the most useful information to policy makers" (p.276). But when a central element of the intervention involves the devolution of authority to a local decision-making group, or what Lehman and Smeeding call "participatory development," the notion of control and intervention subjects, or even control and intervention neighborhoods, becomes difficult for program architects or evaluators to define or hold constant over time.

Despite these and other daunting evaluation questions, practitioners appear to be somewhat optimistic that comprehensive initiatives are on the "right track," a growing number of "naturally occurring experiments" are presenting opportunities, and a sense of urgency prevails about the importance of aggregating the nationwide findings and of scientifically cumulating further knowledge. Otherwise, researchers are recognizing, the field will be unable to provide plausible evidence of strategies that do improve the lives of families and neighborhoods (not because they do not exist but because we cannot document them credibly). And then we will be vulnerable to the despair and public apathy generated by the public perception that "nothing works."

This is the case for substantial investment in research and evaluation that would aim to (1) stimulate the development of new evaluation technologies, (2) place particular emphasis on the how and why of implementation, as well as on what happens, and (3) require a commitment to tracking initiatives over the long run. Corbett (1992, 27) has suggested that we need more synthetic cross-site evaluations, more process analyses and qualitative work, and more attention to the development of common marker variables.

> In the long run, however, we may have to think of a whole new way of doing business. The old form of discrete, impact-focused evaluations, awarded to firms on a competitive basis, may be counterproductive. Longer time lines, less obsession with "what works," and a more collaborative evaluation industry may be needed. The days of the short sprint—one-shot summative evaluations—may be ending. A new paradigm, where the marathon constitutes the more appropriate metaphor, may be emerging.(27)

Despite significant differences, many neighborhood initiatives share many guiding principles, policy concerns, and evaluation challenges; thus, opportunities for cross-site learning need to be exploited. Efforts to accelerate knowledge development in the field might include better documentating the initiatives and thinking more about what data are appropriate to collect at which levels, convening working groups of evaluators from different initiatives, testing similar evaluation instruments and new tools like geocoding and computer mapping across a subset of initiatives, supporting a few exemplary evaluations for initiatives that appear to have the potential to yield substantial learning, and conducting meta-analyses of what is being learned across the field. Every initiative cannot afford a complete multimethod, multilevel data-collection strategy, but the field could benefit from some common data collected in a similar fashion.

Patton (1993) made a relevant distinction between research and evaluation. Research aims to test theory to arrive at findings that are generalizable across time and space, whereas the goal of evaluation is to gather data about program processes and outcomes to inform decision making about specific programs and help improve them. For evaluators, research designs need to be driven by concerns about program utility and policy relevance, rather than testing theory for academic or scholarly purposes. But just as researchers are searching to identify the mechanisms and processes through which neighborhood effects may operate (such as collective socialization and epidemic or contagion mechanisms), so must evaluators, in collaboration with the architects of neighborhood-change initiatives, develop some good theories of community change. For the most part, the new group of neighborhood-change initiatives under way is not research or theory driven, but rather has its roots among funders, social activists, and community-based organizations. In contrast to the years of the War on Poverty, social scientists have had little to do with community development in the past two decades, either as conceptualizers or evaluators of these initiatives. This is one of the reasons why the theory about neighborhood development and its consequences for children and families appears to lag behind the related action. The existence of this new group of initiatives, however, can provide an opportunity for evaluators to contribute to the development of theories of change that are directly informed by what they are learning in targeted neighborhoods.

Clearly, both research and evaluation are needed to maximize learning from current experience and suggest promising directions for future work. Researchers need to view evaluations of neighborhood-change initiatives as a major resource to be mined for what they can contribute to theory. Architects of such initiatives need to specify as concretely as possible their often-implicit theories of change so evaluators can develop the research questions and methods that will yield empirical data to support or refute these theories. Given an organizing theory, the results might well be easier to interpret and could therefore yield stronger policy recommendations.

CONCLUSION

A frustrating distance exists between social science research about how neighborhoods affect child and family development, the experience of a new group of initiatives designed to improve the well-being of children and families through comprehensive neighborhood development, and current policy discussions at the state and local levels. There are, however, two sources of good news. First, the social scientists doing the research presented herein are working within an ecological framework that calls for an interdisciplinary, multi-level understanding of the relationship between person and place. With increasingly sophisticated techniques for collecting and integrating multilevel data on the basis of increasingly complex models of human behavior, these researchers can begin to address an important set of questions about neighborhood effects that are critical to developing policies and initiatives that will improve the lives of children and families living in distressed neighborhoods. The other source of good news is that policy makers, foundation sponsors, and the planners and implementers of the new group of neighborhood initiatives all share a similar ecological perspective in their commitment to comprehensive approaches that try to create synergy between physical, economic, and social development. Given the need to maximize the impact of shrinking resources and to generate public support for investment in poverty-alleviation strategies, those concerned with policy have increasingly recognized the importance of gaining a more sophisticated understanding of how neighborhoods, and the initiatives designed to improve them, affect child and family development.

Despite a shared perspective and a receptiveness to learning from each other, however, both social scientists and policy makers or practitioners face some formidable challenges to combining their interests and needs in a mutually beneficial way. It is not simply a question of adding some new questions to a survey instrument or assessing an initiative's effects over a longer period of time. We need to build an empirical base that includes, but goes beyond, the data sets used in these volumes, and we need to develop new evaluation methodologies so that current initiatives can help us generate and test better-articulated theories of neighborhood effects.

NOTES

1. See chapter 1 and Sampson (1993a) about the relationship among social organization, informal social control, and crime or fear of crime.

2. These descriptions are based on materials from the initiatives, which have evolved substantially since their first inception.

3. For more details about these and other efforts, there are several recent reviews by Eisen (1992), Fishman and Phillips (1993), Jenny (1993), and Rosewater (1992).

11

Communities as Place, Face, and Space: Provision of Services to Poor, Urban Children and Their Families

Tama Leventhal, Jeanne Brooks-Gunn, and Sheila B. Kamerman

The research in these two volumes on neighborhoods, *Neighborhood Poverty*, was undertaken in part as a response to the worsening conditions in poor neighborhoods in America's cities in the 1970s and 1980s and to the cogent analyses by Wilson (1987, 1991a, 1991b) of the causes and consequences of these trends, primarily on inner-city neighborhoods. Consequently, scholars (or policy researchers) from a variety of disciplines who are attempting to understand the effects of low income on children, such as those represented in these volumes, increasingly have begun to focus on the role of neighborhood poverty (most notably in urban areas) in addition to familial poverty. An alarmingly high number of children living in urban neighborhoods are poor, particularly in cities with a population over one million. While poverty is seen in rural and suburban communities as well as urban ones, proportionately, a majority of poor people are living in urban areas: half of poor families with children reside in the eleven largest cities—New York, Los Angeles, Miami, Philadelphia, Baltimore, Boston, Chicago, Houston, San Diego, Detroit, and Dallas (Congressional Research Service 1992; Kahn and Kamerman 1996). The proportion is even higher if all cities with a population of half a million or more are included. Even though large numbers of poor people are located in a relatively small number of cities, services for these children still are provided at the local level (that is, neighborhoods, health districts, and school districts). How do communities, especially those with high concentrations of poor people, actually provide services and strengthen families' efforts to provide food, love, shelter, health care, safe streets, and learning experiences for their children?

Recently, a group of scholars sought to address some of these concerns about poor, urban children and their families and strategies for delivering services to these families. A product of this two-year seminar on big-city children was *Children and Their Families in Big Cities: Strategies for Service*

Reform, edited by Kahn and Kamerman (1996). The seminar focused on the eleven largest cities in the United States.[1] The general issues covered were: How can we provide adequate services to children at a time of limited resources? Do large cities have different problems (and perhaps different strengths) in providing services to children than do smaller entities? Do current ways in which services are delivered to children need to be altered? Two questions raised by the seminar that were particularly relevant to children's development were (1) What family- and child-oriented services are needed in a community and how can they best be delivered? (2) What community supports are needed to complement and buttress the support offered by the family? (Brooks-Gunn 1996). The seminar, like the two volumes, took as its starting point the fact that children are embedded in families in communities (Brooks-Gunn 1995; Brooks-Gunn, Denner, and Klebanov 1995). Additionally, most services (with the exception of the income transfers) were assumed to be delivered locally, and parents were seen as central to service delivery.[2]

The directors of the seminar deliberately chose participants who would consider the overarching issues just specified from conceptual, policy, and programmatic approaches. Accordingly, the seminar members varied in perspectives and disciplines, but all were advocates for better service supports for urban families. Perhaps most noteworthy was the seminar directors' effort to bring together two groups of individuals—those who establish, run, and fund child-oriented initiatives, and those who conduct research on urban children and design evaluations of services for these children and their families. Often seminar members would take varying perspectives, or at least approaches, depending on the issues being discussed. Despite this cross-fertilization of viewpoints, questions were repeatedly raised as to whether or not the existing research was really informative to practitioners and advocates in the field, and further, whether or not the research findings reflected the realities of children's lives or the services they receive. Thus, the seminar acted as a vital bridge between research-evaluators and practitioner-planners.

Drawing on the issues raised by the seminar participants, this chapter focuses on the ways in which the work exemplified by the two volumes may be useful in portraying the lives of urban families, in designing services for children (and indirectly, in reforming or altering the systems in which services are embedded), and in evaluating the outcomes of service initiatives. We make a distinction between four general approaches to delivering services to children in cities: (1) categorical programs, (2) family and community support services, which usually attempt to integrate services, (3) community development corporations (CDCs), and (4) comprehensive community initiatives (CCIs). These approaches to delivering services to urban children and their families can be viewed on a continuum, with categorical programs being the most specific approach and CCIs the broadest (Kubisch 1996).

Services are generally delivered through categorical programs, which consist of federally mandated programs such as Woman, Infants, and Children

(WIC), Head Start, Healthy Start, and Aid to Dependent Families with Children (AFDC; now Temporary Assistance for Needy Families [TANF]). Under recent and pending legislation, some programs will be funded under block grants to states, giving more local autonomy to these programs. (See Lehman and Smeeding [vol. 1] for a review of federal, state, and local legislation.) The second strategy concentrates on integrating services for children and families in a community-based setting and on fostering ties among community residents, often via the provision of family and community support services (Kagan 1996; Schorr with Both 1991). The third service strategy, community development corporations, focuses on housing, job creation, and civic infrastructure (Briggs 1997; Briggs and Mueller, with Sullivan 1997; Sullivan 1993). The fourth approach to delivering services, comprehensive community initiatives (CCIs), integrates the first three approaches to service delivery mentioned earlier. CCIs provide coordinated, integrated services in a neighborhood-based setting and also tend to incorporate housing and community development (chapter 10; Kubisch 1996). Thus, our discussion of urban children and service delivery refers to the four types of programs outlined here: categorical programs, integrated family and community support services, community development corporations, and comprehensive community-based initiatives. Of importance, however, is the degree to which these different strategies are family-oriented or child-oriented, as opposed to individual- or adult-oriented (Wilson, Ellwood, and Brooks-Gunn 1995).

We believe that community-based programs could benefit from research on neighborhoods (as exemplified by these two volumes), and social science would be enriched by a more careful appraisal of what is occurring in communities. Accordingly, this chapter addresses three issues: (1) how urban neighborhoods may be seen as contexts for development of children and for service delivery to them; (2) how social science, generally, and the research in these volumes, specifically, has enhanced our understanding of the lives of urban children; and (3) how the provision of services to poor, urban children varies as a function of the definition of *community* employed, as well as how the research in these volumes informs the design of urban services for children.

INTERSECTION OF URBAN NEIGHBORHOODS AND FAMILY POVERTY

Researchers attempting to understand the causes and consequences of urban poverty have pointed to several historical, social, and political trends underlying changes in America's cities. Wilson (1987, 1991a, 1991b) has convincingly argued that macrolevel changes, including deindustrialization and suburbanization, have led to not only increases in the number of poor and jobless people in urban neighborhoods but also to social isolation, particularly of African Americans and Latinos. Further, Wilson has suggested that these structural changes are associated with behavioral manifestations—out-of-wedlock childbearing, crime, welfare dependency, and school dropout—among the individuals residing in these neighborhoods. Most recently, Wilson's (1996) analysis of urban poverty has focused on the disappearance of jobs in inner-city neighborhoods.

Other scholars, such as Massey and colleagues (Massey 1990; Massey and Denton 1989), while also considering social and geographic isolation, have implicated housing policies as a major factor contributing to concentrated poverty in urban areas. Specifically, the segregation of public housing in cities in predominately poor neighborhoods has resulted in isolated areas of concentrated poverty—in essence, the geographic segregation of neighborhoods by socioeconomic status (SES). Because of the high concentrations of minorities residing in poor, inner-city neighborhoods, these policies have further segregated neighborhoods by race and ethnicity. Discrimination, over and above racial residential segregation, has also played a role (Katz 1989; Mare and Winship 1984; Melendez and Figueroa 1992). Racial discrimination influences urban, minority families in large part by limiting the opportunity structure available to them (MacLeod 1987; Ogbu 1991). Two of the primary contexts in which discrimination operates to undermine the development and well-being of poor, urban, minority families are the labor force (Freeman 1991; Sullivan 1989) and the educational system (Fine 1991; Jencks and Mayer 1990).

Clearly, macrolevel factors have affected urban children's lives. Further, due to institutionalized racism and classism, the policies, programs, and institutions serving urban families may, in subtle ways, not always support families' efforts to provide optimal environments for their children, despite their circumstances. The neighborhood research has focused on community-level effects. At the same time, the findings from neighborhood research, including the six studies in volume 1, clearly point to the prominence of familial factors, such as income, education, and employment, over neighborhood characteristics in predicting child outcomes.

Low income (poverty and near-poverty status) has detrimental effects on child and family well-being across a host of outcomes, such as cognitive and socioemotional development, educational achievement, and parenting (Duncan and Brooks-Gunn 1997; Hauser and Sweeny 1997; Hill and Sandfort 1995). Research on the potential mechanisms by which income may influence children has examined parental irritability and depressed mood, parental conflict, low parental involvement in learning activities, unresponsive parenting, low levels of social support, and inadequate child care (Brooks-Gunn and Duncan 1997; Conger et al. 1992, 1993, 1997; McLoyd et al. 1994). Thus, despite variability in the circumstances of poor families, the confluence of factors often impedes optimal child development. The implication for service delivery to urban children is that neighborhood poverty is likely to coincide with familial poverty, especially for minorities (see Duncan and Aber vol. 1; Duncan et al. 1994).

Again, the importance of families cannot be overstated, because they provide the first learning experiences for children. The provision of learning experiences in the home and emergent literacy and language stimulation are important to children's development, especially their cognitive and verbal abilities (Brooks-Gunn, Liaw, and Klebanov 1995; Snow 1993; Snow et al. 1991). Parental availability and involvement in early school experiences, as well as home learning, are associated with child well-being (Bradley 1995; Lareau 1989; Zigler and Black 1989). Children in less-advantaged families in resource-poor neighborhoods, however, may be less likely to benefit from the provision of learning experiences in the home (Klebanov et al. vol. 1). These findings indicate a need to coordinate family- and neighborhood-level services and interventions.

Concentrating on the intersection of families and neighborhoods, perhaps one of the most important facts is that parents are advocates or brokers for their children's receipt of community resources. Parents must interact with community-level agencies and institutions to garner resources for their children. For example, parents select preschools and schools for their children, obtain health services for them (especially for children with disabilities or risk conditions), and create extracurricular activities for them. Few studies, however, provide information on the process by which families in poor communities obtain, create, and structure opportunities for their children despite scarce resources (chapter 4; Brooks-Gunn, Rauh, and Leventhal forthcoming; Chase-Lansdale and Brooks-Gunn 1995).

In the same vein, federal policy initiatives for children also must be viewed in the context of children in families in communities. Many programs intended to serve (primarily low-income) children, such as immunization campaigns, expanded Medicaid eligibility, and Early Periodic Diagnostic and Screening Test (EPDST), encounter surprisingly low levels of participation (albeit varied levels of outreach), especially among poor families or those residing in poor neighborhoods (Hill, Bartlett, and Brostrom 1993; Lobach 1995; Wolfe 1995). Parental involvement appears to be a missing component to the design and implementation of these services (Lobach 1995). Alternatively, the success of Head Start is often attributed to its efforts to engage parents and local community members in the program (Zigler 1987; Zigler and Valentine 1979). Thus, federal and community programs are important neighborhood resources for families, but their efficacy depends largely on the family and the community.

COMMUNITY INFLUENCES ON CHILDREN AND FAMILIES

Several approaches to understanding community influences on children and families are considered. In this section we address (1) neighborhood effects on children, (2) neighborhood effects on parents, and (3) community socialization.

NEIGHBORHOOD EFFECTS ON CHILDREN

Prior to the undertaking of this project by the Social Science Research Council Working Group in 1990, relatively few studies had considered how neighborhood conditions might affect children's, in distinction to adult's, development (Mayer and Jencks 1989; Shaw and McKay 1969). Models of community-level influences posit both direct and indirect effects of neighborhoods. Neighborhood resources may directly affect children through police presence or access to resources that provide stimulating learning environments such as parks, libraries, and community centers. Research suggests that children's participation in learning-environment activities is associated with enhanced cognitive and emotional development (Bradley 1995; Bradley and Caldwell 1980; Bradley et al. 1989; Gottfried 1984; Wachs and Gruen 1982). Collective socialization models of neighborhoods argue that neighborhood influences indirectly affect children vis-à-vis the presence of adult role models and monitoring (see chapter 2; Wilson 1987). Contagion models focus on problem behavior and are based on the premise that neighborhood effects operate through peer influences, and relative deprivation models posit that neighborhood conditions indirectly affect individuals via their evaluation of their situation relative to neighbors (Jencks and Mayer 1990; 1989). These latter two models may not be as applicable to children as they are to adolescents, because of children's more limited contact with neighborhood and school peers.

Before the six studies described in volume 1 were undertaken, we conducted research on community-level influences and examined the association between neighborhood resources and child outcomes (Brooks-Gunn et al. 1993; Duncan et al. 1994; Klebanov, Brooks-Gunn, and Duncan 1994). Our initial analyses investigated neighborhood affluence (family income more than thirty thousand dollars) and neighborhood low income (family income less than ten thousand dollars). These two measures were chosen because a review of the literature indicated that concentrations of poor and affluent neighbors may have differential effects on child and adolescent development (Mayer and Jencks 1990). This separation was also important in testing the different models of influence. The collective socialization model predicted that the presence of affluent neighbors would have a positive influence on child development, whereas the relative deprivation model predicted negative outcomes. For the presence of low-income neighbors, the contagion model suggested that their presence would have detrimental effects on well-being after a threshold had been passed. These neighborhood effects were examined in relation to family-level variables.

The results of these studies indicated that three- and five-year-olds' IQ scores were positively associated with the presence of affluent neighbors, even when familial-level characteristics (maternal education, maternal age, maternal race, and income-to-needs ratio) were controlled. In addition, several other neighborhood characteristics were explored—joblessness, single mothers, education, and welfare use. Across these three studies, neighborhood affluence was the most powerful predictor of developmental outcomes.

The six studies analyses presented in volume 1 employed more complex measures of neighborhoods than our earlier work. Using data from the Panel Study of Income Dynamic (PSID), five neighborhood factors were identified: low SES, high SES, male joblessness, ethnic diversity, and family concentration (Duncan and Aber vol. 1). These factors were used across the six studies to explore neighborhood effects at different developmental periods. The findings from these studies were consistent with our earlier research on the importance of high SES, particularly its association with IQ (Chase-Lansdale et al. vol. 1). In addition, family residence in ethnically diverse neighborhoods was negatively associated with children's verbal ability, most notably for white children and not for black children.

The effect of neighborhood-level variables on children's behavior problems, including neighborhood affluence, appears to be less powerful and less consistent than for IQ and achievement (Chase-Lansdale et al. vol. 1; Klebanov et al. 1994; Chase-Lansdale and Gordon 1996; vol. 1). However, we did find an association between the male joblessness factor and behavioral functioning, especially for school-aged children. Collective socialization models posit that neighborhood influences operate vis-à-vis social disorganization, absence of role modeling, and lack of routines and monitoring (Wilson 1991a; see also chapter 1). This finding is congruent with research suggesting that residing in a low-income neighborhood is associated with greater externalizing behavior (aggression) in five-year-old children (Brooks-Gunn et al. 1993). As for children living in poor neighborhoods, their aggressive or acting-out behavior may be due in part to the lower-quality schools and child-care settings available to them. Higher adult-to-child ratios may lead to less supervision and increased tolerance toward aggressive behavior (Hayes, Palmer, and Zaslow 1990). Replication of these findings is necessary to draw any firm conclusions about neighborhood effects on children's socioemotional development.

NEIGHBORHOOD EFFECTS ON PARENTING

The effects of neighborhood-level variables on children may operate indirectly through parental behavior and family functioning. Some data support the premise that neighborhood characteristics, over and above sociodemographic factors, influence maternal characteristics and are associated with parenting behavior. The mediator analyses presented in volume 1 found that neighborhood influences on children (aged three to six years) were in part mediated by the effect of neighborhoods on parenting characteristics and behavior (Klebanov et al. vol. 1; see also Klebanov, Brooks-Gunn, and Duncan 1994). For school-aged children, neighborhood economic and ethnic composition characteristics were found to be associated with the quality of the home learning environment, which in turn was associated with children's IQ scores. More specifically, residing in a high-SES neighborhood positively affected the quality of the home environment, which itself was associated with higher academic achievement and verbal abilities and lower behavior-problem scores. Given that neighborhood characteristics affect parenting and the home environment and, consequently, child outcomes, multilevel services seem warranted. Specifically, child-oriented, family-oriented, and community-oriented services should be integrated to reflect their mutual goal—enhancing the lives of children and their families.

Residing in an ethnically diverse neighborhood, on the other hand, had a negative effect on children—namely, low verbal scores—that was mediated by the quality of the home learning environment. Although much of the existing neighborhood research on child development has concentrated on economic resources, much less is known about the effects of ethnic composition. It is argued by some that low- to moderate-income neighborhoods operate more effectively if *not* integrated ethnically (chapters 3 and 4). Community cohesion may be reduced in poor neighborhoods where integration has occurred due to the building of racially segregated public housing, the influx of immigrants, or neighborhoods in the process of either declining or gentrifying (chapter 4). It is not clear whether ethnic or racial groups maintain separate institutional supports (such as social clubs or places of worship) in low-income, racially integrated neighborhoods; however, neighborhood cohesion may be impaired by racial or ethnic groups maintaining separate supports.

Additional neighborhood factors that may affect parenting (beyond economic resources and ethnic integration) are the presence of stressors such as violence, uncertainty, crowding, and daily hassles. All of these stressors are more common in poor neighborhoods (Coulton 1996; Coulton et al. 1995). For example, a study of a poor urban community showed that children are exposed to high levels of violence within both the community and the home (Martinez and Richters 1993; Richters and Martinez 1993). A community-level analysis of child maltreatment revealed a higher occurrence of stressful life events in neighborhoods at greater risk for child maltreatment (Garbarino and Kostelny 1992). Thus, other community characteristics besides low income and ethnic integration can influence parenting. However, such characteristics are not measured by geocoding for census-tract residence.

Consequently, we turn to the work of ethnographers focusing on poor, urban neighborhoods to see how neighborhood conditions impact family processes and, in turn, could influence children. Jarrett (chapter 4) identified four parenting strategies used by low-income African American parents residing in poor neighborhoods: (1) family protective strategies; (2) child-monitoring strategies; (3) parental resource-seeking strategies; and (4) in-home learning strategies. These strategies vary in terms of their ability to maximize familial and neighborhood resources.

Family protection and monitoring emphasize family resources while minimizing exposure to negative neighborhood influences. Because these techniques concentrate primarily on protecting, monitoring, and isolating children from adverse community influences, family resources are not necessarily maximized. Familial protection may be more practical with young children and monitoring more practical with adolescents; both strategies attempt to restrict children to the local neighborhood (chapter 2). (However, see the work by Merriwether–de Vries, Burton, and Eggeletion 1996 on the distinction made between neighborhoods of residence and influence based on teenage girls' sexual behavior.) Restriction tactics illustrate how the cost or benefit of community ties is context specific, and there may be little advantage to socializing with low-functioning families and peers (chapter 7). In general, these types of parenting practices may be particularly influential in reducing problem behaviors; whether or not they would affect verbal ability and school achievement is less clear.

The in-home learning strategy, while maintaining some connection to neighborhood institutions, most notably schools, seeks to tap parental resources—parents attempt to facilitate their children's intellectual development. Many of the behaviors described by Jarrett are similar to those assessed by the Home Observation for Measurement of the Environment (HOME) scale (Bradley 1995; Bradley et al. 1989) used in the analyses by Chase-Lansdale and colleagues in volume 1, such as reading with children or assisting them with homework. Although chapter 6 suggests that family management practices, rather than in-home parenting practices, are affected by neighborhood characteristics, Jarrett's work illustrates how these constructs are not necessarily independent, because family management may involve more-traditional parenting practices such as instruction. This technique may be employed more with preschool and school-aged children rather than adolescents (depending on parents' level of education).

The final technique, parental resource-seeking strategies, maximizes local and extralocal resources. While familial efforts also entail monitoring, parents focus on "bridging" their children to resources both within and outside the neighborhood. In essence, these parents learn to navigate the system to obtain resources and services for their children. This strategy is likely to affect both cognitive and behavioral functioning by restricting children's activities in the neighborhood and providing them with stimulating alternatives outside of the neighborhood. In addition, this technique may be adaptive for young children as well as adolescents.

COMMUNITY SOCIALIZATION

Anderson's (1990, 1991) ethnographic study distinguished alternative socialization strategies operating at the neighborhood level. His work illustrates how neighborhood-level processes may undermine parental efforts to protect children from adverse neighborhood conditions (see also Burton 1990). Multiple role models and socialization processes exist in poor, urban neighborhoods. Two competing forces within neighborhoods are "conventional" adults and youth who are employed and who value work and education and "the street," where unconventional behavior is the norm. An inverse relation exists between the two types of role models such that as the opportunity structure ("conventional" goals) available to youth in the neighborhood declines, the strength of the street increases. These findings, viewed in conjunction with the work in this volume, have implications for parenting older children and youth, who presumably have more direct exposure to neighborhood and school peers (see Newman 1996).

Models of community socialization posit that the effectiveness of individual parents is moderated by the practices of the majority of other parents in the community (chapters 4 and 7). In Coleman's (1988) terms, community socialization may operate through norms and sanctions, which guide parenting practices, peer behavior, and a host of other community processes. For example, according to Darling and Steinberg, peers may be the primary agent through which community socialization influences adolescents. Throughout the childhood years, parents or parental figures manage and supervise children's lives and may play a more salient role in children's development than peers (chapters 2 and 4).[3] Scant research exists, however, on how community socialization might influence parenting practices.

In brief, we have examined several ways in which neighborhoods may influence children. Neighborhood conditions may directly affect children, especially for achievement-related outcomes. Community influences also operate indirectly on child well-being vis-à-vis parenting and community socialization processes. These mechanisms also are associated with school achievement and are related to problem behavior as well. In light of the research findings presented here, the following section provides a more in-depth discussion of strategies for delivering services to poor, urban children.

PROVISION OF SERVICES AS A FUNCTION OF THE DEFINITION OF NEIGHBORHOOD OR COMMUNITY

Defining or operationalizing *community*, as is common practice in neighborhood-based research, is not a high priority for designers of community-based services (Sullivan forthcoming). Definitional disagreements abound, as is seen in the various approaches of social scientists writing for this volume. Predicaments may arise if different definitions of *community* or *neighborhood*[4] are used by family and community support services, community development corporations, comprehensive community initiatives, and categorical programs (and by specific categorical programs such as health districts, police precincts, and school districts). Additional problems confronted by most community-based programs, but not by categorical programs (due to eligibility requirements and federal mandates), are whom to include in a community (exclusion and inclusion) and who speaks for a community.

When considering residents' perceptions in defining *community*, an important fact to acknowledge is that neighborhood boundaries are fluid and differ, depending on the individual's frame of reference. For example, an individual might define *neighborhood* in several ways depending on the function or activity—such as shopping, visiting friends, or going to the doctor—that he or she has in mind (Sullivan forthcoming). Several other chapters in this volume have made a similar point: community can signify a geographic area or a psychological association or both; entities may overlap or be distinct. However, poor families may be more tied geographically to their residential neighborhood than nonpoor families because of fewer resources for traveling to other communities for various activities (Sullivan forthcoming). When designing services, community-based programs will have to assess how residents perceive their community and will have to be prepared to resolve discrepant definitions among residents. Different types of initiatives are likely to be generated from how *community* or neighborhood is defined (for example, a school-based definition versus a hospital-based one versus a block-based one).

Drawing on the work of Kubisch (1996) and Sullivan (forthcoming), we have identified three different approaches to defining communities: (1) communities as "place," (2) communities as "face," and (3) communities as "space." Defining communities as "place" is similar to the six study analyses presented in volume 1, wherein communities are conceived of as neighborhoods (geographic locales) and as bureaucratically defined catchment areas. Viewing communities as "face" emphasizes the psychological associations that residents have within their community; in other words, the community is comprised of relationships and social supports. The last definition, communities as "space," views communities as physical and built environments for living, working, and political organizing. Clearly, these different definitions of *community* have implications for service delivery (Kubisch 1996).

COMMUNITIES AS PLACE

Viewing communities as places—as neighborhoods or as geographical or bureaucratic locales—suggests that communities are manageable units around which to organize and deliver services (Kubisch 1996). Employing a place-based definition of *community* encompasses two main strategies for the provision of services to urban children. The more moderate and ubiquitous approach is categorical programs, and the more ambitious strategy is system reform.

CATEGORICAL PROGRAMS   While categorical programs (such as WIC, Head Start, Healthy Start, Medicaid, and EPDST) are federally mandated, they are delivered at the community level (according to bureaucratic units). Not all communities have the same number, intensity, quality, or availability of ser-vices (for example, physical and mental health, social, recreational, child-care, educational, or job-training services). Research on service use suggests that poor, urban communities typically lack available and high-quality ser-vices (Schorr 1988, Schorr with Both 1991). Thus, a critical issue that most researchers and policy makers have failed to address adequately is how to determine what services are available in the community (the census does not measure availability of services) and whether or not available services are effective (Schorr, Both, and Copple 1991). How parents find out about avail-able services and how they use the services are also unclear.

The effectiveness of categorical programs may depend heavily on how the services are delivered and how families are recruited and informed. In addi-tion, the effectiveness of categorical programs is likely to depend on how families receive the available services, and how much of an attempt is made to provide high-quality services and linkages with other services. It is impor-tant, therefore, to examine differences across neighborhoods in the provision and quality of services and in consumer satisfaction, as well as variation in outcomes by community or catchment area. However, these outcomes are rarely observed for categorical programs; consequently, we know little about how these programs affect children's lives.

Although categorical programs have undergone large-scale research evalu-ations, they are seldom examined for variations in service (provision or qual-ity) or outcome by community, as just noted. To date, most evaluations have concentrated on demonstrating whether or not a program is "successful" (that is, associated with enhanced child outcomes). Data are usually collected by community or catchment area, but community-level analyses are rare.

More in-depth, formative evaluations are being employed at the local level; these efforts emphasize service delivery (and ways to enhance it), outreach to families (and mechanisms to reach families, particularly those who are socially isolated or at high risk), and services tailored to individual children and families (since families differ in the types and intensity of services needed). These efforts exemplify an even more place-based approach to delivering services by adapting programs to meet community needs. For example, an ongoing national evaluation of Early Head Start is attempting to tailor services for each respective community and to incorporate this varia-tion into the program evaluation. Ongoing evaluations, as well as insight from research and existing programs, will be instrumental under new and pending legislation that shifts responsibility and control of service delivery for many categorical programs from the federal to the state and local levels.

SERVICE REFORM   Although categorical programs use geographic definitions of *community*, not all categorical programs define *community* the same way. Consequently, service reform has become a popular, place-based initiative. Kubisch (1996) has suggested that place-based definitions may be more flexible than the bureaucratic systems (that is, categorical programs) in that they represent the local community more precisely. For example, the New Futures initiative funded by the Annie E. Casey Foundation in five cities seeks to restructure the way communities organize, finance, and deliver educational, health, and other services to at-risk youth (Nelson 1996). As exemplified in New Futures, several factors may account for the success of programs that are moving from less bureaucratic to more-flexible, place-based services.

Schorr with Both (1991) attributed the success of system reform programs to their (1) flexibility, comprehensiveness, and responsiveness; (2) child orientations, as well as family and community orientations; (3) high-quality staff; (4) efforts to reach the most at-risk populations and to target services accordingly; (5) superior management; and (6) theoretical approach rooted in client-orientation and long-term prevention. Clearly, these characteristics contrast with the current ways that most bureaucratic institutions and systems deliver services. In particular, categorical funding, standardized program operations, equity in distribution of services, and short-term goals pervade the contemporary culture of human services (Schorr with Both 1991). This discrepancy has fueled the service-reform movement. Home-visiting programs provide a promising avenue for achieving this goal. Findings from several home-visiting intervention programs suggest that home visitors often act as a source of social support to mothers and facilitate access to community services for both mothers and children (Brooks-Gunn 1995; Olds, Henderson, and Kitzman 1994).

In general, the criticisms of categorical programs and limitations of current system reform are relevant *regardless of the age group being served* (Brooks-Gunn 1996). The elements of successful programs that are central to serving children (as opposed to other age groups) have not yet been identified. Clearly, service-reform programs need to target families, not individuals, because even within families, individuals are served by different programs and children themselves also receive services from different programs (Ooms 1996). Thus, viewing communities as places permits modest service reforms that make current categorical services more user friendly and less bureaucratic, but it does not encompass a more coordinated and integrated approach to service delivery, as discussed in the next section. As further evidence of the point, a review of effective programs revealed that most successful programs targeted one specific area (such as health or education) and sometimes incorporated additional services (Kagan and Pritchard 1996).

COMMUNITIES AS FACE

When we define communities as "face," relationships between individuals constitute community. Hence, community in many ways comprises psychological associations more than geographic units. The *community* is perceived of as a system of supports (Kubisch 1996), and this definition, in terms of policies and programs, translates into the integration of services provided to children and families as well as communities, representing a more holistic approach than service reform. Typically, programs consist of community-based multiservice organizations that promote the well-being of children and families (that is, family and community support services). Establishing these programs usually requires system reform—interagency coordination or the creation of an umbrella agency (Kagan and Pritchard 1996). Several relationships are highlighted by this approach: (1) relationships within families, (2) relationships between families and service providers, (3) relationships among service providers, and (4) relationships among members of the community.

RELATIONSHIPS WITHIN FAMILIES   Families are the smallest psychological unit that constitutes community (Brooks-Gunn, Denner, and Klebanov 1995). In our discussion of families in this chapter, we have focused on the parent (mother) and child—specifically, the parent as a provider and overseer of children's learning experiences and linkages with services. This perspective depicts a dyadic, rather unidirectional view of families. However, relationships within families are bidirectional (that is, children influence parents' behaviors) and triadic or higher (that is, fathers, as well as other adult kin, are part of the family system) (Bronfenbrenner and Crouter 1983; Brooks-Gunn and Chase-Lansdale 1995; Crockenberg 1981; Merriwether–de Vries, Burton, and Eggeletion 1996; Parke 1995). Closer appraisal of family functioning by services providers is merited (see for example, Chase-Lansdale, Brooks-Gunn, and Zamsky 1994; Wakschlag et al. 1997). Supports available within the family may play a large role in linking children with community services.

Further, from a life-course perspective, all members of the family are developing, and the intersection of their different life phases and circumstances has implications for the availability of emotional, social, and economic support within the family. Resources available to children are affected by these relational systems. For example, if a parent is caring simultaneously for a child and an older parent, then the parent faces competing demands for time. This situation also may hold true for teenage mothers, as Burton's (1990) ethnographic studies of four-generation families have indicated; teenage mothers often are helping care for their grandmothers, who in some cases raised them. Thus, community-based family support services that meet the multiple needs of family members (rather than specific needs of individuals within the family) are likely to be more effective at strengthening families and enhancing family and child well-being (Kagan 1996; Ooms 1996; Schorr with Both 1991). In sum, building what Ooms (1996) terms "family capital" is an important step in enhancing child development and improving distressed communities.

RELATIONSHIPS BETWEEN FAMILIES AND SERVICE PROVIDERS   Relationships also put a face on families and service providers. Specifically, Ooms (1996) has argued that despite references to children and families, service programs tend to emphasize individuals within the family, rather than family functioning and relational systems. Consequently, a primary means of facilitating services to poor, urban children is for service providers to recognize their embeddedness with family and community systems. Such a notion points to the need to coordinate and integrate community-based services for families—the goal of the family support movement (Kagan 1996). Primary social services, which constitute necessary family supports critical to the promotion and enhancement of child development and family functioning so often lacking in poor, urban neighborhoods, need to be linked with more-specialized, problem-oriented services (Wynn et al. 1994).[5]

The other factor that impinges on the relationship between families and service providers and the need to put a "face" on individuals refers back to the nature of human services as discussed by Schorr with Both (1991). Effective programs alter the context in which families are treated by service providers. Specifically, more client-centered, one-to-one relationships are established between families and service providers, and providers treat families "respectfully, ungrudgingly, and collaboratively" (Schorr with Both 1991, 33). Modifying the relationship between families and service providers is also highly dependent upon having qualified, motivated staff who have relevant life experiences. In addition, increased attention has been placed on cultural sensitivity and the cultural diversity of staff (Allen and Grobman 1996; Gibbs and Huang 1991).

While the service integration model has received widespread support, the related initiatives have primarily been instituted only at the state and local levels. This approach, however, may be overrated in some respects. Programs typically act as entry points to services and do not necessarily deliver services directly to children and families. This fact places increased importance on the relationships among service providers.

RELATIONSHIPS AMONG SERVICE PROVIDERS   The whole notion of service integration is based in part on the premise of putting a face on service providers. In essence, the aim is to build a community among service providers. Again, this goal requires restructuring the context of social services and increasing the flexibility of categorical funding (Schorr with Both 1991). Several other barriers that need to be addressed include relations between federal and local authorities, as well as locus of leadership, technical obstacles (such as creating uniform data systems), and discrepant regulations across systems (Kagan and Pritchard 1996). Ooms (1996) discussed, as an exemplar, a community initiative in which children in the custody of child protective services were placed with neighborhood families rather than with foster-care homes in the suburbs. Thus, the ultimate strength of building relationships between service providers is predicated on maintaining the face of families who receive the respective services.

RELATIONSHIPS WITHIN COMMUNITIES   Community relationships often are placed under the umbrella of family support (Kagan 1996). Often an implicit (rather than explicit) goal of integrated service programs is to build connections among community residents. Coleman (1988) has used the construct "social capital" to describe the intersection of families and neighborhoods. Social capital arises through changes in the relationships among persons (in communities) and is supposed to confer human capital (skills and knowledge) on individuals in communities, which makes it a valuable aspect of community-based programs. Because social relatedness is not economic or tangible, it is not captured by the neighborhood- or family-level variables assessed in the six studies analyses in volume 1 or, for that matter, in most other neighborhood-based analyses. The association between social capital and child well-being has been explored primarily by ethnographers (chapter 2; compare chapter 4; Briggs and Mueller, with Sullivan 1997).

Social capital encompasses several broad dimensions: interpersonal ties and reciprocity, norms and sanctions, information, stability, opportunity, and quality of life (Coleman 1988). Informal social networks (or "weak ties" such as employment networks, membership in a formal organization, and community organization) are often considered the crux of social capital and affect other components. These weak ties are purported to affect feelings of belongingness to one's neighborhood and perceptions of social cohesion and may act as conduits for community relationships and organizations (Granovetter 1985).

Although social relatedness is generally considered advantageous to neighborhoods, perhaps it should not be viewed so monolithically. The analyses in chapter 7 point to contextual variation in the association between structural characteristics and community-level resources (see also Steinberg et al. 1992). These findings are consistent with the ethnographic work of Jarrett (chapter 3) and Furstenberg (1993), which suggests that the benefit for children and families of sociostructural ties to the community depends, in large part, on community characteristics such as danger and safety. As these ethnographic studies indicate, families who reside in poor, dangerous neighborhoods may be less amiable and warm toward their neighbors (that is, they may avoid establishing informal social networks), in order to protect their children from harm. Thus, in neighborhoods where unconventional socialization practices prevail certain forms of social interchange may be considered undesirable (chapter 2).

However, most programs seek to alter neighborhood conditions such as safety and danger, as well as increase social interchanges. For example, although building social networks is not a primary target of community development corporations (or CDCs, which are discussed later), it may be a secondary outcome of these community-based programs. A recent study of three CDCs found that residing in the CDCs affected community social relations (Briggs and Mueller, with Sullivan 1997). Residents of the CDCs were more likely to greet or exchange words with their neighbors than were non-CDC residents. These informal social ties may be especially important, since kin and close family were not likely to live in the residents' neighborhoods. These findings suggest that intimate connections within neighborhoods may be less likely in poor neighborhoods than more middle class neighborhoods.[6] Thus, supportive relations within the community context may be less in close relationships and more in "weak ties" (Granovetter 1985), and such connections probably reduce feelings of isolation. Programs attempting to build such ties have noted that they grow incrementally and are often hard-won (Briggs and Mueller, with Sullivan 1997).

Perhaps, as social scientists, we fall short with respect to advising programs about ways to both measure as well as increase social relatedness (Brooks-Gunn et al. forthcoming). The ability of community support programs (or other community-based programs) to affect causal social ties is likely to affect family life. More importantly, how children are affected by social capital is unclear, but potential domains include child care, schooling, extracurricular activities, mentoring programs, and community-watch programs. These areas may also overlap. For example, in order for parents to attend community organization meetings, a network for child care may be necessary (Stoutland 1995). Outcomes for children may also be affected by the fact that women tend to be more involved than men in community activities (Sullivan forthcoming), which in turn could influence the types of programs organized for children. While methodological work is under way, evaluations of community-based programs are a potential avenue for explicating the role of social capital.

COMMUNITIES AS SPACE

Defining communities as "space" identifies communities as physical and built places for activity—living, working, and political organizing. The primary targets of CDCs and initiatives such as Empowerment Zones and Enterprise Communities have been housing and economic development (Briggs and Mueller, with Sullivan 1997; Fuchs and Thompson 1996). The former activity entails the creation and management of affordable housing, and the latter activity involves both job training and job creation. Organizational governance is another component, but since this aspect of CDCs has more distal effects on children, it is not discussed here. Little research, however, exists on the effect of CDCs on residents (Briggs and Mueller, with Sullivan 1997), and virtually nothing exists regarding their impact on families and children.

This fact reiterates the point that although community development initiatives influence children, they are not typically child oriented. For example, both housing and economic development only indirectly affect children by potentially improving families' economic circumstances. Affordable housing may free up income for other family needs. Economic development vis-à-vis maternal employment also may have positive effects on children despite continued low income and even welfare receipt (Smith, Brooks-Gunn, and Klebanov 1997). Given the salience of familial factors in predicting child outcomes in the research findings presented earlier, the ability of CDCs and other community development initiatives to enhance familial outcomes is likely to have marked benefits for children.

In the previous section, we discussed the fact that many CDCs often have an effect on community building, which appears to influence children as well. CDCs also may influence children's and families' lives by improving the safety of neighborhoods. While programs to improve neighborhood safety are not necessarily considered to belong to the domain of spacial definitions of *community*, CDCs often regard reducing neighborhood danger and, in turn, enhancing safety *instrumental* to improving housing, economic development, and community building. Moreover, safety may be one of the most important direct benefits of CDCs for children.

More specifically, a study of three CDCs found that for two of the three programs examined, real, as well as perceived, safety was higher in CDC neighborhoods and housing than in non-CDC neighborhoods or housing (Briggs and Mueller, with Sullivan forthcoming). In addition, the CDC residents also were more likely to know a neighbor who would intervene in a variety of threatening circumstances (for example, if he or she saw someone selling drugs to the respondent's child) than were non-CDC residents. Thus, neighborhood safety appears to impinge directly on the lives of children and families.

Parental perceptions of safety also affect children indirectly. In the study of three CDCs, for example, satisfaction with housing among younger adults was tied to access to safe play areas (for children) and opportunities for skill development and employment. In contrast, older adults valued privacy and social connections.[7] However, it is important to note that even children residing in CDCs were not immune from crime and danger. Thus, the potential effects of CDCs on children appear to be both economic and noneconomic, but future researchers will need to examine these links more explicitly.

THE INTEGRATION OF PLACE, FACE, AND SPACE

The final strategy for delivering services to poor, urban children and their families—comprehensive community initiatives—takes the most holistic approach by viewing communities as the integration of "place," "face," and "space." Specifically, CCIs are comprehensive, community-based, multiservice organizations that define communities as geographic places around which to organize services ("place"); foundations for social support networks ("face"); and areas of residence, commerce, and civic activity ("space"). Theoretically, such an approach enables poor, urban communities (and the families and children who reside in them) to develop the capacity to address a range of problems they confront (chapter 10; Kubisch 1996). For example, the Center for Family Life in Brooklyn, New York (funded by the Annie E. Casey Foundation as one of four child services programs), is designed to be a preventive, collaborative, comprehensive, flexible, and family-focused community-based initiative (Hess, McGowan, and Meyer 1996). The center runs job-training and job-placement programs, operates advocacy workshops, and offers an emergency food program. In addition, the center administers school-based programs for children, youth, and families in three community schools. A range of services are provided free of charge, including counseling and therapy; neighborhood-based foster-care programs; school-aged child-care and after-school programs; summer programs for children and youth; recreational activities for children, youth, and families; youth employment programs; and parent workshops. As in the example provided, components of these programs that focus on children include education and family support services and provision of extracurricular activities. Other features of CCIs that are less child focused entail housing, commercial revitalization, small-business development, and community organization.

According to Brown and Richman (chapter 10), however, these initiatives are not explicitly research or theory driven. Recently, scholars have used "theories of change" to explain the process through which CCIs may affect communities (Weiss 1995). These models specify a set of nested theoretical assumptions about how a program should work and, accordingly, examine incremental change over time in the designated outcomes. These theories tend to vary by community and by program (Weiss 1995). Models also will differ depending on the aspect of community emphasized—place, face, or space.

Several characteristics of CCIs that are thought to be important vis-à-vis understanding or studying CCI effects include income, identity (boundary recognition), location within urban area, trajectory (going up or down), housing, and local development activities (Sullivan forthcoming). Note that, in general, these are not the dimensions studied by those doing neighborhood-effect research, with the exception of income and, sometimes, trajectory. Populations characteristics—migration, localization of subcultures, demographic composition (age, gender), and social networks—are also essential to understanding the effectiveness of CCIs. Overlap exists here with what is currently being studied by neighborhood scholars. Since we have touched on the types of services likely to be included in CCIs (and have discussed them in detail in the previous three sections), this section addresses a prominent issue facing CCIs and the provision of services to children: the ways in which services may differ as a function of the ages of possible participants (Kahn and Kamerman 1996; see also chapter 10 for examples of current CCIs).

CCIs serve community residents across the age span. Clearly, certain types of services are more applicable to some age groups than to others. Not all services provided by CCIs directly address children (for example, economic rejuvenation), even though they may ultimately affect children by influencing their parents. A review of the CCIs presented in chapter 10 indicates that while children are a target of CCIs, their prominence in the overall mission of CCIs is variable. Also, most CCIs are not family focused (Ooms 1996). Thus, it is reasonable to ask whether children are a primary or a secondary focus of CCIs. A council of providers and citizens or an extension of local government may be necessary to define the needs of the community (Richman, Brown, and Venkatesh 1996). We believe such a council must also ensure that children's needs are considered.

Definitions of community that we discussed earlier may also vary by the age of the residents. For example, children may be more geographically bounded, or place based, than adults (Lewin 1936). Children, in most cases, go to neighborhood schools and play on nearby playgrounds and have friends living nearby (exceptions involve attendance at charter or magnet schools and attendance at schools for desegregation). Adults, in contrast, have more far-flung networks (that is, face-based perceptions of community). In urban communities, few individuals live in neighborhoods around places of work as, in the old working-class neighborhoods (that is, less space-based communities). This discrepancy between children's and adult's geographic boundedness suggests that CCIs have a more critical role to play for children and families with children (as opposed to individuals or families, in general).

If social organizations or place-based institutions are the most salient community for children, then bootstrapping on existing social connections (such as school, playground, neighborhood, or health clinic) may be the most effective route to serving poor, urban children and their families (Sullivan forthcoming). Since schools are among the only institutions that see virtually all children, many comprehensive programs have targeted the school as the center of the community (Comer 1996; Zigler and Styfco 1996). Increasingly, schools have taken on other missions, such as social and health services, in addition to education. It is essential to examine whether or not we can expect schools to provide a range of services and whether or not in doing so, we jeopardize the quality of education provided (Kagan 1997).

CONCLUSION

We have considered, albeit briefly, four general types of service delivery models for poor, urban children and families that vary as a function of the definition of *neighborhood* or *community* employed. The research on neighborhood poverty and child and family well-being was reviewed as well as resultant implications for service delivery to children in urban communities. The current mechanisms for providing services to poor, urban children and families covered were categorical programs, family and community support services, community development corporations, and comprehensive community initiatives. Of the approaches discussed, family and community support services (integrated services) are the most explicitly child focused.

Most income-transfer programs provide money (or food stamps) to parents and do not directly serve children. Current changes in programs are focusing on mothers going to work, not on children's needs (that is, if the mother reaches her welfare time limit, then cash benefits are terminated).[8] Even food stamps are given to parents as is WIC, which supplies milk, cereal, and so on (with the exception being school lunch programs. which provide food to children directly). The Earned Income Tax Credit and minimum wage are aimed at giving families (parents) more disposable income. Child-oriented services for mothers moving off of welfare include a few parenting classes and referrals to local child-care agencies. In addition, mothers making the transition from welfare to work are given vouchers (that is, cash subsidies) to obtain child care. Thus, the lack of a child-centered approach among categorical programs may impede service delivery to poor children. Parental involvement also appears to be a missing link in the design of these programs.

Undoubtedly, the ways in which services are delivered to children and families will be altered by the changes (and additional proposed changes) in the allocation of federal money to the states and the fact that states will not have to match funds for specific programs in the way they have been required to do in the past. At a minimum, the proposed changes will affect the level of dollars allocated to the various programs, which in turn will affect all service delivery programs. Under the 1996 Personal Responsibility and Work Opportunity Bill, the matching of state funds by federal funds is less for TANF (the new welfare program) than it was for AFDC (the pre-1996 program). What seems apparent is that for poor and near-poor urban communities, child- and family-oriented services are likely to be reduced. What remains less clear is how these cuts will affect families and, consequently, the communities in which these families reside. Thus, research on neighborhoods will need to track how poor, urban neighborhoods are affected by declines in benefits to families under the new legislation. Information on changes in both family well-being and, consequently, neighborhood conditions will undoubtedly have broad implications for service delivery to urban families.

Block grants will give states and local governments greater flexibility to administer these programs. In theory, this approach allows communities to tailor programs to meet the needs of their population. Critics, however, argue that block grants give states too much latitude and could jeopardize the well-being of children and families if funds are not used to provide family support and child services and are shifted to other types of programs. One potential advantage of block grants is that they could foster system reform and increased coordination across service delivery systems, since states will have more latitude to run programs. Regrettably, very limited funding has been allocated to evaluate the impact of the new federalism on children and families.

Community development initiatives have as their primary goal housing development, economic rejuvenation (creation of jobs), and job training. Several community-based strategies incorporate a social dimension, although this aim is still not necessarily a child-centered approach. Thus, we recommend that community initiatives address family needs more explicitly. Some recent CCIs—the Casey Foundation's New Futures project, the Ford Foundation's Neighborhood and Family Initiatives, the Chicago Community Trust Initiative, and the New Community Corporation—are attempting to examine children and families more concretely (Kahn and Kamerman 1996). However, it is still important to acknowledge that child-oriented programs are often embedded in the service of adult-oriented programs.

The Carnegie Corporation reports *Starting Points* (1994) and *Years of Promise* (1996) brought attention to the declining status of children in the United States. One of the recommendations is to mobilize communities to support children and their families. Federal, state, and local action as discussed in this chapter were called for to meet the needs of children and families. To date, however, little systematic effort has been initiated at the community level on behalf of children. Despite shifting resources to the community level, children are usually not a primary target of these funds.

We end with several questions that need to be addressed in order to improve service delivery to urban children:

- Why do affluent neighbors have positive effects on child and family well-being, and do we need to look at what relatively affluent families within relatively poor neighborhoods are doing?
- Why are there always much larger family effects than neighborhood effects, and what are the implications of this difference for designing and delivering services?
- What are the effective strategies for obtaining services being used by a small subset of families, and what distinguishes these families?
- Why are some families in urban neighborhoods able to obtain services effectively from their community and other families unable to do so?
- What do individual differences mean for designing programs?
- How does one get a better understanding of families' perceived needs for services in the community?
- How are various neighborhoods being used by individuals to obtain resources?
- Do social networks have direct benefits for children, and what are those benefits? What are the costs of such networks for children and families?
- How are residential neighborhoods different from "hanging-out" neighborhoods?
- What are appropriate neighborhood dimensions (for example, socio-demographic characteristics, presence of stressors, safety, availability and qual-

ity of services) and family characteristics (for example, structure, age, race or ethnicity, stressful events) to examine?

The answers to these questions can strengthen institutional and programmatic resources to children at the neighborhood level.

We would like to thank the Foundation for Child Development and the U.S. Department of Housing and Urban Development for their support of neighborhood programs and the Aspen Institute Roundtable on Comprehensive Community Initiatives for Children and Families, the Russell Sage Foundation, and the Social Science Research Council for their support of neighborhood research. We also would like to acknowledge the National Institute of Child Health and Human Development Research Network on Child and Family Well-being. In addition, we would like to thank Mercer Sullivan for his helpful comments on the manuscript. The authors are particularly grateful to the participants of the Big Cities seminar, organized by A. J. Kahn and S. B. Kamerman, for their stimulating discussion on urban poverty and low-income children and families, particularly strategies for service reform. Portions of this chapter appear in the resultant volume edited by Kahn and Kamerman (1996). We would also like to thank the W. T. Grant Foundation and Robert Wood Johnson Foundation for their support.

NOTES

1. However, the lessons learned from the seminar probably may apply equally well to the additional twelve cities with one-half million to one million residents, as they do to the eleven cities with nearly a million or more in population.

2. Topics discussed by the seminar intended to provide a careful analysis of the seminar's major issues including: What is the historical and political backdrop? What are the interactions of families, children, and neighborhoods, with regard both to problem development and to successful coping? What types of strategies are being pursued? What is the optimum institutional base for the new services delivery strategies? What lessons have been learned? Is there any hope of moving from a successful demonstration to citywide coverage? What leverage does a state government have? What leverage do cities have? What advice does the service practitioner have to offer about needed reform? (See Kahn and Kamerman [1996] for a more detailed discussion). We draw on these findings in our chapter.

3. Similar analyses could probably be done for school as the institution (parallel to family as the institution) and teachers as the adult figures (akin to teachers and schools staff as the parental figures), but such analyses are beyond the scope of this volume.

4. These two terms are used interchangeably in the literature. Thus, it is not clear how the terms neighborhood and community differ.

5. It is beyond the scope of this chapter to provide more detailed models of service integration. We are concerned here with overall approaches to delivering services to poor, urban children and their families.

6. Klebanov, Brooks-Gunn, and Duncan (1994) found that social support was highest in middle-income neighborhoods and usually lower in poor and affluent neighborhoods among families in the Infant Health and Development Program.

7. These findings with respect to younger adults are reinforced by preliminary results from the U.S. Department of Housing and Urban Development's Moving to Opportunity pro-

gram (MTO), in which poor, urban families with children in five of the nation's largest cities are randomly assigned to one of three conditions—staying in public housing, receiving housing vouchers to move to private housing within the city, or receiving vouchers and counseling to move to private housing in low-poverty neighborhoods. A majority of the parents cited danger and safety for children as their primary reason for entering the MTO program (Goering, personal communication).

8. Under the Personal Responsibility and Work Opportunity Bill of 1996, a disregard for up to 20 percent of a state's caseload will be permitted. This provision implies that, at least for a fixed percentage, children will receive cash benefits even if their mothers do not enter the workforce. Also, the disregard families may have counselors manage their money.

REFERENCES

Aaronson, D. 1996. "Using Sibling Data to Estimate the Impact of Neighborhoods on Children's Educational Outcomes." Federal Reserve Board of Chicago. Mimeographed.

Aber, J. L., R. Garfinkel, C. Mitchell, L. Allen, and E. Seidman. (1992). "Indices of Neighborhood Distress: Their Association with Adolescent Mental Health and School Achievement." Paper presented at the Conference on the Urban Underclass: Perspectives from the Social Sciences, University of Michigan. Ann Arbor, Michigan (June 1992).

Aber, J. L., E. Seidman, L. Allen, C. Mitchell, and R. Garfinkel. 1993. *Poverty-Related Risks and the Psychological Adaptation of Urban Youth: Testing Mediational Models.* Unpublished manuscript.

Achenbach, T. M. 1991a. *Manual for the Youth Self-Report and 1991 Profile.* Burlington: University of Vermont, Department of Psychiatry.

———. 1991b. *Manual for the Child Behavior Checklist/4–18 and 1991 Profile.* Burlington: University of Vermont, Department of Psychiatry.

Allen, L., and S. Grobman. 1996. "Multiculturalism and Social Policy." In *Children, Families, and Government: Preparing for the Twenty-first Century,* edited by E. F. Zigler, S. L. Kagan, and N. W. Hall. New York: Cambridge University Press.

Allen, H. M., P. M. Bentler, and B. A. Gutek. 1985. "Probing Theories of Individual Well-being: A Comparison of Quality-of-Life Models Assessing Neighborhood Satisfaction." *Basic and Applied Social Psychology* 6(3): 181–203.

Allison, K., and Y. Takei. 1993. "Diversity: The Cultural Contexts of Adolescents and Their Families." In *Early Adolescence: Perspectives on Research, Policy, and Intervention,* edited by R. M. Lerner. Hillsdale, N.J.: Erlbaum.

Allison, K. W., I. Crawford, R. Echemendia, L. Robinson et al. 1994. "Human Diversity and Professional Competence: Training in Clinical and Counseling Psychology Revisited." *American Psychologist* 49: 792–96.

Altman, I. 1975. *The Environment and Social Behavior.* Monterey, Calif.: Brooks/Cole.

Altonji, J., and T. Dunn. 1995. "The Effects of School and Family Characteristics on the Return to Education." Northwestern University. Mimeographed.

Anderson, E. 1990. *Street Wise: Race, Class, and Change in an Urban Community.* Chicago: University of Chicago Press.

———. 1991. "Neighborhood Effects on Teenage Pregnancy." In *The Urban Underclass,* edited by C. Jencks and P. Peterson. Washington, D.C.: Brookings Institution.

———. 1994. "The Code of the Streets." *Atlantic Monthly,* May, 81–93.

Aschenbrenner, J. 1975. *Lifelines: Black Families in Chicago.* New York: Holt, Rinehart & Winston.

Ashenfelter, O., and A. Krueger. 1994. "Estimates of the Economic Returns to Schooling from a New Sample of Twins." *American Economic Review*: 1157–83.

Auletta, K. 1982. *The Underclass*. New York: Vintage Press.

Baca Zinn, M. 1989. "Family, Race, and Poverty in the Eighties." *Signs* 14: 856–74.

———. 1990. "Minority Families in Crisis: The Public Discussion." In *Women, Class, and the Feminist Imagination: A Socialist-Feminist Reader*, edited by K. Hansen and I. J. Philipson. Philadelphia: Temple University Press.

Baldwin, J. 1974. "Social Area Analysis and Studies of Delinquency." *Social Science Research* 3: 151–68.

———. 1979. "Ecological and Areal Studies in Great Britain and the United States." In *Crime and Justice*, Vol. 1, edited by N. Morris and M. Tonry. Chicago: University of Chicago Press.

Barker, R. 1986. *Ecological Psychology*. Stanford, Calif.: Stanford University Press.

Baum, A., J. E. Singer, and C. S. Baum. 1982. "Stress and the Environment." In *Environmental Stress*, edited by G. Evans. Cambridge, U.K.: Cambridge University Press.

Baumgartner, M. P. 1988. *The Moral Order of the Suburb*. New York: Oxford University Press.

Baumrind, D. 1978. "Parental Disciplinary Patterns and Social Competence in Children." *Youth and Society* 9: 239–76.

Bayne, R., J. Beauchamp, C. Begovich, and V. Kane. 1980. "Monte Carlo Comparisons of Selected Clustering Procedures." *Pattern Recognition* 12: 51–62.

Bell-Scott, P., and R. Taylor. 1989. "The Multiple Ecologies of Black Adolescent Development." *Journal of Adolescent Research* 4: 119–24.

Belsky, J. 1980. "Child Maltreatment: An Ecological Integration." *American Psychologist* 35: 320–35.

Bennett, L. 1993. "Rethinking Neighborhoods, Neighborhood Research, and Neighborhood Policy: Lessons from Uptown." *Journal of Urban Affairs* 15(3): 245–57.

Berg, M., and E. A. Medrich. 1980. "Children in Four Neighborhoods." *Environment and Behavior* 12: 320–48.

Bernard, H. R. 1994. *Research Methods in Anthropology. Qualitative and Quantitative Approaches*, 2d ed. Newbury Park, Calif.: Sage.

Berry, B., and J. Kasarda. 1977. *Contemporary Urban Ecology*. New York: Macmillan.

Blashfield, R. K. 1976. "Mixture Model Tests of Cluster Analysis: Accuracy of Four Agglomerative Hierarchical Methods." *Psychological Bulletin* 83: 377–88.

Blau, P. 1977. *Inequality and Heterogeneity*. New York: Free Press.

Bluebond-Langner, M. 1978. *The Private Worlds of Dying Children*. Princeton, N.J.: Princeton University Press.

Blume, S. S., M. Carley, and C. H. Weiss, eds. *Social Science and Social Policy*. London: Allen & Unwin.

Blyth, D., J. P. Hill, and K. P. Thiel. 1982. "Early Adolescents' Significant Others." *Journal of Youth and Adolescence* 11: 425–50.

Boone, M. 1989. *Capital Crime: Black Infant Mortality in America*. Newbury Park, Calif.: Sage.

Borgatta, E., and J. Hadden. 1977. "The Analysis of Social Areas: A Critical Review and Some Empirical Data." In *The Outlook Tower*, edited by J. Ferreira and S. Jha. Bombay: Popular Prakashan.

Borjas, G. 1995. "Ethnicity, Neighborhoods, and Human Capital Externalities." *American Economic Review*: 365–90.

Bound, J., and B. Freeman. 1992. "What Went Wrong? The 1980's Erosion of the Economic Well-being of Black Men." *Quarterly Journal of Economics* 107(1): 201–32.

Bradley, R. H. 1995. "Environment and Parenting." In *Handbook of Parenting*, edited by M. Bornstein. Hillsdale, N.J.: Erlbaum.

Bradley, R. H., and B. M. Caldwell. 1980. "The Relation of the Home Environment, Cognitive Competence, and IQ among Males and Females." *Child Development* 51: 1140–48.

Bradley, R. H., and B. M. Caldwell, S. L. Rock, C. T. Ramey, K. E. Barnard, C. Gray, M. A. Hammond, S. Mitchell, A. W. Gottfried, L. Sigel, and D. L. Johnson. 1989. "Home Environment and Cognitive Development in the First Three Years of Life: A Collaborative Study Involving Six Sites and Three Ethnic Groups in North America." *Developmental Psychology* 25(2): 217–35.

Brett, J. M., L. K. Stroh, and A. H. Reilly. 1993. "Pulling Up Roots in the 1990s: Who's Willing to Relocate?" *Journal of Organizational Behavior* 14: 49–60.

Brewster, K. L., J. O. G. Billy, and W. R. Grady. 1993. "Social Context and Adolescent Behavior: The Impact of Community on the Transition to Sexual Activity." *Social Forces* 71: 713–40.

Briggs, X. S. 1997. "Moving Up Versus Moving Out: Neighborhood Effects in Housing Mobility Programs." *Housing Policy Debate* 8(1): 195–234.

Briggs, X. S., and E. Mueller, with M. L. Sullivan. 1997. *From Neighborhood to Community: Evidence on the Social Effects of Community Development*. New York: Community Development Research Center, Graduate School of Management and Urban Policy, New School for Social Research.

Bronars, S., and J. Grogger. 1994. "The Economic Consequences of Unwed Motherhood: Using Twin Births as a Natural Experiment." *American Economic Review*: 84(5): 1141–56.

Bronfenbrenner, U. 1977. "Toward an Experimental Ecology of Human Development." *American Psychologist* 32: 513–31.

———. 1979. *The Ecology of Human Development: Experiments by Nature and Design*. Cambridge, Mass.: Harvard University Press.

———. 1986. "Ecology of Family as a Context for Human Development." *Developmental Psychology* 22(6): 732–42.

———. 1988. "Foreword." In *Ecological Research with Children and Families: from Concepts to Methodology*, edited by A. Pence. New York: Teachers College Press.

———. 1993. "The Ecology of Cognitive Development: Research Models and Fugitive Findings." In *Development in Context*, edited by R. H. Wozniak and K. W. Fischer. Hillsdale, N.J.: Erlbaum.

Bronfenbrenner, U., and A. Crouter. 1983. "The Evolution of Environmental Models in Developmental Research." In *Handbook of Child Psychology*. Vol. 1, *History, Theory, and Methods*, 4th ed., edited by P. H. Mussen. New York: Wiley.

Bronfenbrenner, U., P. Moen, and J. Garbarino. 1984. "Child, Family, and Community." In *Review of Child Development Research*, edited by R. Parke. Chicago: University of Chicago Press.

———. 1985. "Child, Family, and Community." In *The Family*, edited by R. Parke. Chicago: University of Chicago Press.

Brooks-Gunn, J. 1995. "Children and Families in Communities: Risk and Intervention in The Bronfenbrenner Tradition." In *Examining Lives in Context: Perspective on the Ecology of Human Development*, edited by P. Moen, G. H. Elder, and K. Lusher. Washington, D.C.: American Psychological Association Press.

———. 1996. "Big City Kids and Their Families: Integration of Research and Practice." In *Children and Their Families in Big Cities: Strategies for Service Reform*, edited by A. J. Kahn and S. B. Kamerman. New York: Cross-National Studies Program.

Brooks-Gunn, J., and P. L. Chase-Lansdale. 1995. "Adolescent Parenthood." In *Handbook of Parenting*, edited by M. Bornstein. Mahwah, N.J.: Erlbaum.

Brooks-Gunn, J., J. Denner, and P. K. Klebanov. 1995. "Families and Neighborhoods as Contexts for the Education." In *Changing Populations, Changing Schools: Ninety-fourth Yearbook of the National Society for the Study of Education, Part II*, edited by E. Flaxman and A. H. Passow. Chicago: National Society for the Study of Education.

Brooks-Gunn, J., and G. J. Duncan, eds. 1997. *Consequences of Growing Up Poor.* New York: Russell Sage Foundation Press.

Brooks-Gunn, J., G. J. Duncan, P. K. Klebanov, and N. Sealand. 1993. "Do Neighborhoods Influence Child and Adolescent Development?" *American Journal of Sociology* 99(2): 353–95.

Brooks-Gunn, J., P. K. Klebanov, and G. J. Duncan. 1996. "Ethnic Differences in Children's Intelligence Test Scores: Role of Economic Deprivation, Home Environment, and Maternal Characteristics." *Child Development* 67: 396–408.

Brooks-Gunn, J., P. K. Klebanov, and F. Liaw. 1994. "The Learning, Physical, and Emotional Environment of the Home in the Context of Poverty: The Infant Health and Development Program." *Children and Youth Services Review.* 17: 251–76.

Brooks-Gunn, J., P. K. Klebanov, F. Liaw, and G. J. Duncan. 1995. "Toward an Understanding of the Effects of Poverty upon Children. In *Children of Poverty: Research, Health, and Policy Issues*, edited by H. E. Fitzgerald, B. M. Lester, and B. Zuckerman. New York: Garland Press.

Brooks-Gunn, J., V. Rauh, and T. Leventhal. Forthcoming. "Equivalence and Conceptually-Anchored Research with Children of Color." In *Children of Color*, edited by H. E. Fitzgerald, B. M. Lester, and B. Zuckermen. New York: Garland Press.

Brown, L. P. 1988. "Crime in the Black Community." In *The State of Black America*, edited by J. Dewart. New York: National Urban League.

Bryant, B. K. 1985. "The Neighborhood Walk: Sources of Support in Middle Childhood." *Monographs of the Society for Research in Child Development* 50(210). Chicago: University of Chicago Press.

Bryk, A. S., and S. W. Raudenbush. 1992. Hierarchical Linear Models: Applications and Data Analysis Methods. Newbury Park, Calif.: Sage Publications.

Bryk, A. S., and Y. M. Thum. 1989. The Effects of High School Organization on Dropping Out: An Exploratory Investigation. *American Educational Research Journal*, 26; 353–83.

Bullard, R. D., and B. H. Wright. 1987. "Blacks and the Environment: Special Issue, Black America in the Eighties." *Journal of Social Relations* 14: 165–84.

Bunting, T. E., and L. R. Cousins. 1985. "Environmental Dispositions Among School-Age Children: A Preliminary Investigation." *Environment & Behavior* 17: 725–68.

Bursik, R. J., Jr. 1986. "Ecological Stability and the Dynamics of Delinquency." In *Communities and Crime*, edited by A. J. Reiss Jr. Chicago: University of Chicago Press.

———. 1988. "Social Disorganization and Theories of Crime and Delinquency: Problems and Prospects." *Criminology* 26: 519–52.

———. 1989. "Political Decision-making and Ecological Models of Delinquency: Conflict and Consensus." In *Theoretical Integration in the Study of Deviance and Crime*, edited by S. Messner, M. Krohn, and A. Liska. Albany: State University of New York at Albany Press.

Bursik, R. J., Jr., and H. G. Grasmick. 1992. "Longitudinal Profiles in Delinquency: The Decomposition of Change." *Journal of Quantitative Criminology.* 8: 247–64.

———. 1993. *Neighborhoods and Crime: The Dimensions of Effective Community Control.* New York: Lexington.

Bursik, R. J., and J. Webb. 1982. "Community Change and Patterns of Delinquency." *American Journal of Sociology* 88: 24–42.

Burstein, L., R. L. Linn, and F. J. Capell. 1978. "Analyzing Multilevel Data in the Presence of Heterogeneous Within-Class Regressions." *Journal of Educational Statistics* 3: 347–83.

Burton, L. M. 1990. "Teenage Childbearing as an Alternative Life-Course Strategy in Multi-generational Black Families." *Human Nature* 1(2): 123–43.

———. 1991. "Caring for Children: Drug Shifts and Their Impact on Families." *American Enterprise* 2: 34–37.

Burton, L. M., K. W. Allison, and D. Obeidallah. 1995. "Social Context and Adolescence: Perspectives on Development among Inner-City African-American Teens." In *Pathways Through Adolescence: Individual Development in Relation to Social Context*, edited by L. Crockett and A. C. Crouter. Hillsdale, N.J.: Erlbaum.

Burton, L., and G. J. Duncan. 1993. "Effects of Residential Mobility on Adolescent Behavior." Paper presented at the meeting of the Society for Research in Child Development. New Orleans (1993).

Burton, L. M., and R. L. Jarrett. 1991. "Studying African-American Family Structure and Process in Underclass Neighborhoods: Conceptual Considerations." Paper presented at the American Sociological Association Conference. Cincinnati, Ohio (August 1991).

Burton, L. M., D. A. Obeidallah, and K. Allison. 1996. "Ethnographic Insights on Social Context and Adolescent Development among Inner-City African-American Teens." In *Ethnography and Human Development: Context and Meaning in Social Inquiry*, edited by D. Jessor, A. Colby, and R. Shweder. Chicago: University of Chicago Press.

Byrne, J., and R. J. Sampson. 1986. "Key Issues in the Social Ecology of Crime." In *The Social Ecology of Crime*, edited by J. Byrne and R. J. Sampson. New York: Springer-Verlag.

Calinski, T., and J. Harabasz. 1974. "A Dendrite Method for Cluster Analysis." *Communications in Statistics* 3: 1–27.

Campbell, D. T., and D. W. Fiske. 1959. "Convergent and Discriminant Validation by the Multitrait-Multimethod Matrix." *Psychological Bulletin* 56: 81–85.

Campbell, K. E., and B. A. Lee. 1991. "Name Generators in Surveys of Personal Networks." *Social Networks* 13: 203–21.

———. 1992. "Sources of Personal Neighbor Networks: Social Integration, Need, or Time?" *Social Forces* 70: 1077–1100.

Carnegie Corporation. 1994. *Starting Points: Meeting the Needs of Our Youngest Children.* New York: Carnegie Corporation.

Carnegie Corporation. 1996. *Years of Promise: A Comprehensive Learning Strategy for America's Children.* New York: Carnegie Corporation.

Carnegie Council on Adolescent Development (1996). *Great Transitions: Preparing Adolescents for a New Century.* New York: Carnegie Corporation.

Case, A. C., and L. F. Katz. 1991. "The Company You Keep: The Effects of Family and Neighborhood on Disadvantaged Youths." Working Paper 3705. Cambridge, Mass.: National Bureau of Economic Research.

Cattell, R. B. 1949. "*Rp* and Other Coefficients of Pattern Similarity." *Psychometrika* 14: 279–98.

Center for Population and Family Health. 1991. Columbia University. Unpublished manuscript.

Chamberlain, G. 1980. "Analysis of Covariance with Dualitative Data." *Review of Economic Studies*: 225–38.

Chase-Lansdale, P. L., and J. Brooks-Gunn, eds. 1995. *Escape from Poverty: What Makes a Difference for Children?* New York: Cambridge University Press.

Chase-Lansdale, P. L., J. Brooks-Gunn, and E. S. Zamsky. 1994. "Young African-American Multigenerational Families in Poverty: Quality of Mothering and Grandmothering." *Child Development* 65(2): 373–93.

Chase-Lansdale, P. L., and R. A. Gordon. 1996. "Economic Hardship and the Development of Five- and Six-Year-Olds: Neighborhood and Regional Perspectives." *Child Development* 67(6): 3338–67.

Chaskin, R. J. 1994. "Defining Neighborhood." Background paper prepared for the Neighborhood Mapping Project of the Annie E. Casey Foundation.

Chilton, R. 1964. "Continuity in Delinquency Area Research: A Comparison of Studies for Baltimore, Detroit, and Indianapolis." *American Sociological Review* 29: 71–83.

Chow, J., and C. Coulton. 1992. "Was There a Social Transformation of Urban Neighborhoods in the 1980s?: A Decade of Changing Structure in Cleveland, Ohio." Case Western Reserve University, Center for Urban Poverty and Social Change. Unpublished manuscript.

Cicchetti, D., and M. Lynch. 1993. "Toward an Ecological/Transactional Model of Community Violence and Child Maltreatment: Consequences for Children's Development." *Psychiatry* 56: 96–118.

Clark, R. L., and D. A. Wolf. 1992. "Do Neighborhoods Matter? Dropping Out among Teenage Boys." Paper presented at the Annual Meeting of the Population Association of America. Denver (May 1992).

Clark, R. M. 1983. *Family Life and School Achievement: Why Poor Black Children Succeed or Fail*. Chicago: University of Chicago Press.

Clinard, M. B., ed. 1964. *Anomie and Deviant Behavior: A Discussion and Critique*. Glencoe, Ill. Free Press.

Cloward, R. A., and L. E. Ohlin. 1960. *Delinquency and Opportunity: A Theory of Delinquent Gangs*. Glencoe, Ill.: Free Press.

Cohen, A. K. 1955. *Delinquent Boys*. Glencoe, Ill.: Free Press.

Cohen, S., G. W. Evans, D. S. Krantz, and D. Stokols. 1980. "Physiological, Motivational, and Cognitive Effects of Stressors on Children." *American Psychologist* 35: 231–43.

Coleman, J. S. 1987. "Families and Schools." *Educational Researcher* 16:32–38.

———. 1988. "Social Capital in the Creation of Human Capital." *American Journal of Sociology* 94: S95–S120.

Coleman, J. S., and T. Hoffer. 1987. *Public and Private High Schools: The Impact of Communities*. New York: Basic Books.

Comer, J. P. 1990. "Educating Poor Minority Children." *Scientific American* 259: 231–43.

———. 1996. *Rallying the Whole Village: The Comer Process of Reforming Education*. New York: Teachers College Press.

Conger, R. D., K. J. Conger, G. H. Elder, F. D. Lorenz, R. L. Simons, and L. B. Whitbeck. 1992. "A Family Process Model of Economic Hardship and Adjustment of Early Adolescent Boys." *Child Development* 63(3): 526–41.

Conger, R. D., G. H. Elder, F. D. Lorenz, R. L. Simons, L. B. Whitbeck. 1994. *Families in Troubled Times: Adapting to Change in Rural America*. New York: Aldine De Gruyter.

Conger, R. D., X. Ge, G. H. Elder Jr., F. D. Lorenz, and R. L. Simons. 1994. "Economic Stress, Coercive Family Process, and Developmental Problems of Adolescents." *Child Development* 65(2): 541–61.

Conger, R., K. J. Conger, and G. H. Elder, Jr., 1997. "Family Economic Hardship and Adolescent Adjustment: Mediating and Moderating Processes." In *Consequences of Growing Up Poor*, edited by G. J. Duncan & J. Brooks-Gunn. New York: Russell Sage Foundation.

Congressional Research Service. 1992. *Selected Brief Facts about Poverty and Welfare among Urban Families with Children*. Washington, D. C.: Congressional Research Service.

Cook, T. D., F. F. Furstenberg Jr., J. R. Kim, J. O. Teitler, L. M. Geitz, J. Eccles, G. H. Elder Jr., and A. Sameroff. 1994. "Neighborhood Differences in Resources for Promoting the Positive Development of Adolescents: The Roles of Financial, Human, Social, Cultural and Psychological Capital." Manuscript in preparation.

Cooper, M. C., and G. W. Milligan. 1988. "The Effect of Error on Determining the Number of Clusters." *Proceedings of the International Workshop on Data Analysis, Decision Support, and Expert Knowledge Representation in Marketing and Related Areas of Research*. 319–28.

Corbett, T. 1992. *Focus*. Madison, Wisc.: Institute for Research on Poverty.

Corcoran, M., R. Gordon, D. Laren, and G. Solon. 1992. "The Association between Men's Economic Status and Their Family and Community Origins." *Journal of Human Resources* 27(4): 575–601.

Coulton, C. J. 1996. "Effects of Neighborhoods on Families and Children: Implications for Services." In *Children and Their Families in Big Cities: Strategies for Service Reform*, edited by A. J. Kahn and S. B. Kamerman. New York: Columbia University, School of Social Work, Cross-National Studies Program.

Coulton, C., J. Korbin, and M. Su. 1996. "Measuring Neighborhood Context for Young Children in an Urban Area." *American Journal of Community Psychology* 24(1): 5–32.

Coulton, C. J., J. Korbin, M. Su, and J. Chow. 1995. "Community Level Factors and Child Maltreatment Rates." *Child Development* 66: 1262–76.

Coulton, C. J., and S. Pandey. 1992. "Geographic Concentration of Poverty and Risk to Children in Urban Neighborhoods." *American Behavioral Scientist* 35(3): 238–57.

Coulton, C. J., S. Pandey, and J. Chow. 1990. "Concentration of Poverty and the Changing Ecology of Low-Income, Urban Neighborhoods: An Analysis of the Cleveland Area." *Social Work Research and Abstracts* 26: 5–16.

Crane, J. 1991a. "Effects of Neighborhoods on Dropping Out of School and Teenage Childbearing." In *The Urban Underclass*, edited by C. Jencks and P. P. Peterson. Washington, D.C.: Brookings Institution.

———. 1991b. "The Epidemic Theory of Ghettos and Neighborhood Effects on Dropping Out and Teenage Childbearing." *American Journal of Sociology* 96(5): 1226–59.

———. 1991c. "The Pattern of Neighborhood Effects on Social Problems." *American Journal of Sociology* 96: 1226–59.

Craven, P., and B. Wellman. 1973. "The Network City." *Sociological Inquiry* 43: 57–88.

Crockenberg, S. G. 1981. "Infant Irritability, Mother Responsiveness, and Social Support Influences on the Security of Infant–Mother Attachment." *Child Development* 52: 857–65.

Currie, J., and D. Thomas. 1995. "Does Head Start Make a Difference?" *American Economic Review* 85(3): 341–64.

Darling, N., and M. Gringlas. 1994. "Neighborhood Parenting, Peer Characteristics, and Social Integration as Predictors of Adolescent Socialization." Poster presented at the Society for Research on Adolescence meeting. San Diego (February 1994).

Darling, N., S. F. Hamilton, and S. Niego. 1994. "Adolescents' Relations with Adults outside the Family." In *Advances in Adolescent Development*. Vol. 6, *Adolescent Close Relationships*, edited by R. Montemayor, G. R. Adams, and T. P. Gullotta. Newbury Park, Calif.: Sage.

Darling, N., L. Steinberg, and M. Gringlas. 1993. "Community Integration and Value Consensus as Forces for Socialization: A Test of the Functional Community Hypothesis." Paper presented at the meeting of the Society for Research on Child Development. New Orleans (March 1993).

Darling, N., L. Steinberg, M. Gringlas, and S. M. Dornbusch. 1995. "Community Influences on Adolescent Achievement and Deviance: A Test of the Functional Community Hypothesis." Manuscript submitted for publication.

DeSena, J. N. 1990. *Protecting One's Turf: Social Strategies for Maintaining Urban Neighborhoods*. New York: University Press of America.

Donovan, J., and R. Jessor. 1985. "Structure of Problem Behavior in Adolescence and Young Adulthood." *Journal of Consulting and Clinical Psychology* 53: 890–904.

Dornbusch, S., P. Ritter, H. Leiderman, D. Roberts, and M. Fraleigh. 1987. "The Relation of Parenting Style to Adolescent School Performance." *Child Development* 56: 326–41.

Downs, A. 1981. *Neighborhoods and Urban Development*. Washington, D.C.: Brookings Institution.

Downs, R. M., and L. S. Liben. 1993. "Mediating the Environment: Communicating, Appropriating, and Developing Graphic Representations of Place." In *Development in Context: Acting and Thinking in Specific Environments*, edited by R. H. Wozniak and K. W. Fischer. Hillsdale, N.J.: Lawrence Erlbaum Associates, Inc.

Duda, R. O., and P. E. Hart. 1973. *Pattern Classification and Scene Analysis*. New York: Wiley.

Duncan, G. J. 1994. "Families and Neighborhoods as Sources of Disadvantage in the Schooling Decisions of White and Black Adolescents." *American Journal of Education* 103(1): 20–53.

Duncan, G. J., J. Brooks-Gunn, and P. K. Klebanov. 1994. "Economic Deprivation and Early Childhood Development." *Child Development* 65(2): 296–318.

Duncan, G. J., and J. Brooks-Gunn, eds. 1997. *Consequences of Growing Up Poor*. New York: Russell Sage Foundation.

Dunn, J., and R. Plomin. 1990. *Separate Lives: Why Siblings Are So Different*. New York: Basic Books.

Edgerton, R. 1993. *The Cloak of Competence*. Rev. ed. Berkeley: University of California Press.

Eisen, A. 1992. *A Report on Foundations' Support for Comprehensive Neighborhood-Based Community Empowerment Initiatives*. New York: New York Community Trust.

Elliott, D. S., and D. Huizinga. 1990. "The Mediating Effects of Social Structure in High Risk Neighborhoods." Paper presented at the annual meeting of the American Sociological Association. Washington, D.C. (August 1990).

Elliott, D. S., S. Menard, B. Rankin, A. Elliott, W. J. Wilson, and D. Huizinga. Forthcoming. *Overcoming Disadvantage: Successful Youth Development in High Risk Neighborhoods*. Chicago: University of Chicago Press.

Elliott, D. S., W. J. Wilson, D. Huizinga, R. Sampson, A. Elliott, and B. Rankin. 1994. "The Effects of Neighborhood Disadvantage on Adolescent Development." Paper in progress.

Emirbayer, M., and J. Goodwin. 1994. "Network Analysis, Culture, and the Problem of Agency." *American Journal of Sociology* 99(6): 1411–54.

Evans, W., W. Oates, and R. Schwab. 1992. "Measuring Peer Group Effects: A Study of Teenage Behavior." *Journal of Political Economy* 100: 966–91.

Fine, G. A. 1987. *With the Boys*. Chicago: University of Chicago Press.

Fine, M. 1991. *Framing Dropouts*. New York: State University of New York Press.

Fischer, C. S. 1982. *To Dwell among Friends: Personal Networks in Town and City*. Chicago: University of Chicago Press.

Fischer, C. S., R. M. Jackson, C. A. Stueve, K. Gerson, L. McCallister Jones, and M. Baldassare. 1977. *Networks and Places: Social Relations in the Urban Setting*. New York: Free Press.

Fishman, N., and M. Phillips. 1993. *A Review of Comprehensive, Collaborative Persistent Poverty Initiatives*. Evanston, Ill.: Northwestern University, Center for Urban Affairs and Policy Research.

Fordham, S., and J. U. Ogbu. 1986. "Black Students' School Success: Coping with the Burden of Acting White." *Urban Review* 18: 176–206.

Foster, E. M., and S. McLanahan. 1996. "An Illustration of the Use of Instrumental Variables: Do Neighborhood Conditions Affect a Young Person's Chance of Finishing High School?" Mimeographed. Vanderbilt University.

Freeman, R. B. 1991. "Employment and Earnings of Disadvantaged Young Men in a Labor Shortage Economy." In *The Urban Underclass*, edited by C. Jencks and P. E. Peterson. Washington, D.C.: Brookings Institution.

Fuchs, E., and J. P. Thompson. 1996. "Urban Community Initiatives and Shifting Federal Policy: The Case of the Empowerment Zones." In *Children and Their Families in Big Cities: Strategies for Service Reform*, edited by A. J. Kahn and S. B. Kamerman. New York: Columbia University, School of Social Work, Cross-National Studies Program,

Furstenberg, F. F., Jr. 1992. "Adapting to Difficult Environments: Neighborhood Characteristics and Family Strategies." Paper presented at the annual meetings of the Society for Research on Adolescents. Washington, D.C. (March 19–22, 1992).

———. 1993. "How Families Manage Risk and Opportunity in Dangerous Neighborhoods." In *Sociology and the Public Agenda*, edited by W. J. Wilson. Newbury Park, Calif.: Sage.

Furstenberg, F. F., Jr., T. D. Cook, J. Eccles, G. H. Elder Jr., and A. Sameroff. *Managing to Make It: Urban Families in High-Risk Neighborhoods*. Unpublished Manuscript.

Furstenberg, F. F., Jr., J. Eccles, G. H. Elder, T. D. Cook, and A. Sameroff, eds. Forthcoming. *Urban Families and Adolescent Success*.

Furstenberg, F. F., Jr., and M. E. Hughes. 1995. "Social Capital and Successful Development in Early Adulthood." Journal of Marriage and the Family 57(3):580–92.

Gans, H. J. 1962. *The Urban Villagers*. New York: Free Press.

Garbarino, J. 1977. "The Human Ecology of Child Maltreatment: A Conceptual Model for Research." *Journal of Marriage and the Family* 39: 721–35.

———. 1992. *Children and Families in the Social Environment*, 2d ed. New York: Aldine De Gruyter.

Garbarino, J., and A. Crouter. 1978. "Defining the Community Context for Parent–Child Relations: The Correlates of Child Maltreatment." *Child Development* 49: 604–16.

Garbarino, J., N. L. Galambos, M. C. Plantz, and K. Kostelny. 1992. "The Territory of Childhood." In *Children and Families in the Social Environment*, 2d ed., edited by J. Garbarino. New York: Aldine De Gruyter.

Garbarino, J., and K. Kostelny. 1992. "Child Maltreatment as a Community Problem." *Child Abuse and Neglect* 16: 455–64.

Garbarino, J., K. Kostelny, and N. Dubrow. 1991. "What Children Can Tell Us about Living in Danger." *American Psychologist* 46(4): 376–83.

Garbarino, J., and D. Sherman. 1980. "High-Risk Neighborhoods and High-Risk Families: The Human Ecology of Child Maltreatment." *Child Development* 51: 188–98.

Gardner, J. W. 1991. *Building Community*. Washington, D.C.: Independent Sector.

Gephart, M. A., A. O'Connor, and R. R. Peterson. 1993. "Persistent Urban Poverty: Integrating Research, Policy, and Practice." Paper presented at the Social Science Research Council Policy Conference on Persistent Poverty. Washington, D.C. (Nov. 9–10, 1993).

Geronimus, A., and S. Korenman. 1992. "The Socioeconomic Consequences of Teen Childbearing Reconsidered." *Quarterly Journal of Economics:* 1187–1215.

Gibbs, J. T., and L. N. Huang. 1991. "A Conceptual Framework for Assessing and Treating Minority Youth." In *Children of Color: Psychological Interventions with Minority Youth*, edited by J. T. Gibbs and L. N. Huang. San Francisco: Jossey-Bass.

Gordon, R. 1967. "Issues in the Ecological Study of Delinquency." *American Sociological Review* 32: 927–44.

Gottfried, A. W., ed. 1984. *Home Environment and Early Cognitive Development*. Orlando, Fla.: Academic Press.

Granovetter, M. 1985. "Economic Action and Social Structure: The Problem of Embeddedness." *American Journal of Sociology* 91(3): 481–510.

Grantmakers for Children, Youth and Families. 1992. *Vulnerable Children and Families: Philanthropic Perspectives on New Collaborations*. Washington D.C.: Council on Foundations.

Greenberger, E., R. Josselson, C. Knerr, and B. Knerr. 1974. "The Measurement and Structure of Psychosocial Maturity." *Journal of Youth and Adolescence* 4: 127–43.

Griliches, Z. 1977. "Sibling Models and Data in Economics: Beginnings of a Survey." *Journal of Political Economy*: S37–S64.

Guest, A. M. 1974. "Neighborhood Life Cycles and Social Status." *Economic Geography* 50: 228–43.

Guest, A. M., and B. A. Lee. 1984. "How Urbanites Define Their Neighborhoods." *Population and Environment* 7: 32–56.

Hagedorn, J., with P. Macon. 1988. *People and Folks: Gangs and the Underclass in a Rustbelt City*. Chicago: Lake View Press.

Hambrick-Dixon, P. J. 1990. "The Effect of the Physical Environment on the Development of Black Children." *Journal of Environmental Psychology* 8: 299–314.

Haney, W. G., and E. S. Knowles. 1978. "Perception of Neighborhoods by City and Suburban Residents." *Human Ecology* 6(2): 201–14.

Hannerz, U. 1969. *Soulside: Inquiries into Ghetto Culture and Community*. New York: Columbia University Press.

Harris, C. D., and E. Ullman. 1945. "The Nature of Cities." *Annals of the American Academy of Political and Social Sciences* 242: 7–17.

Hart, R. 1979. "The Spatial World of the Child." In *The Child in the City*, edited by W. Michelson, S. V. Levine, and E. Michelson. Toronto: University of Toronto Press.

Hauser, R. M., B. Brown, and W. Prosser, eds. 1997. *Indicators of Children's Well-Being*. New York: Russell Sage Foundation.

Hauser, R. M., and M. M. Sweeney. 1997. "Does Poverty in Adolescence Affect the Life Chances of High School Graduates?" In *Consequences of Growing Up Poor*, edited by G. J. Duncan and J. Brooks-Gunn. New York: Russell Sage Foundation.

Hawley, A. H. 1950. *Human Ecology: A Theory of Community Structure*. New York: Ronald.

Hayes, C. D., J. L. Palmer, and M. E. Zaslow. 1990. *Who Cares for America's Children? Child Care Policy for the 1990's*. Washington, D.C.: National Academy Press.

Heckler, M. 1985. *Report of the Secretary's Task Force on Black and Minority Health*. Washington, D.C.: U.S. Government Printing Office.

Hess, P., B. G. McGowan, and C. H. Meyer. 1996. "Practitioners' Perspectives on Family and Child Services." In *Children and Their Families in Big Cities: Strategies for Service Reform*, edited by A. J. Kahn and S. B. Kamerman. New York: Columbia University, School of Social Work, Cross-National Studies Program.

Hill, I. T., L. Bartlett, and M. B. Brostrom. 1993. "State Initiatives to Cover Uninsured Children." *Futures of Children* 3(2): 142–63.

Hill, M. 1989. "The Role of Social Networks in the Care of Young Children." *Children and Society* 3(3): 195–211.

Hill, M. S., and J. R. Sandfort. 1995. "Effects of Childhood Poverty on Productivity Later in Life: Implications for Public Policy." *Children and Youth Service Review* 12(1 and 2): 91–126.

Hillery, G. A., Jr. 1995. "Definitions of Community: Areas of Agreement." *Rural Sociology* 20:111–23.

Hippler, A. E. 1971. *Hunter's Point: A Black Ghetto*. New York: Basic Books.

Hirsch, A. 1983. *Making the Second Ghetto: Race and Housing in Chicago 1940–1960*. New York: Cambridge University Press.

Hogan, D. P., and E. M. Kitagawa. 1985. "The Impact of Social Status, Family Structure, and Neighborhood on the Fertility of Black Adolescents." *American Journal of Sociology* 90: 825–55.

Holloman, R. E., and F. E. Lewis. 1978. "the 'Clan': Case Study of a Black Extended Family in Chicago." In *The Extended Family in Black Societies*, edited by D. Shimkin, E. Shimkin, and D. A. Frate. The Hague: Mouton.

Hormuth, S. E. 1990. "The Ecology of the Self. Relocation and Self-concept Change." *European Monographs in Social Psychology*. Cambridge, U.K.: Cambridge University Press.

Howell, J. 1973. *Hard Living on Clay Street*. Prospect Heights, Ill.: Peter Smith Publishers.

Hoyt, H. 1939. *The Structure and Growth of Residential Neighborhoods in American Cities*. Washington, D.C.: Federal Housing Administration.

Huckfeldt, R. R. 1983. "Social Contexts, Social Networks, and Urban Neighborhoods: Environmental Constraints on Friendship Choice." *American Journal of Sociology* 89: 651–69.

Hunter, A. 1974. *Symbolic Communities: The Persistence and Change of Chicago's Local Communities*. Chicago: University of Chicago Press.

Hyson, M. C., and G. C. Bollin. 1990. "Children's Appraisal of Home and Neighborhood Risks: Questions for the 1990s." *Children's Environment Quarterly* 7(3): 50–60.

Jacob, J. E. 1990. "Black America: An Overview." *The State of Black America, 1990*. New York: National Urban League.

Jargowsky, P. A. 1996. "Beyond the Street Corner: The Hidden Diversity of High-Poverty Neighborhoods." *Urban Geography* 17:579–603

Jarrett, R. L. 1990. *A Comparative Examination of Socialization Patterns among Low-Income African-Americans, Chicanos, Puerto Ricans, and Whites: A Review of the Ethnographic Literature*. New York: Social Science Research Council.

———. 1992b. "A Family Case Study: An Examination of the Underclass Debate." In *Qualitative Methods in Family Research*, edited by J. Gilgun, G. Handel, and K. Daley. Newbury Park, Calif.: Sage.

——— . 1994. "Living Poor: Family Life among Single-Parent, African-American Women." *Social Problems* 41: 30–49.

———. 1995. "Growing Up Poor: The Family Experiences of Socially Mobile Youth in Low-Income African-American Neighborhoods." *Journal of Adolescent Research* 10: 111–35.

Jeffers, C. 1967. "Living Poor: A Participant Observer Study of Choices and Priorities." Ann Arbor, Mich.: Ann Arbor Publishers.

Jencks, C., and S. Mayer. 1990. "The Social Consequences of Growing Up in a Poor Neighborhood." In *Inner-City Poverty in the United States*, edited by L. E. Lynn and M. F. H. McGeary. Washington, D.C.: National Academy Press.

Jencks, C., and P. E. Peterson, eds. 1991. *The Urban Underclass*. Washington, D.C.: Brookings Institution.

Jenny, P. 1993. *Community Building Initiatives: A Scan of Comprehensive Neighborhood Revitalization Programs*. New York: New York Community Trust.

Jessor, R. 1993. "Successful Adolescent Development among Youth in High Risk Settings." *American Psychologist* 48(2): 117–26.

Jessor, R., and S. L. Jessor. 1973. "The Perceived Environment in Behavioral Science." *American Behavioral Scientist* 16(6): 801–27.

Kagan, S. L. 1996. "America's Family Support Movement: A Moment of Change." In *Children, Families, and Government: Preparing for the Twenty-first Century*, edited by E. F. Zigler, S. L. Kagan, and N. W. Hall. New York: Cambridge University Press.

———. 1995. "Support Systems for Children, Youth, Families, and Schools in Inner City Situations." *Education and Urban Society* 29(3): 277–95.

Kagan, S. L., and E. Pritchard. 1996. "Linking Services for Children and Families: Past Legacies, Future Possibilities." In *Children, Families, and Government: Preparing for the Twenty-first Century*, edited by E. F. Zigler, S. L. Kagan, and N. W. Hall. New York: Cambridge University Press.

Kahn, A. J., and S. B. Kamerman, eds. 1996. *Children and Their Families in Big Cities: Strategies for Service Reform*. New York: Columbia University, School of Social Work, Cross-National Studies Program.

Kasarda, J., and M. Janowitz. 1974. "Community Attachment in Mass Society." *American Sociological Review* 39: 328–39.

Katz, M. B. 1989. *The Undeserving Poor*. New York: Pantheon Books.

Keiser, R. L. 1969. *The Vice Lords: Warriors of the Street*. New York: Holt, Rinehart & Winston.

Keller, S. 1986. *The Urban Neighborhood*. New York: Random House.

Kenny, D., and C. M. Judd. 1984. "Estimating the Nonlinear and Interactive Effects of Latent Variables." *Psychological Bulletin* 96: 201–10.

Keyes, L. C. 1992. *Strategies and Saints: Fighting Drugs in Subsidized Housing*. Washington D.C.: Urban Institute Press.

Klebanov, P. K., J. Brooks-Gunn, and G. J. Duncan. 1994. "Does Neighborhood and Family Poverty Affect Mothers' Parenting, Mental Health, and Social Support?" *Journal of Marriage and the Family* 56(2): 441–55.

Kochman, T. J. 1992. "The Relationship between Environmental Characteristics and the Psychological Functioning of the African American Youth." Unpublished honors thesis, Psychology Department, Emory University.

Korbin, J., and C. Coulton. 1994. "Neighborhood Impact on Child Abuse and Neglect." Final Report of Grant #90-CA1494. Washington: U. S. Government Printing Office for National Center on Child Abuse and Neglect, Health and Human Services.

———. 1996. "Neighbors, Neighborhood, and Child Maltreatment." *Journal of Social Issues* 52(3): 163–76.

Kornblum, W. 1974. *Blue Collar Community*. Chicago: University of Chicago Press.

Kornhauser, R. 1978. *Social Sources of Delinquency*. Chicago: University of Chicago Press.

Kostarelos, F. 1989. "A Social and Cultural Account of an Evangelical Storefront Church in a Black Ghetto." Ph.D. diss., Department of Anthropology, University of Chicago.

Kotlowitz, A. 1991. *There Are No Children Here*. New York: Anchor.

Kubisch, A. C. 1996. "On the Term Community: An Informal Contribution." In *Children and Their Families in Big Cities: Strategies for Service Reform*, edited by A.J. Kahn and S.B. Kamerman. New York: Columbia University, School of Social Work, Cross-National Studies Program.

Kuiper, F., and L. Fisher. 1975. "A Monte Carlo Comparison of Six Clustering Procedures." *Biometrics* 31: 777–83.

Ladner, J. A. 1971. *Tomorrow's Tomorrow: The Black Woman*. New York: Anchor Books.

Land, K., P. McCall, and L. Cohen. 1990. "Structural Covariates of Homicide Rates: Are There Any Invariances across Time and Space?" *American Journal of Sociology* 95: 922–63.

Lareau, A. 1989. "Family School Relationships: A View from the Classroom." *Educational Policy* 3(3): 245–57.

LaRuffia, A. L. 1988. *Monte Carmelo: An Italian-American Community in the Bronx*. New York: Gordon & Breach.

Lee, B. A., K. E. Campbell, and, O. Miller. 1991. "Radical Differences in Urban Neighboring" *Social Forum* 6(3): 525–50.

Lee, B. A., R. S. Oropesa, and J. W. Kanan. 1994. "Neighborhood Context and Residential Mobility." *Demography* 31: 249–70.

Lemert, E. M. 1951. *Social Pathology: A Systematic Approach to the Theory of Sociopathic Behavior*. New York: McGraw-Hill.

LeVine, R., P. Miller, and M. Maxwell West, eds. 1988. *Parental Behavior in Diverse Societies*. San Francisco: Jossey-Bass.

Lewin, K. 1935. *A Dynamic Theory of Personality*. New York: McGraw-Hill.

———. 1936. *Principles of Topological Psychology*. New York: McGraw-Hill.

———. 1951. *Field Theory in Social Science*. New York: Harper & Row.

Lewin-Epstein, N. 1985. "Neighborhoods, Local Labor Markets, and Employment Opportunities for White and Non-white Youth." *Social Science Quarterly* 66: 163–71.

Liebow, E. 1966. *Talley's Corner*. Boston: Little, Brown.

Little, R. J. A. and D. B. Rubin. 1987. *Statistical Analysis with Missing Data*. New York: Wiley.

Lobach, K. S. 1995. "Health Policy in the Family Support Act: Implications for Quality of Health Services to Children." In *Escape from Poverty: What Makes a Difference for Poor Children?* edited by P. L. Chase-Lansdale and J. Brooks-Gunn. New York: Cambridge University Press.

Logan, J., and H. Molotch. 1987. *Urban Fortunes: The Political Economy of Place*. Berkeley, Calif.: University of California Press.

Lynch, K., ed. 1977. *Growing Up in Cities*. Cambridge, Mass.: MIT Press.

Lynn, L. E., and M. G. H. McGeary. 1990. *Inner-City Poverty in the United States*. Washington, D.C.: National Academy Press.

Maccoby, E., J. Johnson, and R. Church. 1958. "Community Integration and the Social Control of Juvenile Delinquency." *Journal of Social Issues* 14: 38–51.

MacLeod, J. 1995. *Ain't No Makin' It: Leveled Aspirations in a Low-Income Community*, 2d ed. Boulder, Colo.: Westview Press.

Manski, C. F. 1993. "Identification Problems in the Social Sciences." *Sociological Methodology* 23: 1–56.

Mare, R. D., and C. Winship. 1984. "The Paradox of Lessening Racial Inequality and Joblessness among Black Youth: Enrollment, Enlistment, and Employment, 1964–1981." *American Sociological Review* 49: 39–55.

Markstrom-Adams, C., and M. B. Spencer. 1994. "A Model for Identity Intervention with Minority Adolescents." In *Interventions for Adolescent Identity Development*, edited by S. Archer. Beverly Hills, Calif.: Sage.

Marsden, P. V. 1987. "Core Discussion Networks of Americans." *American Sociological Review* 52: 122–31.

Martin, E., and J. M. Martin. 1978. *The Black Extended Family*. Chicago: University of Chicago Press.

Martinez, J. E., and P. Richters. 1993. "The NIMH Community Violence Project: II. Children's Distress Symptoms Associated with Violence Exposure." *Psychiatry* 56: 22–35.

Maryland—National Capital Park and Planning Commision 1993. *Selected 1990 Census Statistics*. Prince George's County, Maryland, Profile Area VII, vol. 7. Series no. 92693152801.

Massey, D. S. 1990. "American Apartheid: Segregation and the Making of the Underclass." *American Journal of Sociology* 96: 338–39.

Massey, D. S., and N. A. Denton. 1989. "Hypersegregation in U.S. Metropolitan Areas: Black and Hispanic Segregation along Five Dimensions." *Demography* 26: 373–91.

———. 1993. *American Apartheid: Segregation and the Making of the Underclass*. Cambridge, Mass.: Harvard University Press.

Massey, D., and M. Eggers. 1990. "The Ecology of Inequality: Minorities and the Concentration of Poverty, 1970–1980." *American Journal of Sociology* 95: 1153–88.

Massey, D., and S. Kanaiaupuni. 1993. "Public Housing and the Concentration of Poverty." *Social Science Quarterly* 74: 109–22.

Matza, D. 1964. *Delinquency and Drift*. New York: Wiley.

Maurer, R., and J. C. Baxter. 1972. "Images of the Neighborhood and City among Black-, Anglo-, and Mexican-American Children." *Environment and Behavior* 4(4): 351–87.

Mayer, S. E., and C. Jencks. 1989. "Growing Up in Poor Neighborhoods: How Much Does It Matter?" *Science* 243: 1441–45.

McDermott, P. A. 1980. "Prevalence and Constituency of Behavioral Disturbance Taxonomies in the Regular School Population." *Journal of Abnormal Child Psychology* 8: 523–36.

———. 1995. "Sex, Race, Class, and Other Demographics as Explanations for Children's Ability and Adjustment: A National Appraisal." *Journal of School Psychology* 33: 75–91.

McDermott, P. A., J. J. Glutting, J. N. Jones, and J. V. Noonan. 1989. "Typology and Prevailing Composition of Core Profiles in the WAIS-R Standardization Sample." *Psychological Assessment* 1: 118–23.

McHenry, D. F. 1990. "A Changing World Order: Implications for Black America." In *The State of Black America, 1990*, edited by J. Dewart. New York: National Urban League.

McLoyd, V. C., T. Jayaratne-Epstein, R. Ceballo, and J. Borquez. 1994. "Unemployment and Work Interruption among African American Single Mothers: Effects on Parenting and Adolescent Socioemotional Functioning." *Child Development* 65(2): 562–89.

Medrich, E. A., J. Roizen, V. Rubin, and S. Buckley. 1982. *The Serious Business of Growing Up.* Berkeley: University of California Press.

Melendez, E., and J. B. Figueroa. 1992. "The Effects of Local Labor Market Conditions on Labor Force Participation of Puerto Rican, White, and Black Women." *Hispanic Journal of Behavioral Sciences* 14(1): 76–90.

Merriwether–de Vries, C. 1994. "Exploring the Relationship between Neighborhood Quality and Adolescent Depression among Urban Resident Adolescents." Master's thesis, Pennsylvania State University.

Merriwether–de Vries, C., L. M. Burton, and L. Eggeletion. 1996. "Early Parenting and Intergenerational Family Relationships within African-American Families." In *Transitions through Adolescence: Interpersonal Domains and Context*, edited by J. A. Graber, J. Brooks-Gunn, and A. C. Petersen. Mahwah, N.J.: Erlbaum.

Merry, S. E. 1981. *Urban Danger: Life in a Neighborhood of Strangers.* Philadelphia: Temple University Press.

Milligan, G. W. 1980. "An Examination of the Effect of Six Types of Error Perturbation of Fifteen Clustering Algorithms." *Psychometrika* 45: 325–42.

Mitchell, J. C. 1969. "The Concept and Use of Social Networks." In *Social Networks in Urban Situations*, edited by J. C. Mitchell. Manchester: University of Manchester Press.

Moen, P., G. H. Elder, and K. Lusher, eds. 1995. *Examining Lives in Context: Perspective on The Ecology of Human Development.* Washington, D.C.: American Psychological Association Press.

Mojena, R. 1977. "Hierarchical Grouping Methods and Stopping Rules: An Evaluation." *Computer Journal* 20: 359–63.

Moore, W., Jr. 1969. *The Vertical Ghetto: Everyday Life in an Urban Project.* New York: Random House.

Moynihan, D. P. 1965. *The Negro Family: The Case for National Action.* Washington, D.C.: Office of Policy Planning and Research, U.S. Department of Labor.

Mundlak, Y. 1978. "On the Pooling of Time Series and Cross Sectional Data." *Econometrica* 46(1): 69–86.

Myers, D., and A. Doyle. 1990. "Age-Specific Population-per-Household Ratios: Linking Population Age Structure with Housing Characteristics." In *Housing Demography: Linking Demographic Structure and Housing Markets*, edited by D. Myers. Madison: University of Wisconsin Press.

Myers, H. F. 1989. "Urban Stress and Mental Health in Black Youth: An Epidemiological and Conceptual Update." In *Black Adolescents*, edited by R. L. Jones. Berkeley, Calif.: Cobb & Henry.

Nelson, D. 1996. "The Path of Most Resistance: Lessons Learned from New Futures." In *Children and Their Families in Big Cities: Strategies for Service Reform*, edited by A. J. Kahn and S. B. Kamerman. New York: Columbia University, School of Social Work, Cross-National Studies Program.

Newman, K. S. 1992. *"The View from the Corner": Neighborhood Influences on Children and Adolescents.* New York: Social Science Research Council.

———. 1996. " 'The View from the Corner': Neighborhood Influences on Children and Adolescents." In *Transitions through Adolescence: Interpersonal Domains and Context*, edited by J. A. Graber, J. Brooks-Gunn, and A. C. Petersen. Hillsdale, N.J.: Erlbaum.

———. 1996. "Working Poor: Low Wage Employment in the Lives of Harlem Youth. In *Transitions through Adolescence: Interpersonal Domains and Context*, edited by J. A. Graber, J. Brooks-Gunn, and A. C. Petersen. Hillsdale, N.J.: Erlbaum

Newmann, F. M. 1981. "Reducing Student Alienation in High School: Implications of Theory." *Harvard Educational Review* 51(4): 546–64.

Noack, P., and R. K. Silbereisen. 1988. "Adolescent Development and the Choice of Leisure Settings." *Children's Environments Quarterly* 5: 25–33.

Ogbu, J. 1974. *The Next Generation: An Ethnography of Education in an Urban Neighborhood.* New York: Academic Press.

———. 1991. "Minority Coping Responses and School Experience." *Journal of Psychohistory* 18(4): 433–56.

Olds, D., C. R. Henderson, and H. Kitzman. 1994. "Does Prenatal and Infancy Nurse Home Visitation Have Enduring Effects on Qualities of Parental Caregiving and Child Health at Twenty-five to Fifty Months of Life?" *Pediatrics* 93(1): 89–98.

Oliver, M. L. 1988. "The Urban Black Community as Network: Toward a Social Network Perspective." *Sociological Quarterly* 29: 623–45.

Olson, P. 1982. "Urban Neighborhood Research: Its Development and Current Focus." *Urban Affairs Quarterly* 17: 491–518.

Ooms, T. 1996. *Where Is the Family in Comprehensive Community Initiatives for Children and Families?* Washington, D.C.: Family Impact Seminar.

Orleans, P. 1969. "Robert Park and Social Area Analysis: A Convergence in Urban Sociology." In *Urbanism, Urbanization and Change: Comparative Perspectives*, edited by P. Meadows and E. Mizruchi. Reading, Mass.: Addison-Wesley.

Overall, J. E., J. M. Gibson, and D. M. Novy. 1993. "Population Recovery Capabilities of 35 Cluster Analysis Methods." *Journal of Clinical Psychology* 49: 459–70.

Overall, J. E., and K. N. Magee. 1992. "Replication as a Rule for Determining the Number of Clusters in Hierarchical Cluster Analysis." *Applied Psychological Measurement* 16: 119–28.

Overton, W., and H. W. Reese. 1977. "General Models for Man–Environment Relations." In *Ecological Factors in Human Development*, edited by H. McGurk. New York: Elsevier North-Holland.

Park, R. 1916. "The City: Suggestions for the Investigations of Human Behavior in the Urban Environment." *American Journal of Sociology* 20: 577–612.

———. 1936. "Human Ecology." *American Journal of Sociology* 42: 1–15.

Park, R. E., and E. W. Burgess. 1924. *Introduction to the Science of Sociology.* Reprint, Chicago: University of Chicago Press, 1984.

———. 1925. *The City.* Chicago: University of Chicago Press.

Parke, R. D. 1995. "Fathers and Families." In *Handbook of Parenting.* Vol. 3, *Status and Social Conditions of Parenting*, edited by M. H. Bornstein. Mahwah, N.J.: Erlbaum.

Patterson, G., and M. Stouthamer-Loeber. 1984. "The Correlation of Family Management Practices and Delinquency." *Child Development*, 55: 1299–1307.

Patton, M. Q. 1993. *The Aid to Families in Poverty Program: A Synthesis of Themes, Patterns and Lessons Learned.* Minneapolis, Minn.: McNight Foundation.

Pedhazur, E. J. 1982. *Multiple Regression in Behavioral Research*, 2d ed. New York: Holt, Rinehart & Winston.

Pence, A., ed. 1988. *Ecological Research with Children and Families: From Concepts to Methodology.* New York: Teachers College Press.

Philpott, T. L. 1991. *The Slum and the Ghetto: Immigrants, Blacks, and Reformers in Chicago, 1880–1930.* Belmont, Calif.: Wadsworth.

Plomin, R., and D. Daniels. 1987. "Why Are Children in the Same Family So Different from One Another?" *Behavioral and Brain Sciences*: 1–60.

Polansky, N. A., J. M. Gaudin, P. W. Ammons, and D. B. Davis. 1985. "The Psychological Ecology of the Neglectful Mother." *Child Abuse and Neglect* 9: 265–75.

Powell, L. 1990. "Factors Associated with the Under-representation of African Americans in Mathematics and Science." *Journal of Negro Education* 59: 292–98.

Price-Spratlen, T., and L. M. Burton. 1995. "Theoretical Models and the 'Hood: Considering the Effect of Research Strategies on Our Understanding of African-American Neighborhoods." Unpublished manuscript.

Proctor, E. K., N. R. Volser, and E. A. Sirles. 1993. "The Social-Environmental Context of Child Clients: An Empirical Exploration." *Social Work* 38(3): 256–62.

Proshansky, H. M., and A. K. Fabian. 1987. "The Development of Place Identity in the Child." In *Spaces for Children*, edited by C. S. Weinstein and T. G. David. New York: Plenum.

Putnam, R. 1993. "The Prosperous Community: Social Capital and Public Life." *American Prospect* 25 (March/April): 26–28.

Rainwater, L. 1970. *Behind Ghetto Walls*. Chicago: Aldine.

Rank, M. R. 1992. "The Blending of Qualitative and Quantitative Methods in Understanding Childbearing among Welfare Recipients." In *Qualitative Methods in Family Research*, edited by J. Gilgun, K. Daly, and G. Handel. Newbury Park, Calif.: Sage.

Raudenbush, S. W., B. Rowan, and S. J. Kang. 1991. Multi-level, Multi-Variate Model for Studying School Climate with Estimation Via the EM Algorithm for Application to U.S. High School Data. *Journal of Educational Statistics* 16: 295–330.

Reiss, A. J., Jr. 1986. "Why Are Communities Important in Understanding Crime?" In *Communities and Crime*, edited by A. J. Reiss Jr. and M. Tonry. Chicago: University of Chicago Press.

Richman, H. S., P. Brown, and S. Venkatesh. 1996. "The Community Base for New Service Delivery Strategies." In *Children and Their Families in Big Cities: Strategies for Service Reform*, edited by A. J. Kahn and S. B. Kamerman. New York: Columbia University, School of Social Work, Cross-National Studies Program.

Richters, P., and J. E. Martinez. 1993. "The NIMH Community Violence Project: I. Children as Victims of and Witnesses to Violence." *Psychiatry* 56: 7–21.

Ricketts, E. R., and I. V. Sawhill. 1988. "Defining and Measuring the Underclass." *Journal of Policy Analysis and Management* 7: 316–25.

Rivlin, L. G. 1982. "Group Membership and Place Meanings in an Urban Neighborhood." *Journal of Social Issues* 38(3): 75–93.

Roberts, K. H., and L. Burstein, eds. 1980. *Issues in Aggregation*. San Francisco: Jossey-Bass.

Robinson, W. S. 1950. "Ecological Correlations and the Behavior of Individuals." *American Sociological Review* 15: 351–57.

Rosenbaum, J. E., and S. J. Popkin. 1992. "The Gautreaux Program: An Experiment in Racial and Economic Integration." *Center Report: Current Policy Issues* 2(1).

Rosenthal, R., and D. B. Rubin. 1982. "A Simple, General Purpose Display of Magnitude of Experimental Effect." *Journal of Educational Psychology* 74: 166–69.

Rosenzweig, M., and K. Wolpin. 1995. "Sisters, Siblings, and Mothers: The Effect of Teen-age Childbearing on Birth Outcomes in a Dynamic Family Context." *Econometrica* 303–26.

Rosewater, A. 1992. *Comprehensive Approaches for Children and Families: A Philanthropic Perspective*. Washington, D. C.: Grantmakers for Children and Families.

Roundtable on Effective Services. 1993. *Summary of Planning Meeting on Evaluation of Geographically-Targeted Cross-Systems Reform Efforts.* Washington, D.C.: National Academy of Sciences.

Ruffins, P. 1989. "Black America: Awakening to Ecology." *Washington Post*, December 24, 1989, p. C3.

Saegart, S., and R. Hart. 1977. "The Development of Environmental Competence in Girls and Boys." In *Play: Anthropological Perspectives*, edited by M. A. Salter. West Point, N.Y.: Leisure Books.

Sampson, R. J. 1985. "Neighborhood and Crime: The Structural Determinants of Personal Victimization." *Journal of Research in Crime and Delinquency* 22: 7–40.

———. 1988. "Community Attachment in Mass Society: A Multilevel Systemic Model." *American Sociological Review* 53: 766–69.

———. 1991. "Linking the Micro- and Macrolevel Dimensions of Community Social organization." *Social Forces* 70: 43–64.

———. 1992. "Family Management and Child Development: Insights from Social Disorganization Theory." In *Advances in Criminological Theory: Facts, Frameworks, and Forecasts*, Vol. 3, edited by J. McCord. New Brunswick, N.J.: Transaction.

———. 1993a. "Crime and Community Social Disorganization: Implications for Social Policy." Memorandum prepared for the Social Science Research Council and HUD Roundtable. Washington, D.C.

———. 1993b. "Family and Community-Level Influences on Delinquency in the Inner City." Paper presented at the annual meeting of the Society for Research on Child Development. New Orleans (1993).

———. 1996. "What 'Community' Supplies." Paper prepared for the Brookings Institution National Community Development Policy Analysis Network (November 1996).

Sampson, R. J., and W. B. Groves. 1989. "Community Structure and Crime: Testing Social-Disorganization Theory." *American Journal of Sociology* 94(4): 774–802.

Sampson, R. J., and W. J. Wilson. 1994. "Race, Crime, and Urban Inequality." In *Crime and Inequality*, edited by J. Hagan and R. Petersen. Stanford, Calif.: Stanford University Press.

Scheibler, D., and W. Schneider. 1985. "Monte Carlo Tests of the Accuracy of Cluster Analysis Algorithms—A Comparison of Hierarchical and Nonhierarchical Methods." *Multivariate Behavioral Research* 20: 283–304.

Schiavo, S. R. 1988. "Age Differences in Assessment and Use of a Suburban Neighborhood among Children and Adolescents." *Children's Environment Quarterly* 5(2): 4–9.

Schmid, C. 1960. "Urban Crime Areas: Part I." *American Sociological Review* 25: 527–42.

———. 1961. "Urban Crime Areas: Part II." *American Sociological Review* 25: 655–78.

Schorr, L. B. 1988. *Within Our Reach: Breaking the Cycle of Disadvantage.* New York: Anchor.

Schorr, L. B., with D. Both. 1991. "Attributes of Effective Services for Young Children: A Brief Survey of Current Knowledge and Its Implications for Program and Policy Development." In *Effective Services for Young Children*, edited by L. B. Schorr, D. Both, and C. Copple. Washington, D.C.: National Academy Press.

Schorr, L. B., D. Both, and C. Copple, eds. 1991. *Effective Services for Young Children.* Washington, D.C.: National Academy Press.

Schulz, D. 1969. *Coming Up Black: Patterns of Ghetto Socialization.* Englewood Cliffs, N.J.: Prentice-Hall.

Shaw, C. 1949. "Rejoinder." *American Sociological Review* 14: 614–17.

———. 1969. *Juvenile Delinquency and Urban Areas*. Chicago: University of Chicago Press.

Shaw, C., and H. McKay. 1931. *Report of the Causes of Crime*. Vol. 2, *Social Factors in Juvenile Delinquency*. Washington, D.C.: U.S. Government Printing Office.

———. 1942. *Juvenile Delinquency and Urban Areas*. Chicago: University of Chicago Press.

———. 1969. *Juvenile Delinquency and Urban Areas; A Study of Rates of Delinquency in Relation to Differential Characteristics of Local Communities in American Cities*. Chicago: University of Chicago Press.

Shaw, C., F. Zorbaugh, H. McKay, and L. Cottrell. 1929. *Delinquency Areas*. Chicago: University of Chicago Press.

Shevky, E., and W. Bell. 1955. *Social Area Analysis: Theory, Illustration, Application and Computational Procedures*. Stanford: Stanford University Press.

Shinn, M. 1988. "Mixing and Matching: Levels of Conceptualization, Measurement, and Statistical Analysis in Community Research." Paper presented at the Conference on Researching Community Psychology: Integrating Theories and Methodologies. De Paul University (September 1988).

Silverstein, B., and R. Krate. 1975. *Children of the Dark Ghetto: A Developmental Psychology*. New York: Praeger.

Simcha-Fagan, O., and J. Schwartz. 1986. "Neighborhood and Delinquency: An Assessment of Contextual Effects." *Criminology* 24: 677–704.

Skjaeveland, O., T. Garling, and J. G. Maeland. 1996. "A Multidimensional Measure of Neighboring." *American Journal of Community Psychology* 24: 413–35.

Skogan, W. 1990. *Disorder and Decline: Crime and the Spiral of Decay in American Neighborhoods*. New York: Free Press.

Smith, H. L. 1989. "Integrating Theory and Research on the Institutional Determinants of Fertility." *Demography* 26(2): 171–84.

Smith, J. R., J. Brooks-Gunn, and P. K. Klebanov. 1997. "The Consequences of Living in Poverty for Young Children's Cognitive and Verbal Ability and Early School Achievement." In *Consequences of Growing Up Poor*, edited by G. J. Duncan and J. Brooks-Gunn. New York: Russell Sage Foundation.

Snow, C. 1993. "Families as Context for Literacy Development." In *The Development of Literacy through Social Interaction*, edited by C. Daiute. San Francisco: Jossey-Bass.

Snow, C. E., W. S. Barnes, J. Chandler, L. Hemphill, and I. F. Goodman. 1991. *Unfulfilled Expectations: Home and School Influences on Literacy*. Cambridge, Mass.: Harvard University Press.

Spencer, M. B. 1985. "Cultural Cognition and Social Cognition as Identity Factors in Black Children's Personal-Social Growth." In *Beginnings: Social and Affective Development of Black Children*, edited by M. B. Spencer, G. K. Brookins, and W. R. Allen. Hillsdale, N.J.: Erlbaum.

———. 1988. "Persistent Poverty of African American Youth: A Normative Study of Developmental Transitions in High-risk Environments." Unpublished proposal submitted to and funded by the Spencer and Ford Foundations, Emory University, Atlanta, Georgia.

———. 1995. "Old Issues and New Theorizing about African American Youth: A Phenomenological Variant of Ecological Systems Theory." In *Black Youth; Perspectives on Their Status in the United States*, edited by R. L. Taylor. Westport, Conn · Praeger.

Spencer, M. B., and A. Glymph. 1993. "The Development of Context: Violent Behaviors in American Youth Contexts." Paper presented to the meeting of the American Criminality Society, Phoenix, Arizona.

Spencer, M. B., P. McDermott, L. Burton, T. J. Kochman, and D. Neuwirth, 1997. *An Alternative Neighborhood Assessment Measure.* Unpublished paper. Philadelphia: University of Pennsylvania.

Spradley, J. P. 1979. *The Ethnographic Interview.* New York: Holt, Rinehart & Winston.

Stack, C. B. 1974. *All Our Kin: Strategies for Survival in a Black Community.* New York: Harper & Row.

Stack, C. B., and L. M. Burton. 1993. "Kinscripts." *Journal of Comparative Family Studies* 24: 157–70.

Steinberg, L. 1989. "Communities of Families and Education." In *Education and The American Family: A Research Synthesis*, edited by W. Weston. New York: University Press.

———. 1990. "Autonomy, Conflict, and Harmony in the Family Relationships." In *At the Threshold: The Developing Adolescent*, edited by S. S. Feldman and G. R. Elliott. Cambridge, Mass.: Harvard University Press.

Steinberg, L., N. Darling, and A. Fletcher. 1993. *Authoritative Parenting and Adolescent Adjustment: An Ecological Journey.* Paper presented at the Urie Bronfenbrenner Symposium. Ithaca, New York (September 1993).

Steinberg, L., S. D. Lamborn, S. M. Dornbusch, and N. Darling. 1992. "Impact of Parenting Practices on Adolescent Achievement: Authoritative Parenting, School Involvement, and Encouragement to Succeed." *Child Development* 63: 1266–81.

Stokols, D., and S. A. Shumaker. 1981. "People in Places: A Transactional View of Settings." In *Cognition, Social Behavior, and the Environment*, edited by J. Harvey. Hillsdale, N.J.: Erlbaum.

Stoutland, S. 1995. "Neither Urban Jungle nor Urban Village: Informal and Formal Collective Strategies in Multi-ethnic Community-Based Subsidized Housing." Ph.D. diss., University of Minnesota, St. Paul.

Sudman, S. 1988. "Experiments in Measuring Neighborhood and Relative Social Networks." *Social Networks* 10: 93–108.

Sugland, B. W., M. Zaslow, J. R. Smith, J. Brooks-Gunn, D. Coates, C. Blumenthal, K. A. Moore, T. Griffin, and R. Bradley. 1995. "The Early Childhood HOME Inventory and HOME–Short Form in Differing Racial/Ethnic Groups: Are There Differences in Underlying Structure, Internal Consistency of Subscales, and Patterns of Prediction?" *Journal of Family Issues* 16: 632–63.

Sullivan, M. L. 1989. *Getting Paid: Youth, Crime and Work in the Inner City.* Ithaca, N.Y.: Cornell University Press.

———. 1993. *More than Housing: How Community Development Corporations Go about Changing Lives and Neighborhoods.* New York: New School for Social Research, Graduate School of Management and Urban Policy, Community Development Research Center.

———. Forthcoming. "Local Knowledge and Local Participation: Lessons from Community Studies for Community Initiatives." In *Applying a Theories of Change Approach to the Evaluation of Comprehensive Community Initiatives: Progress, Prospects, and Problems*, edited by J. P. Connell, A. C., and Kubisch. Washington, D.C.: Aspen Institute.

Summers, A., and B. Wolfe. 1977. "Do Schools Make a Difference?" *American Economic Review* 67(4): 639–52.

Super, C. M., and S. Harkness. 1986. "The Developmental Niche: A Conceptualization at the Interface of Child and Culture." *International Journal of Behavioral Development* 9: 545–69.

Super, C. M., and S. Harkness, eds. 1980. *New Directions for Child Development*. No. 8, *Anthropological Perspectives on Child Development*. San Francisco: Jossey-Bass.

Susser, I. 1982. *Norman Street: Poverty and Politics in an Urban Neighborhood*. New York: Oxford University Press.

Sutherland, E. H. 1937. *The Professional Thief: By a Professional Thief*. Chicago: the University of Chicago Press.

———. 1939. *Principles of Criminology*. New York: Lippincott.

Suttles, G. 1968. *The Social Order of the Slum*. Chicago: University of Chicago Press.

———. 1972. *The Social Construction of Communities*. Chicago: University of Chicago Press.

Swidler, A. 1986. "Culture in Action: Symbols and Strategies." *American Sociological Review* 51: 273–86.

Tannenbaum, F. 1938. *Crime and Community*. New York: Columbia University Press.

Tepperman, L., and R. J. Richardson. 1986. *The Social World: An Introduction to Sociology*. Toronto: McGraw-Hill Ryerson.

Tatje, T. A. 1974. "Mother–Daughter Dyadic Dominance in Black American Kinship." Ph.D. diss., Department of Anthropology, Northwestern University.

Tatum, B. 1987. *Assimilation Blues*. New York: Greenwood Press.

Taub, R. 1990. *Nuance and Meaning in Community Development: Finding Community Development*. New York: New School for Social Research, Community Development Research Center.

Taub, R., G. Taylor, and J. Dunham. 1984. *Paths of Neighborhood Change: Race and Crime in Urban America*. Chicago: University of Chicago Press.

Thorndike, R. L. 1939. "On the Fallacy of Imputing the Correlations Found for Groups to the Individuals or Smaller Groups Composing Them." *American Journal of Psychology* 52: 122–24.

Thorne, B. 1993. *Gender Play: Girls and Boys in School*. New Brunswick, N.J.: Rutgers University Press.

Thrasher, F. M. 1927. *The Gang*. Chicago: University of Chicago Press.

Tienda, M. 1991. "Poor People and Poor Places: Deciphering Neighborhood Effects on Poverty Outcomes." In *Macro–Micro Linkages in Sociology*, edited by J. Huber. Newbury Park, Calif.: Sage.

Torrell, G., and A. Biel. 1985. "Parental Restrictions and Children's Acquisition of Neighborhood Knowledge." In *Children Within Environments: Toward a Psychology of Accident Prevention*, edited by T. Garling and J. Valsiner. New York: Plenum.

Tryon, B. C., and D. E. Bailey. 1970. *Cluster Analysis*. New York: McGraw-Hill.

U.S. Bureau of the Census. 1991. *State and Metropolitan Area Date Book*. Washington, D.C.: U.S. Government Printing Office.

Valentine, B. L. 1978. *Hustling and Other Hard Work: Life Styles of the Ghetto*. New York: Free Press.

Van Den Wollenberg, A. L. 1977. "Redundancy Analysis: An Alternative for Canonical Correlation Analysis." *Psychometrika* 42(2): 207–19.

van Vliet, W. 1981. "Neighborhood Evaluations by City and Suburban Children." *Journal of the American Planners Association* 47(4): 458–66.

Vidal, A. C. 1992. *Rebuilding Communities: A National Study of Urban Community Development Corporations*. New York: New School for Social Research, Graduate School of Management and Urban Policy, Community Development Research Center.

von Andel, J. 1990. "Places Children Like, Dislike, and Fear." *Children's Environment Quarterly* 7(4): 24–31.

Wachs, T. D., and G. E. Gruen. 1982. *Early Experience and Human Development*. New York: Plenum Press.

Wainer, H. 1976. "Estimating Coefficients in Linear Models: It Don't Make No Nevermind." *Psychological Bulletin* 83: 213–17.

Wakschlag, L. S., P. L. Chase-Lansdale, and J. Brooks-Gunn. 1997. "Not Just 'Ghosts in the Nursery': Contemporaneous Intergenerational Relationships and Parenting in Young African American Families." *Child Development, 67*(5): 2131–2147.

Walker, K., and F. F. Furstenberg, Jr. 1994. "Neighborhood Settings and Parenting Strategies." Paper presented at the annual meeting of the American Sociological Association. Los Angeles, California (August 1994).

Ward, J. H., Jr. 1963. "Hierarchical Grouping to Optimize an Objective Function." *American Statistical Journal* 58: 236–44.

Washington, V., and V. LaPointe. 1989. *Black Children and American Institutions: An Ecological Review and Resource Guide*. New York: Garland.

Wehlage, G., R. Rutter, G. Smith, N. Lesko, and R. Fernandez. 1989. *Reducing the Risk: Schools as Communities of Support*. London: Falmer.

Weisner, T. 1984. "Ecocultural Niches of Middle Childhood: A Cross-Cultural Perspective." In *Development during Middle Childhood. The Years from Six to Twelve*, edited by W. A. Collins. Washington, D.C.: National Academy Press.

Weiss, C. H. 1995. "Nothing as Practical as Good Theory: Exploring Theory-Based Evaluation for Comprehensive Community Initiatives for Children and Families." In *New Approaches to Evaluating Community Initiatives: Concepts, Methods, and Contexts*, edited by J. P. Connell, A. C. Kubisch, L. B. Schorr, and C. H. Weiss. Washington, D.C.: Aspen Institute.

Wellman, B. 1979. "The Community Question: The Intimate Networks of East Yorkers." *American Journal of Sociology* 84: 1201–31.

Wellman, B., and B. Leighton. 1979. "Networks, Neighborhoods, and Communities: Approaches to The Study of the Community Question." *Urban Affairs Quarterly* 14: 363–90.

White, Michael. 1987. *American Neighborhoods and Residential Differentiation*. New York: Russell Sage Foundation.

Whiting, B. B., ed. 1963. *Children of Six Cultures. Studies of Child Rearing*. New York: Wiley.

Whiting, B., and C. Edwards. 1988. *Children of Different Worlds. The Formation of Social Behavior*. Cambridge, Mass.: Harvard University Press.

Whiting, B. B., and J. W. M. Whiting. 1975. *Children of Six Cultures. A Psychocultural analysis*. Cambridge, Mass.: Harvard University Press.

Whyte, W. F. 1955. *Street Corner Society*, 2d ed. Chicago: University of Chicago Press.

Widaman, K. F. 1993. "Common Factor Analysis versus Principal Component Analysis: Differential Bias in Representing Model Parameters?" *Multivariate Behavioral Research* 28: 263–311.

Williams, M. 1981. *On the Street Where I Lived*. New York: Holt, Rinehart & Winston.

Williams, T., and W. Kornblum. 1985. *Growing Up Poor*. Lexington, Mass.: Lexington Books.

———. 1994. *The Uptown Kids: Struggle and Hope in the Project*. New York: Putnam.

Wilson, J. B., D. T. Ellwood, and J. Brooks-Gunn. 1995. "Welfare to Work through the Eyes of Children: The Impact on Parenting of Movement from AFDC to Employment." In *Escape from Poverty: What Makes a Difference for Children?* edited by P. L. Chase-Lansdale and J. Brooks-Gunn. New York: Cambridge University Press.

Wilson, W. J. 1987. *The Truly Disadvantaged: The Inner City, the Underclass, and Public Policy*. Chicago: University of Chicago Press.

———. 1991a. "Public Policy Research and *The Truly Disadvantaged*." In *The Urban Underclass*, edited by C. Jencks and P. E. Peterson. Washington, D.C.: Brookings Institution.

———. 1991b. "Studying Inner-City Social Dislocations: The Challenge of Public Agenda Research." *American Sociological Review* 56(1): 1–14.

———. 1996. *When Work Disappears: The World of the New Urban Poor*. New York: Alfred A. Knopf.

Wilson, W. J., R. Aponte, J. Kirschenman, and L. Wacquant. 1988. "The Ghetto Underclass and the Changing Structure of American Poverty." In *Quiet Riots: Race and Poverty in the United States*, edited by F. Harris and R. W. Wilkins. New York: Pantheon.

Wireman, P. 1984. *Urban Neighborhoods, Networks, and Families: New Forms for Old Values*. Lexington, Mass.: Lexington Books.

Wirth, L. 1938. "Urbanism as a Way of Life." *American Journal of Sociology* 44: 1–24.

Wohlwill, J. F. 1985. "The Confluence of Environmental and Developmental Psychology: Signpost to an Ecology of Development?" *Human Development* 23: 354–58.

Wohlwill, J. F., and H. Heft. 1987. "The Physical Environment and the Development of the Child." In *Handbook of Environmental Psychology*, Vol. 1, edited by D. Stokols and I. Altman. New York: Wiley.

Wohlwill, J. F. and Van Vliet, W. 1985. *Habitats for Children: The Impact of Destiny*. Hillsdale, N. J.: Lawrence Erlbaum Associates.

Wolfe, B. L. 1995. "Health Policy for Children of AFDC Families: Economic Issues." In *Escape from Poverty: What Makes a Difference for Poor Children?* edited by P. L. Chase-Lansdale and J. Brooks-Gunn. New York: Cambridge University Press.

Wrobel, P. 1979. *Our Way: Family, Parish, and Neighborhood in a Polish-American Community*. Notre Dame, Ind.: University of Notre Dame Press.

Wrong, D. 1961. "The Oversocialized Conception of Man in Modern Society." *American Sociological Review* 26: 183–93.

Wynn, J. R., J. Costello, R. Halpern, and H. Richman. 1994. *Children, Families, and Communities: A New Approach to Social Services*. Chicago: University of Chicago, Chapin Hall Center for Children.

Wynn, J. R., H. Richman, R. A. Rubenstein, and J. Littell. 1988. *Communities and Adolescents: An Exploration of Reciprocal Supports*. Washington, D.C.: Youth and America's Future: William T. Grant Foundation, Commission on Work, Family and Citizenship.

Zigler, E. F. 1987. "The Effectiveness of Head Start: Another Look." *Educational Psychologist* 13: 71–77.

Zigler, E. F., and K. B. Black. 1989. "America's Family Support Movement: Strengths and Limitations." *American Journal of Orthopsychiatry* 59(1): 6–17.

Zigler, E. F., and S. Styfco. 1996. "Head Start and Early Childhood Intervention: The Changing Course of Social Science and Social Policy." In *Children, Families, and Government: Prepar-*

ing for the Twenty-first Century, edited by E. F. Zigler, S. L. Kagan, and N. W. Hall. New York: Cambridge University Press.

Zigler, E. F., and J. Valentine. 1979. *Education's Project Head Start: A Legacy of the War on Poverty*. New York: Macmillan.

Zollar, A. C. 1985. *A Member of the Family: Strategies for Black Family Continuity*. Chicago: Nelson-Hall.

Zorbaugh, H. [1929] 1976. *The Gold Coast and the Slum*. Chicago: University of Chicago Press.

Index